About the CD-ROM

This CD and the software included on it have been designed to run on Windows systems using a Web browser. System requirements vary depending on what you download from the CD. Please review all software readme files before installing or running any of the software included on this CD.

For more information about this CD please refer to the CD appendix at the back of this book.

Windows System Requirements

- ▶ Computer: 386 IBM PC-compatible
- ▶ Memory: 8MB of RAM
- ▶ Platform: Windows 3.1, NT, or 95
- ▶ Software: Web browser
- ▶ Hardware: 2X CD-ROM drive

CD Start Instructions

1 Place the CD-ROM in your CD-ROM drive.

2 Launch your Web browser.

3 From your Web browser, select Open File from the File menu. Select the CD-ROM (usually drive D), then select the file called Welcome.htm.

How to Program

JavaBeans

How to Program

JavaBeans

**Peter Coffee,
Michael Morrison,
Randy Weems,
and Jack Leong**

Ziff-Davis Press
An imprint of Macmillan Computer
Publishing USA
Emeryville, California

Publisher	Stacy Hiquet
Associate Publisher	Steven Sayre
Acquisitions Editor	Brett Bartow
Development Editor	Paula Hardin
Copy Editor	Bill Cassell and Nicole Clausing
Technical Reviewer	Selim Tuvi
Production Editor	Edith Rex
Proofreader	Jeff Barash
Cover Illustration and Design	Megan Gandt
Book Design	Bruce Lundquist
Page Layout	M. D. Barrera
Indexer	Valerie Perry

Ziff-Davis Press, ZD Press, and the Ziff-Davis Press logo are trademarks or registered trademarks of, and are licensed to Macmillan Computer Publishing USA by Ziff-Davis Publishing Company, New York, New York.

Ziff-Davis Press imprint books are produced on a Macintosh computer system with the following applications: FrameMaker®, Microsoft® Word, QuarkXPress®, Adobe Illustrator®, Adobe Photoshop®, Adobe Streamline™, MacLink®Plus, Aldus® FreeHand™, Collage Plus™.

Ziff-Davis Press, an imprint of
Macmillan Computer Publishing USA
5903 Christie Avenue
Emeryville, CA 94608

ISBN 1-56276-521-3

Manufactured in the United States of America
10 9 8 7 6 5 4 3 2 1

About the Authors

Michael Morrison is a freelance software developer and author. He has written or contributed to numerous titles, including: *Late Night Microsoft Visual J++, Presenting JavaBeans, Tricks of the Java Programming Gurus,* and *Java Unleashed.* Michael currently resides in Nashville, TN with his lifelong love, Mansheed. In his spare time, he enjoys adding to his hard-earned collection of cuts and bruises on the skateboard ramps.

Randy Weems is a senior software engineer for Electronic Product Information Corporation (EPIC), an ISV specializing in pricing and configuration systems for complex products. He is responsible for software design, programming, and maintenance of expert systems. He is also responsible for design and documentation of internal tools and systems, and research of new technologies, such as: ActiveX and Java. He is coauthor of SAMS' *Win95 Game Developer's Guide Using the Game SDK.*

Peter Coffee is the Advanced Technologies Analyst for *PC Week Labs* and works with *PC Week's* industry-leading technical staff to keep readers on the cutting edge of information technology. Peter's own work focuses on software development methods and tools, processor architectures and programming models, and operating systems and environments. Peter authored Ziff-Davis Press's recent *How to Program Java.*

Jack Leong was first exposed to Java in 1995 and has subsequently become addicted to the language. He has explored several areas of Java, including large scale intranet development, evaluating bugs for the JDK 1.0.2 and researching JavaBeans. He is currently a Consulting Engineer in the Opcom Group of Sun Microsystems Canada.

Table of Contents

Acknowledgments

This book would have taken far longer to write if it weren't for the extraordinary efforts of the people at Sun Microsystems, who brought JavaBeans from concept to reality even more quickly than they said they would—and who documented their work with thoroughness and clarity, letting us bring you this tutorial with confidence in its foundations. We stand on the shoulders of giants, and cast the spells conceived by exceptional wizards.

—PC

Early in the development cycle of this book, I fractured my left forearm skateboarding and subsequently had my entire arm placed in a cast for six weeks. Without my wife, Mahsheed, I wouldn't have been able to survive the trials of getting through everyday activities with a full arm cast. You are absolutely the best—thanks!

I also want to thank Brett Bartow, the acquisitions editor for this book, who was far more supportive and understanding than I deserved as I adjusted to working with one arm less than I am accustomed to using.

I also want to thank my parents, who were so generous to step in and lead the renovation of our house while I was busy writing with my one good hand.

Finally, I would like to thank my very good friend Randy Weems, who was willing to join this project amidst a heavy workload at his day job. You've always come through when it counts and I appreciate it!

—MM

I'd like to thank Eduardo Pelegri-Llopart of Sun for his explanations of the BeanBox. Thanks to Joe Thompson and everyone else at EPIC for allowing me to juggle writing with my real job. And thanks to all our editors for being very patient while we authors figured out what we were doing.

—RW

To my wife Kit for her support, understanding, and continual encouragement throughout those long hours into the night.

—JL

Introduction

Objects, components, GUIs, rapid application development, and visual programming: These are all buzzwords the computer industry has thrown around to the point of inducing nausea. Unfortunately, for most software developers, these buzzwords often don't make life as easy as we are led to believe they will. It's one thing to envision a world of well-organized, completely self-contained software that can be integrated and used to build applications in a highly visual manner; it's quite another thing to deliver on such a vision.

Although no technology has so far fulfilled this vision, Sun's new JavaBeans software-component technology is by far the closest to emerge yet. Built upon the immensely successful Java programming language and runtime system, JavaBeans delivers on Sun's promise to deliver a technology for creating fully reusable, platform-independent software. JavaBeans marks a significant step forward for Java, since software-component support was one of the noticeably missing pieces of the original Java puzzle.

This book explores the JavaBeans technology from a number of different angles. Not only will you learn a great deal of theory behind JavaBeans technology and how it relates to the core Java API, but you will also learn how to build your own JavaBeans components, also known as Beans. In addition, you will learn about some of the future directions the JavaBeans technology may take, including their relationship to Microsoft's ActiveX technology.

We've tried hard to make this book not only a solid introduction to the JavaBeans technology, but also a practical guide to JavaBeans component development. Our goal is for you to put this book down with the knowledge and confidence to go about developing your own JavaBeans components. We hope you find JavaBeans as exciting a technology as we did. Have fun!

—Michael Morrison

Part 1

Getting Started with JavaBeans

Chapter 1

JavaBeans: Java Meets Components

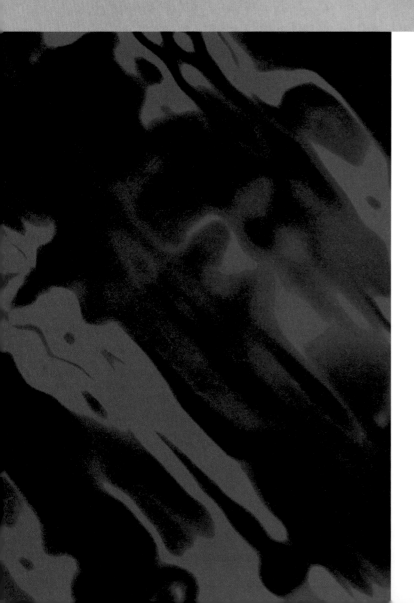

- ▶ **Why Creators Need Components**
- ▶ **The Goals of JavaBeans**
- ▶ **The Java Software Platform**

You create for a living. You know that there's nothing worse than the moment before you type that first line of code. It's a lot like typing "Chapter One" at the top of a page: it means taking on a large set of challenges.

It doesn't matter if your work is going to be read by a person, or interpreted in some way by a machine. In either case, you're offering a contract to identify a set of needs, and to offer useful solutions.

Either way, that's a big promise. This book is about JavaBeans, a better way to keep that promise. JavaBeans is the technology of choice for giving users of programs quicker, more flexible, and more reliable solutions by easing the process of packaging and reusing code so that a good solution can go wherever it's needed.

This first chapter will cover some of the basic concepts behind JavaBeans, including:

▶ The logic of component-based development

▶ The risks of using purchased software components

▶ The goals of JavaBeans: reusability, visual development, and tools

▶ The Java software platform: the language and the Java Virtual Machine

Why Creators Need Components

We said that writers of code and writers of words faced similar challenges. Writers of words, though, have long enjoyed a huge advantage over writers of machine-readable works.

That's because a human reader has a variety of resources, such as the dictionary and the body of well-known literature, that provide a valuable context that a writer can assume to be on hand. Even when looking at a blank page, a writer of words knows that the reader has a running start on understanding what's to come.

In particular, the writer of words can rely on the reader to understand (or be able to find out) the standard definitions of words, and to recognize (or be able to find out) the origins and associations of hundreds or thousands of figures of speech. If a human reader doesn't understand a word, there's a uniform process that the reader can follow for looking up the word and fitting its meaning into the text.

Note that the writer of words doesn't need to know tricky details, such as what dictionary the reader might be using. The writer need only spell the word correctly and use it as it is generally understood. There's a standard interface, so to speak, for using that "component" in many different roles. It's more than just a matter of simple definitions. If the writer knows a lot about the reader, huge economies of effort may result. For example, the concise phrase "pointy-haired manager" conveys a wealth of images and associations to any reader who's familiar with the comic strip "Dilbert"—as readers of this book are likely to be! The writer who knows the audience can therefore add a lot of content, in effect, with a much smaller effort than the writer who has to spell out everything from scratch.

Why not give writers of software the same kind of leverage? Software authors should have the same ability to call on collections of prebuilt units, and to count on standard mechanisms that will make those units work together wherever they're needed.

That's the goal of component-based software technologies: to let a software writer invoke whole libraries of known and tested work with a few well-chosen lines.

Component-based application development and deployment lets software users get the benefit of those libraries many times, in many different tasks, while paying for those software components just once. That payment may be in money, or in network retrieval time: either way, components offer welcome runtime economies.

Component technology lowers the cost, and potentially raises the quality, of the software that we use to communicate with each other; to analyze the world around us; and to control the complex systems that we build. Sun's Java language is helpful in doing these things, making Java-based components a welcome arrival.

Component Technologies Meet a Long-Felt Need

The arrival of components lets us deal with issues raised ten years ago in an article by Frederick Brooks, one of the elder statesmen of software development. A software project, wrote Brooks, all too often becomes "a monster of missed schedules, blown budgets, and flawed products." This is so, he continued, because software is inherently complex: it has a kind of complexity that's only appreciated once you've designed or built a substantial application.

Think about a mechanical system with 1,000 parts. It will have many identical units, such as fasteners, whose design cost is spread across dozens or hundreds of uses in that one system. Once a mechanical component, like a bolt, is designed and tested, it's relatively cheap to make many copies that can be used in many different places.

A software system that has 1,000 parts will be more complex and far more costly to design. This is because no two of those 1,000 components will be identical. When the same function is needed at more than one point in a software system, a single module does all of those jobs: it just gets called from more than one point.

Yes, there are functions that are common to many software systems, such as locating and opening files. Some of these functions have begun to migrate out of individual applications and into operating environments such as Windows. In an application domain such as manufacturing, though, there are common notions such as the idea of a Customer or a Shipment that it would be useful to share across many projects: you won't see these things in the operating environment, and it takes a significant effort to package such ideas so that one piece of code can be used in every likely situation. The discipline involved has not been a tradition among many programmers.

Component technologies offer software developers economies of reuse by defining the frameworks, and establishing the rules, for spreading costs of design across dozens or hundreds of uses. A component that provides a basic function, such as formatted data entry, can be employed by developers in many different departments of a company—or even in many different industries, if that component is sold on the open market.

Third-party component developers have a commercial motivation to provide a more complete, more thoroughly tested, more easily usable module than would normally be created by an in-house developer trying to meet an incidental need. This way of doing things offers benefits to all involved. The third-party developer makes money; the in-house developer is able to concentrate scarce resources on the task-specific parts of an application that demand more specialized knowledge; and the end-user gets a better solution. A strong component technology makes a software development platform far more competitive than it would be without that on-ramp to a profitable software industry.

Developers Want Rules

Frederick Brooks, who was cited above, noted that software is also hard to write because of its need to conform to arbitrary rules and standards where one piece of software interacts with another. In other disciplines, systems become more similar at their lowest levels; for example, a civil engineer can safely assume that steel beams will bend before they break. But software has no such set of inherently common rules.

A component technology specification offers developers such a set of rules, making software interactions far more systematic. This makes it easier to update one piece of a system without causing unintended side effects in other parts of the system. Rigorous studies have identified such "breakage" of previously working code as a major cause of software defects. By reducing the effort wasted on solving such problems, component technologies increase the resources available to improve software function and ease of use.

Is It Safe Not to Do It Yourself?

Despite all its advantages, the notion of using software components produced by some outside agency has its dark side. Especially in a networked environment, it's a questionable practice to run a piece of code that you didn't write yourself, unless you've given it a line-by-line audit for defects or malicious behaviors (accidental or otherwise).

1

> CAUTION: *What bad things could an externally written component do to you?*
>
> ▶ *Destroy or alter data (example: transfer funds from one account to another)*
>
> ▶ *Violate privacy mechanisms (example: read confidential messages)*
>
> ▶ *Deny service to legitimate users (example: saturate a processor with high-priority tasks, slowing or halting normal activities)*
>
> ▶ *Annoy legitimate users (example: make annoying noises using a client system's multimedia hardware)*

In a networked environment, a software developer may be working with tools that download frequent updates from a remote location such as a vendor's Web site. In a classic paper on software risks, Ken Thompson showed that when a critical tool such as a compiler comes from an outside source, it is entirely possible for that tool to embed undesired behaviors in the applications that it builds. Such behaviors might include, for example, providing a trapdoor password in an access-control routine. It is even possible that these behaviors may go undetected by someone scrutinizing the source code of either the application or the compiler, if an untrusted executable version of that compiler is used to compile the compiler itself.

And like networks themselves, problems caused by undesired behaviors go both ways. Malicious code may extract information from a computer and send it to some other location. It may originate messages that will appear to be sent by the user of the target system. It may even use the resources of the target system to mount an attack on yet another networked resource, with any blame for that attack falling on the victimized machine and its user.

When proposing to move a software development community away from its established practice of rolling its code on a task-by-task basis, one must therefore have an answer for those who point out these genuine and potentially costly risks. The Java platform provides such answers, making Java-based components intrinsically more attractive than those produced by other software development technologies.

The Goals of JavaBeans

Unlike other component technologies, such as Microsoft's Object Linking and Embedding (which evolved into the current ActiveX), JavaBeans was conceived in the modern era of visual programming tools. These let a developer compose the appearance, and visualize the behavior, of an application under construction using a graphical environment.

This difference between JavaBeans and older component models shows up in the first and most minimal definition offered by the JavaBeans specification:

> *A Bean in JavaBeans is a reusable software component that can be manipulated visually in a builder tool.*

Let's look at those goals one by one.

Goal 1: A Reusable Component, Not a Puzzle Piece

JavaBeans components can't lower the cost of software development unless the typical component is used again and again. This means that Beans can't merely be used as a way of carving up one application into modules.

When an application is designed in a pre-component fashion, then divided up into objects, you wind up with a block diagram of the one task at hand. That's not the same thing as developing a collection of objects that each encapsulate a recurring task and wiring those objects together with a small amount of custom code to deliver a particular solution.

To be reusable, and more attractive than writing new code from scratch, components must invite refinement and reuse in other applications. Specifically, they must appeal to programmers other than those who originally built the components.

> **CAUTION:** *It is not enough to take an application, carve it up into pieces, encapsulate each piece in a JavaBeans component, and call the result a component-based application. Such an application will have identifiable pieces, but so does a jigsaw puzzle. Such after-the-fact partitioning will probably produce a set of pieces, like those of a puzzle, that only fit together in one useful way.*

To be made reusable, a component must first be envisioned from the outside in; that is, from the point of view of an entire family of present and prospective applications. Reusability is *not* very likely to come from wrapping a task-specific collection of functions and data fields in a barely adequate interface. Most of the C++ code that's been written to date probably meets the latter description.

Compared to other tools that claim to be object-oriented, Java does a better job of enabling programmers to do objects right and to get their full benefits in the long run.

For example, the full-strength object orientation of the Java language enables subclassing. This means that a solid foundation can easily be tailored to a new use, rather than being replaced from the ground up (as it has to be in Visual Basic). Java also supports interfaces, giving the conceptual benefits of multiple inheritance without the ambiguities of this feature as it's implemented in C++.

The doctrine of writing components so that they're useful to other programmers is impossible to enforce, though, with any technology or tool. As Ed Post said in his classic 1982 essay, "Real Programmers Don't Use Pascal" (http://www.mit.edu: 8001/afs/athena.mit.edu/activity/h/humor/www/Computers/real.programmers), some things require actual talent.

At least the design of JavaBeans doesn't get in the way of good design.

Goal 2: Visual Manipulation During Design

JavaBeans is meant to support visual manipulation, but Beans are more than graphical user interface components like push buttons and text boxes. Beans are meant for brewing stronger stuff as well. A Bean might be meant for server-side use, for example, in which case it would not appear directly to the user. But it should still have some kind of graphical appearance at design time. A stored-procedure Bean might have some kind of graphical canvas, for example, to let a developer draw the connections between server-resident tables to support a custom query definition.

At this point, the alert developer will wonder if every Bean has to carry around the overhead of graphical embellishments that it doesn't actually need to do its job. This would increase network transfer times and memory requirements, making JavaBeans less attractive on heavily used networks and making it quite impractical for consumer-electronics information appliances. But Beans are not so burdened. Design-time interfaces, such as those required for an elaborate "wizard" automation tool, can be encapsulated in a separate class from the runtime interfaces that must be supported for a Bean to do its job.

> **TIP:** *Encapsulation is one of the linchpins of object-oriented programming. It means that aspects of a program aren't accessible unless they're meant to be.*
>
> *If a data structure is implemented as an array, for example, then other code might directly operate on an element of that array, possibly confusing another part of the program that was using that array as a stack. Encapsulation might block any operations on that array other than those using the authorized, stack-flavored methods* push *and* pop.
>
> *JavaBeans technology relies on encapsulation to make sure that a component carries the code that's needed to do its job (and all of that code) without dragging along facilities that are only needed during design.*

Design-time interfaces give Java a notable advantage over other component technologies such as Microsoft's COM. Design-time interfaces eliminate the need for a separate definition language like that provided, in effect, by Microsoft's Active Template Library (by which a programmer persuades a C++ compiler to generate the code of a COM or ActiveX component).

It's true that the latest edition of Microsoft's Visual C++, version 5.0, incorporates editing and code-generation facilities that reduce the burden of this bilingualism. Java's introspection APIs, however, avoid the problem entirely: The design language of JavaBeans components is Java. Yes, life really can be that simple.

Chapter 9 will explore Introspection APIs and Chapter 10 will cover other design-time interfaces, specifically those called the Customization APIs in JavaBeans.

TIP: *It's perfectly possible to deliver a Bean without employing advanced options like the Customization API facilities. For any JavaBeans component, an application builder tool will always be able to construct a plain-vanilla property sheet that lists the properties exported by that Bean. It will be able to offer basic editing tools for modifying those properties' values. JavaBeans doesn't rely on the kindness of strangers: The architecture ensures that a component can be inspected and used, adequately if not elegantly, with even a minimal implementation.*

Where complexity warrants, the Customization APIs allow a Bean's developer to offer a customizer class. This might be something as simple as a distinctively styled or conveniently laid out property sheet, or it might be something as elaborate as a GUI application (written in Java, of course!) that interacts with a developer and makes a complex set of design-time trade-off decisions. This flexibility lets a component's designer offer, for example, low-cost versions of a component with basic facilities, and more expensive versions that are packaged with elaborate automated aids.

Goal 3: Working with Builder Tools

JavaBeans is meant to be a widely used model for building a wide variety of software, and is meant to be usable by programmers of widely varying backgrounds—from systems-level programmers to graphically sophisticated content authors with minimal programming backgrounds. Realizing these goals will create market opportunities for a wide variety of programming tools. This is especially true because the JavaBeans standard guarantees that programming tools will be able to make new strides toward actively anticipating what a developer might want to do. Using facilities that we'll explore in chapters to come, a Java development tool may actually be able to compare the capabilities of components on hand and assist the developer in choosing the best available options.

Despite the recent vintage of Java itself, and the even more recent emergence of this Java-based component model, many companies are wrapping some of their most innovative development systems around JavaBeans development, mostly for Windows platforms but also in some cases for Macintosh and Solaris. Here's a preview of the JavaBeans tools that were on the way when this book was written, representing the leading edge of many more to come.

Sun Microsystems' JDK 1.1, BDK 1.0, and Java WorkShop

Most JavaBeans tools were still forthcoming at the time this chapter was written. At their foundation, however, are the Java Development Kit (JDK) 1.1 and the Beans Development Kit (BDK), both of which are distributed freely by Sun Microsystems, Inc. to evangelize and standardize the Java technologies. The BDK contains extensive documentation in HTML format for convenient viewing in Web browsers (like the one pictured in Figure 1.1 that serves as the shell for the collection of tools that make up Sun's own Java WorkShop development system).

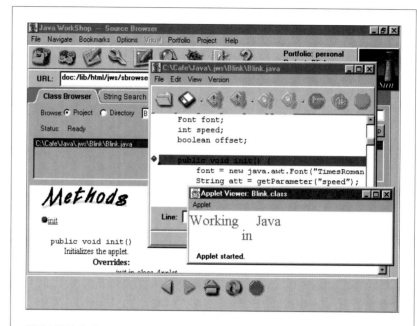

FIGURE 1.1

Sun's Java WorkShop development system unifies its tools within a Web browser environment

The BDK includes both compiled and source code files for the BeanBox, a "reference Bean container" for use in testing newly developed components (see Figure 1.2 for an example of the BeanBox in action). The JavaBeans API classes are provided in the same two formats. A dozen example Beans, also included in the BDK, provide additional exposure to the technique and style of coding a conforming Bean.

> **TIP:** *It's likely that any full-strength development tool for JavaBeans programming will include both JDK and BDK documentation and code files. Even so, it's worth the effort to find your way to the Sun Microsystems Web sites, http://www.javasoft.com/products/JDK/1.1/index.html and http://splash.javasoft.com/beans/bdk_download.html, where updates and technical discussions will appear. Java evolves at the speed of the Web, and any code old enough to be on a CD in a package is almost certainly out of date in tiny but crucial respects.*

Symantec Visual Café

Leading the wave of more elaborate, fully integrated Beans-based development systems is Symantec Corp.'s Visual Café, already shipping (with preliminary

JavaBeans support based on the JDK 1.0.2) as of mid-winter 1997.

Visual Café conclusively demonstrates the benefits of a fully object-oriented language that retains information about objects and data types well into the cycle of application delivery (unlike C++, which discards most object information long before it finishes building the executable file). Visual Café lets a developer manipulate both visual and textual representations of an application under construction, maintaining synchronized views in several concurrently open tools as shown in Figure 1.3. It does so even as the developer uses first one tool, then another, to make changes to various portions of a user interface or its underlying logic.

It takes a good deal of effort to bring an externally developed Bean into Visual Café's integrated development environment as a fully supported component. Specifically, the component developer must create a rather elaborate description file. Once that's been done, though, another programmer will be able to work with the new component and make it part of an application without any conventional

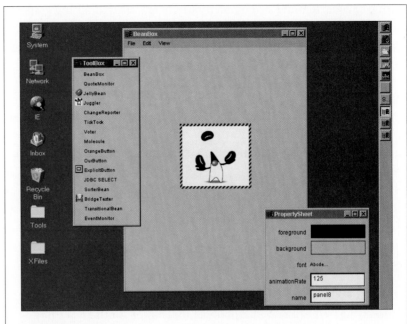

FIGURE 1.2

The BeanBox, a "reference Bean container" for use in testing newly developed components

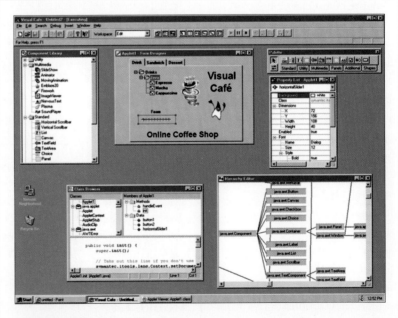

FIGURE 1.3

Visual Café tools

writing of code. Reusing a component merely requires a dragging gesture with the mouse to activate Visual Café's Interaction Wizard, a somewhat overdone but quite intuitive tool: It offers lists of events that might trigger an interaction between two components, and generates the code that's needed to handle the details.

ParcPlace-Digitalk

The leading-edge feel of Visual Café is far more pronounced during initial application design than it is during subsequent maintenance. The interactions between an application's components are easy to create, but not so easy to visualize after the fact.

Visual Café would do well to incorporate the kind of graphical view of object interactions that has long been a feature of visual Smalltalk programming tools from vendors such as ParcPlace-Digitalk. That company, a long-time bastion of Smalltalk, made mid-winter 1997 promises to deliver Java versions of its tools at about the time this book is due to appear.

Borland JBuilder

Unlike Symantec, Borland International Inc. waited for the real thing—that is, for a shipping JDK 1.1—before delivering its JavaBeans development system, JBuilder, promised early in 1997 but not yet available at this writing.

JBuilder does not "demo" as well as does Visual Café, but it may prove the better choice for "industrial development" shops that build and maintain applications over long periods of time using constantly changing teams. Visual Café has a "gee whiz" appeal during initial design and assembly of an application but is less impressive over the long haul. JBuilder offers a repository feature for fragments of a project and has a streamlined development environment that may prove the better choice for many development tasks. An early look at JBuilder appears in Figure 1.4.

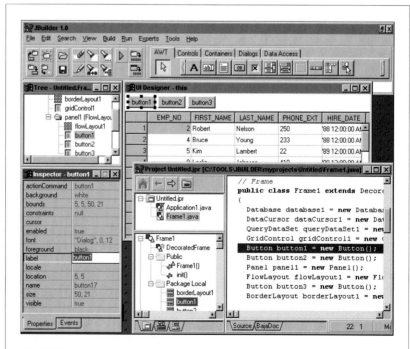

FIGURE 1.4

Borland International's JBuilder has the integrated tools of the company's popular Pascal-based Delphi development system

Sybase Powersoft PowerJ

To make the choice still more interesting, Sybase Inc. will be offering a Java variation on Power++, its extraordinary C++ development tool (formerly called Optima++) for exploring and assembling ActiveX components. The Java version, PowerJ, takes a different approach than that taken by Visual Café. While Symantec's tool essentially asks, "What do you want?", the Powersoft product's greeting is more like "Here's what this component can do." PowerJ displays each component's facilities in a well-organized and searchable onscreen "reference card" (as shown in Figure 1.5).

Dragging with the mouse from the reference card to the source-code editing window causes PowerJ to generate the appropriate event-handling code. This exposes the code-generation process more fully than it's shown during development with Visual Café, and it seems likely that a developer will learn Java by example more quickly with the Powersoft product.

PowerJ will also have the exceptionally well-integrated debugging tools of Optima. If PowerJ is installed on the same machine as Power++, the developer will have a single integrated environment for programming both C++ (with ActiveX controls) and Java (with JavaBeans components).

Microsoft Visual J++

Speaking of unified development systems for C++ and Java, Microsoft continues to confound its critics by offering

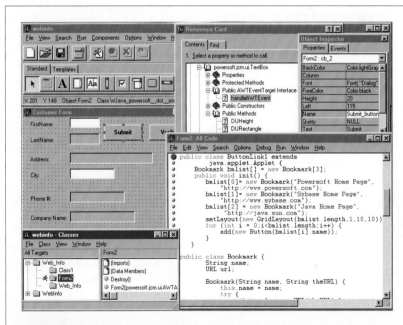

FIGURE 1.5

The well-organized, searchable "reference card" of components highlights Sybase's Powersoft PowerJ development system

1

first-rate Java tools even while promoting the ActiveX technology that many see as Java's biggest competition.

Microsoft's Developer Studio integrated development environment just keeps on accumulating new languages, having debuted as Microsoft's C++ editor but now supporting Java, SQL, HTML, ATL, and probably a few more notations by the time this book appears.

Visual J++ gave developers the capability to debug running applets in a browser, as shown in Figure 1.6. This lets a developer probe, for example, the interactions between concurrent applets in a single Web page. If you want to develop primarily for Windows platforms, mixing and matching the strengths of both Java and ActiveX, Visual J++ is a top contender.

NOTE: *The debugging API used by Microsoft's Internet Explorer is being licensed by other toolmakers, so don't assume that this feature is still unique to Visual J++.*

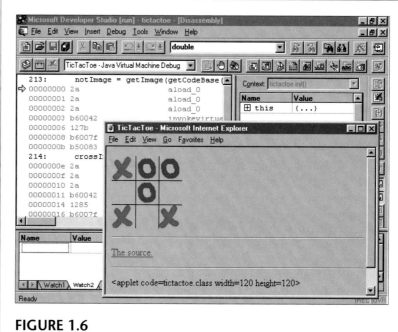

FIGURE 1.6

Debugging running applets in a browser with Microsoft's Visual J++

The Java Software Platform

These development tools for JavaBeans would not be attractive unless the Java technology provided a strong foundation for component-based development. But even without components, the Java family of technologies already offered many attractions to software developers in the era of the information appliance.

This book assumes that the reader is a programmer or an Internet content creator who already knows at least the essentials of the Java programming language—but Java, which also encompasses the portable elegance of the Java Virtual Machine and the powerful encapsulations provided by the API class libraries, is much more than a language alone. And although the Java language is the starting point for most Java developers, it need not be the only way to access Java technology's many benefits.

The Java Language

The Java language is still quite young compared to veterans (or geezers?) like COBOL, FORTRAN, or BASIC, but Java has already earned a similar level of "mind share" among both professional software developers and incidental programmers.

Many Java programmers come to the language with previous experience in writing C++, which Java resembles in many ways—especially in its syntax, which looks like line noise to those who prefer more English-like languages such as COBOL, BASIC, or REXX. Key advantages of Java over C++ include:

▶ Standardized primitive data types whose size and behavior are defined independently of the hardware

▶ True arrays, with bounds checking and type enforcement, unlike the syntactically sugared pointer arithmetic that passes for arrays in C++

▶ Strong protection of private data, achieved in part by eliminating the arbitrary manipulations through untyped pointers that are endemic in C and C++

▶ Automatic recovery of memory freed by disposal of temporary objects, eliminating the laborious and error-prone memory management that makes C and C++ programs infamously unreliable

▶ Multitasking facilities defined at the level of the language (rather than by outside libraries), and fully integrated (through object-oriented treatment of threads) into Java's type-safety and memory-management facilities.

▶ Implementation of multiple interfaces (as opposed to the multiple inheritance model of C++), eliminating the ambiguities that arise in C++ when a subclass inherits a member variable from more than one base class.

NOTE: *Components are risky because they require developers to rely on outside writers of software whose testing and other quality-assurance procedures may not be as stringent as the developer might prefer. Java is attractive for components because the Java language itself eliminates many common causes of programming error.*

Java's strengths make it a contender for any programming project. Do not be misled by Java's close associations with the Internet: This is no mere scripting language, and Java has arguably displaced both Smalltalk and Ada as the language that one should learn first on the path to any kind of programming career.

1

This is because Java, with its combination of object orientation and language-level multitasking, provides an excellent frame of reference for understanding other languages with comparable power but more encumbered designs. It can't be said too often, though, that there's more to Java than a language, and the dimensions of this larger world of Java are often overlooked when the language is described and taught.

The Java Virtual Machine

Java is associated with the Internet not only because the language is excellent for Internet-related purposes, but also because it is part of a platform that's largely independent of the underlying hardware.

The Java language is designed to execute in an environment, called the *Java Virtual Machine*, that can itself be implemented as a combination of a program and a set of supporting classes of software object. The resulting environment uses only small amounts of machine-specific code.

This makes it easy to rehost Java on many different types of computer, or even on devices that bear little resemblance to any conventional idea of what a computer should look like or how it should work. If the hardware has the resources needed to run a Java Virtual Machine, then code written in Java can run on that hardware.

> **TIP:** *Don't confuse the Java language with the Java Virtual Machine. The latter does not read Java source code files, but processes the compiled file of byte codes (a* `.class` *file) that's produced by a Java compiler. A Java byte-code (J-code) file can also be produced by some other tool, one that does not use the Java language at all but instead uses a comparably powerful language such as Ada 95 (http://www.appletmagic.com/). Intermediate approaches compile another language to Java, then let a standard Java compiler finish the job: This can be done with programs written in Microsoft's Visual Basic (http://www.tvobjects.com/, http://www.blackdirt.com/bdvbtojava.htm) or in IBM's NetREXX language (http://www2.hursley.ibm.com/netrexx/).*

When a Java Virtual Machine loads a .class file, it goes through a sophisticated process of data-flow and theorem-proving analysis that prevent ill-formed code from running. A Java program (referring now to anything that's running on a Java Virtual Machine, no matter what language was used to write it) can only operate on data with an instruction that is appropriate to that data's type; it can only execute instructions that are in the region of memory that's owned by that program; it can only operate on "stack" data structures within the limits of stack size and content, closing the loopholes that create security risks in less disciplined processing environments.

For these reasons, deploying software in the form of Java applets and/or Beans is inherently attractive to users who might otherwise be reluctant to trust an unknown source.

Playing in the "Sandbox"

Perhaps most important of all, the Java Virtual Machine takes an active role in assuring the user that Java-based software won't do more harm than good. Any Java environment can limit, in a finely detailed manner, the privileges of executing programs.

This means that a user, or the person who designs a runtime environment for a user, can determine the precise desired mix of utility and risk. For example, an application designer can trade the performance of working with the local hard disk for the greater safety of using only an applet's "home" server storage, while the user or the user's representative still gets to veto the higher-risk option.

How does the Java Virtual Machine limit the possible actions of a running Java program? It defines a subclass of the standard Java API class `SecurityManager`. That subclass is tailored to the privileges that the programmer wishes to grant.

The controls that are implemented in this manner, through the Java Virtual Machine, are not well understood. Many users, and some developers, have the impression that Java is intrinsically a crippled language because the privileges of Internet-based "applets" are so tightly controlled.

It is true that in a properly designed implementation of a typical Java-enabled Internet browser, it's normal for a browser-hosted applet to be barred from writing or reading any files that don't reside on the server from which the applet came. Applets cannot normally open network connections to any host but their own. Applets cannot normally cause other local programs to run, nor can they even open a window on the screen without having the runtime environment label that window as "untrusted." (This prevents, for example, the display of a window that looks like a normal login prompt, but which actually steals the user's login name and password for mailing to some other address.)

This is known as running an applet "in the sandbox," but it is not a design limitation. It is a policy decision.

It is possible to build a Java-enabled Internet browser that does not impose these restrictions. But it would be very risky, since this would allow an untrusted piece of code to download and run on a user's machine, perhaps as an invisible side effect of their viewing an innocent-looking Web page. That program would be able to do anything that the user's own privileges allowed.

Walk on the Wild Side

The privileges of a Java program aren't attributes of the program, as they are in the Unix environment. The facilities available to a program are determined by the subclass of `SecurityManager` that's instantiated by the Java runtime environment.

A Java runtime environment does not normally install any security manager at all. A Java "application" (that is, a Java program running on a Java Virtual Machine that runs as a stand-alone task) will normally have access to all of the facilities available to its user. Any files that can be read or written (or deleted), any connections that can be made, and any peripheral devices that the user can normally access are going to be available to that code.

But it's not an all-or-nothing deal. Browsers don't allow very much and a stand-alone Java environment like Sun's appletviewer utility allows everything, but there are infinite shades of gray in between.

How do you pick a point on that continuum? Table 1.1 shows the permission-checking methods of the `SecurityManager` class and briefly describes the function each one has when a security manager is installed.

Note that this mechanism can do anything that you can describe in Java. If you want to give your program permission to write files with names beginning with "Q," but only in months whose names include the letter "r," you can do that by writing a version of the `checkWrite()` method such as

```
public void checkWrite(String filename)
  { int thismonth = (Calendar.getInstance()).get(Calendar.MONTH);
    if (!(filename.startsWith("Q")
          & (thismonth < 4 | thismonth > 7)))
      throw new SecurityException("File write denied");
  }
```

By designing and instantiating a suitable subclass of the default (everything forbidden) SecurityManager class, a Java environment gains extraordinary control over what a running piece of code can do.

> **NOTE:** *It is, quite literally, impossible to add this kind of security to a component model such as Microsoft's ActiveX, since ActiveX code is native code that has direct access to the operating system (and in some cases even to hardware).*

At the same time, it would be wrong to conclude this opening chapter without pointing out that bugs or oversights in an implementation of Java may leave broken links in this chain of security mechanisms. Java *can* be made secure, which is more than one can say for ActiveX, but verifying the security of any given Java implementation is a job for experts.

TABLE 1.1   Permission-Checking Methods of the `SecurityManager` Class

SecurityManager Method Name	Function
`checkAccept()`	The arguments to this method are a host name and a remote port number. The method throws an exception if it has not been coded to permit acceptance of a socket connection from that combination of host and port.
`checkAccess()`	The argument to this method call may be a thread or a thread group. The method throws an exception if the current execution context is not authorized to stop, rename, change priority, or perform other operations on the specified thread(s).
`checkAwtEventQueueAccess()`	Tests if a client can get access to the AWT event queue.
`checkConnect()`	Determines if the current execution context is allowed to establish a socket connection.
`checkCreateClassLoader()`	Throws an exception if the current execution context is not authorized to create a new class loader (an act with major security implications, since it might allow replacement of critical system classes with malicious substitutes).
`checkDelete()`	Determines if a named file may be deleted.
`checkExec()`	Determines if a named local program may be executed.
`checkExit()`	Determines if the Virtual Machine may be exited with a specified status code.
`checkLink()`	Determines if a named library may be loaded and linked, with security implications like those of creating a new class loader.
`checkListen()`	Determines if a local port may be bound for monitoring.
`checkMemberAccess()`	Tests if a client is allowed to access members.
`checkMulticast()`	Tests if the current execution context is allowed to use (join/leave/send/receive) IP multicast.
`checkPackageAccess()`	Determines if classes in a named package may be used by the current execution context.
`checkPackageDefinition()`	Throws an exception if the current execution context is not allowed to add classes to a named package.
`CheckPrintJobAccess()`	Tests if a client can initiate a print job request.
`checkPropertiesAccess()`	Determines if system properties may be read and updated.
`checkPropertyAccess()`	Determines if a particular property may be accessed, and optionally if a particular default value may be returned if that property is not defined.
`checkRead()`	Determines if a file (or another object attached to a file descriptor) may be read.
`checkSecurityAccess()`	Tests access to certain operations for a security API action.
`checkSetFactory()`	Determines if a "factory" for network-related objects may be created.
`CheckSystemClipboardAccess()`	Tests if a client can get access to the system clipboard.
`checkTopLevelWindow()`	Determines if a top-level window may be created, optionally with a warning banner since a window like this can mimic a security mechanism such as a login password prompt.
`checkWrite()`	Determines if a named file may be written.

1

Summary

We began this chapter by exploring the need for software components to enhance programming productivity, and hence to reduce the cost and boost the quality of end-user software solutions. Like writers of human-readable works, writers of code will work more efficiently when the end-user's machine can be expected to look things up in a dictionary of predefined units that perform common functions, instead of requiring every application to define every little thing that it wants to do in excruciating, redundant, error-prone detail.

As developers contemplate the notion of using components built by others, they're wise to consider the risks. Code may have accidental defects or malicious behaviors, and it's desirable for a component model to be based on a programming technology that makes accidents less likely while blocking common modes of attack. The Java language and the Java Virtual Machine combine to deliver both of these desirable features.

Additionally, the Java .class file format is portable to any implementation of the Java Virtual Machine, meaning that JavaBeans components maximize the economic benefits of reusability.

JavaBeans components aren't just a new layer on top of the 1.0 version of Java. Some of the core facilities of the language have been dramatically enhanced to let components ask each other questions, or to let a JavaBeans development tool inspect a component even if its developer did not provide elaborate tools for its convenient customization. JavaBeans tools can even integrate the JavaBeans model with other component models such as ActiveX.

Components are needed, and Java makes their benefits easier to obtain. That combination is the essence of JavaBeans.

Chapter 2

An API Primer for JavaBeans Development

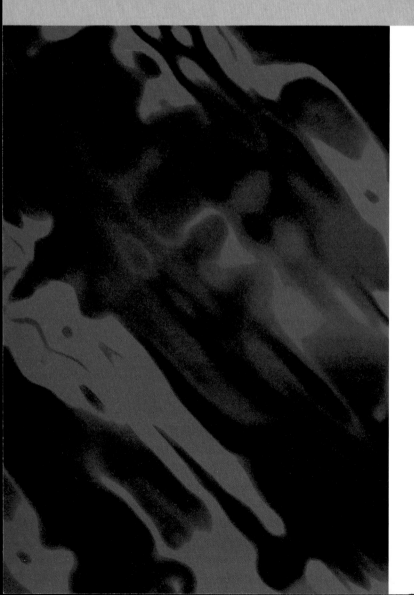

- ▶ **Picking a Place to Begin**

- ▶ **A Nice Reflection on You**

- ▶ **The JavaBeans APIs**

If you spend any time in technical pursuits, you eventually run into "Murphy's Laws." This is the list of wry remarks that's famous for the classic lament, "Anything that can go wrong, will go wrong." Less well known is Murphy's tenth law: "Before you can do anything, you have to do something else first." In the process of adding a robust component model to the Java platform, Java's designers must often have felt that Murphy's tenth law was written with them in mind. As we'll see in this chapter, many prerequisites for a good component model needed to be fitted into the foundations of the language, rather than being added as part of the remodeling work upstairs.

In this chapter, we'll look at the Application Programming Interface (API) that defines the possibilities of JavaBeans components. Before we can do that, though, we—like Java's designers—will develop the foundations that we'll need for our components to work together in flexible, dynamic arrangements. This is much more useful than the fragile house of cards that can easily emerge from a less thorough approach to modular software construction.

In this chapter, the main topics will be

▶   Components versus modules: The Core Reflection APIs

▶   Information and customization: The JavaBeans APIs

The Core Reflection APIs let JavaBeans components inspect each other and their surroundings, so that off-the-shelf components can be designed to handle a wide range of situations. The JavaBeans APIs let a component creator offer application developers the best of both worlds: components that are rich in design-time aids, without being burdened by unacceptable runtime overheads.

Picking a Place to Begin

This chapter will lay a foundation for the tightly focused discussions in the chapters that follow: It will explore the collection of capabilities that combine to create the JavaBeans environment, emphasizing the interactions and the mutual dependencies between the new API enhancements that all work together within the Java Virtual Machine.

It will seem as if everything depends on everything else, but we have to choose a starting point. We'll make that choice based on what we said in Chapter 1, where we argued that a component architecture is pointless if the components only fit together in one useful way. Such a result would be like a jigsaw puzzle: It would be modular, aiding program maintenance, but it wouldn't promote reusability. It's reusability that's essential to spreading the initial costs of development across the largest possible number of projects, and that's why we're going to the trouble of developing a component architecture in the first place.

2

The creator of a JavaBeans component will know, of course, what the component can do and how to use its capabilities, but that's not the real point. What's essential (remember the JavaBeans specification) is that a JavaBeans component be something that's easily reusable, based on convenient manipulation in a visual tool. Browsing the source code of a component may appeal to some developers, and, in general, reading code written by other developers is an excellent and underused practice, but a JavaBeans tool like Borland's JBuilder or Sybase's PowerJ has to offer the developer a higher-level view as well: a view that it can construct merely by interrogating the component's .class file.

Remember, commercial components have to be usable without distribution of their precious source code! A developer should not need to read a JavaBeans component's code to figure out what it does; neither should a JavaBeans-based tool require source-code access to make a component's facilities and interactions easily accessible. Some components, as we discussed in Chapter 1, may be accessorized with elaborate design-time tools, taking advantage of proprietary knowledge to accelerate the process of tailoring a component to a particular task. Well and good, but any conforming component must disclose its essential nature in a way that's available from the compiled .class file alone. Building the needed information directly into the .class file lets any JavaBeans development tool offer its own distinctive approach to making a component's services available for new uses.

If you're a client/server or database maven, you may be able to guess what's coming. In relational database design, one of the cardinal rules is that all of the information that describes a database must itself be accessible in the same form as the contents of the database. If you're thinking in terms of tables, for example, it must be possible to make database-style queries (as if querying a table of your tables) so that an application program can learn about the structure of the database, as well as learning about the content of the records within. Java's designers recognized the need for a self-referential approach as they moved toward the 1.1 version of their language, which supports (among other things) the JavaBeans component model. The result was the addition of the Core Reflection APIs. The word "reflection" isn't used here in the sense of something bouncing off something else like a reflection from a mirror, but in the more abstract sense of "reflect" that Webster's New Collegiate Dictionary defines as "to make manifest or apparent: SHOW <the pulse ~s the condition of the heart>." In the same way, the Core Reflection APIs give the Java developer or the JavaBeans toolmaker indirect but effective ways of determining what's inside an object. Core Reflection is not, properly speaking, a JavaBeans API, but it's something that we need before we can build a component technology that's transparent; that is, a technology that can serve the component-assembling developer who *doesn't* want to read other people's code.

The Core Reflection APIs might be said to complete the job that Java's designers promised to do when they said, in the original Java documents, that they would deliver "a general-purpose concurrent class-based object-oriented programming language." There weren't many lapses from idealized object-oriented design in Java 1.0, but they turned out to be notable flaws when the language designers sought to make the leap to JavaBeans. In addition to its major innovations, therefore, Java 1.1 fills in those gaps.

A Nice Reflection on You

If we're going to investigate a JavaBeans component, and perhaps even manipulate that component through behind-the-scenes operations of a complex visual tool, we need to have object-oriented handles on things that developers used to figure out by reading code. We especially need to get answers to the fundamental questions, "What does this component know? What can this kind of component do? How do I make more of them?"

To answer questions about a component's contents and capabilities, without jumping out of Java's object-oriented discipline, we need classes that will correspond to the data fields of a component object; to the methods of a component's class of objects; and to the constructors of a component's class. The following sections describe the major classes of the Core Reflection APIs.

The Field Class

With the fully qualified name of `java.lang.reflect.Field`, the `Field` class is declared as public and final, extending `Object` and implementing `Member`. As a public class, it can be accessed from other packages as well as from its own. As a final class, it cannot be subclassed and its methods cannot be overridden. A `Field` is a `Field` is a `Field`.

The `Field` class has no superclass other than the generic root class `Object`, which means that `Field` inherits only a minimal set of methods for operations like comparing values and synchronizing threads. Since `Field` implements `Member`, however, any other object can know that any `Field` will define certain variables and methods—even though `Field` does not inherit those things from its parent class `Object`.

To support the `Member` interface, `Field` must have the public static final variables DECLARED and PUBLIC, whose values are (respectively) the set of declared members and the set of public members of that class.

> **TIP:** *Note that PUBLIC is not simply the public subset of DECLARED, because PUBLIC includes inherited members that have public access while DECLARED excludes inherited members of any kind.*
>
> *To determine if an entity has a non-public field that it inherited from a superclass (not that this is really useful knowledge), code can climb the inheritance tree and inspect each superclass in turn.*

For Members Only

The Member interface also requires Field to respond to several methods that we'll be glad to have when a JavaBeans component needs to get its bearings, so to speak (see Figure 2.1). A component will use these methods when it needs to determine the situation in which it is being asked to contribute useful work.

The Member interface requires implementation of three methods. The first, getDeclaringClass(), returns a Class object corresponding to the class that declared the entity (or declared the constructor of the entity) on which the method is invoked. Returning a Class object enables quite general manipulations of the results, using other Core Reflection APIs. It will often be sufficient, though, merely to know the name of the class that declared the entity at hand: for this purpose, Member includes the method getName() to return that name as a String.

A more complex method is getModifiers(), which returns an integer value that might seem unnecessarily cryptic. This is an example, however, of Java's designers leaving room for the technology to evolve. The integer value returned by getModifiers() encodes information on whether the corresponding Field has one or more of the attributes listed below. (We render these names in capitals because we're following the usual Java convention for final static variables.) Each of these attributes has a value that is encoded in this way.

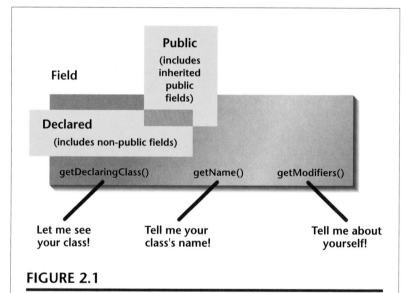

FIGURE 2.1

The variables and methods required by the Member interface guarantee that we'll get answers to the questions we'll ask of an instance of the Core Reflection class Field.

- ► ABSTRACT

- ► FINAL

- ► INTERFACE

- ► NATIVE

- ► PRIVATE

- ► PROTECTED

- ► PUBLIC

- ► STATIC

- ► SYNCHRONIZED

- ► TRANSIENT

- ► VOLATILE

The codes defined for the access modifier attributes are public final static integer fields of the class `java.lang.reflect.Modifier`. The only role of this class is to serve as a clearinghouse for identifying the characteristics of fields. Being public, the modifier code names are accessible everywhere; being final, they can't be changed; being static, they can be used outside any instance of their owning class. They are Java's version of the global constant, enabling safe and convenient use of symbolic names without the overhead of handling a complex data type such as a character string.

Rather than working directly with the integer code values, therefore, readable Java programs will use these named constants (in the same way that graphical programs use named constants such as BOLD for a font style). To decode the values, the `Modifier` class provides the corresponding set of methods `isAbstract()`, `isFinal()`, and so on through `isVolatile()`. This mechanism can be modified and extended in the future without breaking code that has followed good style by using names and method calls rather than numeric values and low-level equality tests.

Like any well-written class, `Modifier` provides an appropriate implementation of `toString()` that returns a description of the modifiers of the field. The modifier keywords are returned in the order defined by §19.7 of *The Java Language Specification*; for example, `public final synchronized` or `private transient volatile`.

TIP: *Overriding the inherited version of* `toString()` *with a class-appropriate implementation is a basic part of the etiquette of writing reusable classes in Java. An informative string representation of any instance of a class serves as a*

2

convenient—if crude—debugging tool, and gives new Java developers valuable insight into the language's mechanics.

Like `Modifier`, the `Field` class has its own tailored version of `toString()`, returning the modifiers followed by the fully qualified name of the declaring class and then the field name; for example, `public static final int java.lang.Thread.MIN_PRIORITY`.

As with `toString()`, it's good Java practice to override the method `equals()`—more formally, `public boolean equals(Object obj)`—so that it does something semantically useful in the context of a given class. For example, two `Field` objects will be identified as "equal" in the sense of this method if they refer to underlying fields with the same name that have the same declaring class.

Is This Field Secure?

Only the Java Virtual Machine is permitted to create `Field` objects. This security measure protects the integrity of Java's field-access privilege modifiers. A Java program acquires a reference to an instance of the `Field` class by well-defined access methods, according to the discipline of an object-oriented environment.

As with other access privileges in Java, a check method of a subclass of `SecurityManager` can veto any request for information about the internals of an application—that is, if a `SecurityManager` has been installed by the runtime environment. Specifically, the new method `public void checkMemberAccess(Class clazz, int which)` takes a class object and an integer value (either of the static values Member.PUBLIC or Member.DECLARED) as its arguments: if access to the specified subset of the fields of that class is allowed, the check method does nothing; otherwise it throws a SecurityException.

After `checkMemberAccess()` has given its blessing, the Java Virtual Machine will still perform its normal checks for protected or private status (or the default, package-level access) when a member is accessed in any way—including, for example, being accessed through a method of class `Field`. Why have two levels of checking? Because the designers of Java are trying to open a fast lane for more efficient execution of "trusted" code (such as code whose source has been verified through cryptographic signing). The Core Reflection APIs contemplate the possibility that trusted code would be allowed to bypass the second level of checking that we just described.

Finally: the Field

It seems as if every time we try to talk about the reason for having a `Field` class, we wind up talking about foundation layers that had to be merged into Java 1.0.x to make a Java 1.1 that could support this new class in a robust way. We warned you that it would seem as if there could be no logical starting point, because the dependencies among JavaBeans facilities within the Java environment all go in so many directions. But we're finally ready to address the `Field` class's reasons for being.

`Field` objects will normally be available to Java programs through methods of the class `java.lang.Class`. Like instances of `Field`, instances of `Class` are created by the Java Virtual Machine as .class files are loaded under the supervision of an instance of `ClassLoader`.

When a `Class` object is at hand, we can invoke the method `getFields()` to obtain an array of `Field` objects. This array will contain objects for all of the public fields of the class or interface to whose `Class` object we applied the `getFields()` call. It will include both the public fields declared by the target class or interface, and the public fields that the target inherits from its superclasses or superinterfaces.

The `getFields()` method returns an array of length zero if the target `Class` object represents a primitive type or an array. It's handy to have this method of detecting that a target entity is an instance of a primitive type, but to use that approach we'll need to have `Class` objects for every entity. That includes the instances of the primitive types that had no wrapper class defined in Java 1.0.x.

Java 1.1 therefore adds wrapper classes for the `byte`, `short`, and `void` types. As long as this is being done at all, it might as well be done right: the new wrapper classes, like the established wrapper classes for `int` and the other primitive types, provide reference information such as maximum and minimum numeric values supported by the corresponding primitives. This information is stored in static variables such as Byte.MAX_VALUE.

TIP: *Java arrays have always been objects, with every array belonging to a class that comes into being automatically and that represents all arrays with the same element type and number of dimensions. An array class has an instance variable representing the length of the array, which is a great convenience in operations such as looping over the elements of an array.*

But in the context of `getFields()`*, the length of an array is not considered a field, and an array object does not return an instance of* `Field` *that represents its length attribute.*

The methods `getDeclaredFields()` and `getDeclaredField()` are analogous to `getFields()` and `getField()`, but, on the one hand, the "Declared" methods ignore inherited fields; on the other hand, they include non-public fields.

The "Declared" field reflectors cannot be used to obtain otherwise forbidden access to a private field. Their broader scope only means that they will return a `Field` object corresponding to such a field, where applicable, if they are not

2

getFields() Gets Personal!

As noted above, the getFields() method throws a SecurityException if access to sensitive information is not authorized. Like other SecurityManager behaviors, this one defaults to denial.

If you have defined a subclass of SecurityManager for a custom runtime environment that you've been using since before the advent of core reflection, be prepared to go back and do some additional overriding of inherited methods to enable the use of reflective method calls; otherwise you'll inherit the default implementations of the checking methods and you won't be able to ask these probing questions.

Note also that a program may use a character string that contains the name of a field as an argument to getField(), getting in return a single Field object representing a public field (either declared or inherited) of the target class. This can, however, lead to an ambiguous situation, since this use of getField() calls for a simple field name and a class can inherit more than one field with the same simple name (from any combination of its superclass and/or one or more interfaces). In such a case, any reference to that simple field name will produce a compile-time error, even in a case where both interpretations can be guaranteed to yield the same value (for example, when both of the inherited fields are final and of of identical type and value).

Working with an array of Field objects returned by getFields(), rather than taking a shortcut through the simple field name alone, will avoid the ambiguity of same-named fields, and will result in more robust code.

prevented from doing so by the SecurityManager checkMemberAccess() method described above.

After a getDeclaredField() call gets its hands on an object that represents a private field, the usual access controls will then get their chance to determine if a program is allowed to do anything useful with that Field object—unless those controls are bypassed by something like the prospective "trusted code" facility.

Getting and Setting Field Values

With an instance of Field finally at hand, a program will usually wish to determine or change the value that's held by that field. We'll want to use simple verbs, like "get" and "set," to invoke such operations in several different contexts: We get the freedom to do this from *polymorphism*, as it's termed in the world of object-oriented programming. Java, like other object-oriented languages, will let us use the same name for different behaviors that all give the same result even though different low-level operations are required.

The universal methods get() and set() are formally defined as follows:

```
public Object get(Object obj)
throws NullPointerException, IllegalArgumentException,
IllegalAccessException
```

and

```
public void set(Object obj, Object value)
throws NullPointerException, IllegalArgumentException,
IllegalAccessException
```

The performance and reliability of your Java code may depend on your understanding the behavior of these important methods.

The get() method is the simpler of the two. As shown in its declaration, get() returns an Object (with a capital O); that is, an instance of some subclass of the root of the Java class hierarchy.

It would be wrong for get() to return a primitive type, so get() automatically packages any primitive type that it finds in a target field within an instance of that type's corresponding wrapper class. But there may be situations in which this is a waste of time.

To avoid the overhead of wrapping a primitive value in an object, only to unwrap the result when it's delivered in another time-consuming operation, every primitive Java type has a corresponding type-specific variation of get(). These variations range from getBoolean() through getLong() and getDouble(), with other versions for all the intermediate primitive types in between.

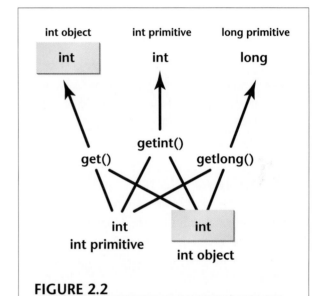

FIGURE 2.2

The get() method makes it irrelevant whether a retrieved value is stored as primitive data type or as an instance of a wrapper class, and where allowed converts as needed.

The type-specific get*X*() methods will automatically perform allowable type-widening conversions, if necessary, to return the value of the field in the specified primitive form, without a wrapper class. That is, a getInt() will return a primitive int even if the target of the call was a field that contained a byte or a short primitive value (see Figure 2.2).

If you're really thinking in Java, you'll wonder what you have to provide as the Object-type argument to get() if the field in question is a static field—that is, one owned by a class rather than by an instance of the class. The answer is that it doesn't matter. If get() is invoked on an instance of Field that encapsulates a static field of the Field's declaring class, the result will be that static field's value—whether or not an instance of that class is supplied as an argument. The Object argument can even be null.

If the Field does not refer to a static field, then get() does expect an Object argument that is an instance of the Field's declaring class. An instance of another

2

class will result in an IllegalArgumentException; a `null` argument will result in a NullPointerException; a valid argument with a field that is not normally accessible will result in an IllegalAccessException.

The converse method, `set()`, has the same semantics as `get()`, but transforms its arguments in the opposite ways. It will, if necessary, unwrap the supplied object to produce a primitive type, if that's what's expected by the target field; it will, if necessary and allowable, perform a widening conversion in the event of a primitive type mismatch.

In the same way that `get()` has type-specific variants that return a primitive type rather than its wrapped equivalent, `set()` has type-specific variants that accept a primitive argument instead of an `Object` argument as the value to be stored in the target field. Like `get()`, `set()` ignores the target `Object` argument if the `Field` in question is static.

The Method Class

We've reached a point now where we can really pick up speed. This is because many of the things that we've had to explain in the course of exploring the `Field` class also apply to the new Core Reflection classes `Method` and `Constructor`. For example, both of these classes implement the interface `Member`, and we've already explained what that requires.

The nature of reflection is most obvious when we start talking about things like "the methods of `Method`." One has the sense of seeing an infinite series of images, like the images of an object placed between two parallel mirrors. Using Java's facilities to investigate themselves is powerful and addictive; a non-reflective language seems extremely limiting by comparison.

Investigating a Method

The first three distinctive methods of `Method` are `getReturnType()`, `getParameterTypes()`, and `getExceptionTypes()`. These let us write code that can interrogate other classes in the system and can decide, or even negotiate, matters such as which class will handle a particular kind of exception. When components can interact with each other at runtime to investigate each other's abilities, that opens up liberating options for writing systems that deal in sensible ways with circumstances that could not be envisioned at the time that a program was written.

The `getReturnType()` method returns a `Class` object; `getParameterTypes()` returns an array of `Class` objects, one for each parameter (in declaration order), which may be an array of length zero; `getExceptionTypes()` also returns an array of `Class` objects, possibly of length zero.

For a given declaring class, we can use names and parameter types to determine if two different instances of Method are actually referring to the same thing. This intuitive notion of equality is captured in the Method class's version of equals().

Invoking a Method

In the same way that fields exist for storage and retrieval of values, methods exist so that we can invoke them. It's therefore no surprise that the Method class provides a method called invoke() that gives us the same kind of polymorphic convenience as the get() and set() methods of Field.

```
public Object invoke(Object obj, Object[] args)
throws NullPointerException, IllegalArgumentException,
IllegalAccessException, InvocationTargetException
```

The invoke() method sends the message of the represented method to the specified object, supplying that method call with the supplied parameters. In a continuing spirit of transparent conversion between objects and primitive values, this method will unwrap parameter objects for any case where the underlying method expects primitive arguments, making widening conversions as needed and permitted; returned primitive values, if any, are wrapped into matching objects.

If you were paying attention during the discussion of get() and set(), you don't need to be told how invoke() handles static methods. In these cases, invoke() simply ignores the supplied Object argument, which may be null.

Importantly, the throwing of exceptions by an invoked method also gets a new layer of object abstraction. Any exception thrown by an invoked method is caught and captured in an instance of a new class, InvocationTargetException. In the spirit of Java's established exception-handling model, this leaves the invoking code free to inspect, handle, and/or re-throw the result.

TIP: *If you're familiar with the conventions of Unix and other hierarchical environments, you may wonder if invoking a method is like invoking a program with an absolute path, instead of letting the normal process decide which of several identically named programs will be executed. That's not the case. Whether a method is called in the usual way, or through the new* invoke() *method of* Method, *the usual Java dynamic lookup process decides which version of the method by that name will actually be used.*

2

The Constructor Class

It might seem as if `Constructor` should be a subclass of `Method`, since a constructor is a special case of a method that returns an instance of the method's declaring class. But that's not the way `Constructor` has been defined. Like `Method`, `Constructor` extends `Object` and implements `Member`.

The fact that it implements the `Member` interface means that `Constructor` has several of the characteristics that we've already discussed. `Constructor` differs from `Method` in that it does not implement the method `getReturnType()`, logically enough since the return type of a constructor is by definition the type of the declaring class.

The distinctive method of class `Constructor` is `newInstance()`, or formally:

```
public Object newInstance(Object[] initargs)
throws InstantiationException, IllegalArgumentException,
IllegalAccessException, InvocationTargetException
```

In the same polymorphic spirit as `get()`, `set()`, and `invoke()`, `newInstance()` handles wrapping and widening transparently where required and allowed.

There are some special issues to address with a constructor, such as an attempt to create an instance of an abstract class, which throws an InstantiationException. Other possible errors, such as trying to use a constructor that's blocked by normal Java access controls, throw corresponding exceptions: IllegalAccessException for the case just described, IllegalArgumentException if the numbers or types of supplied arguments are incorrect, InvocationTargetException if the underlying constructor throws an exception (as described for class `Method` above).

On a good day, `newInstance()` just returns an initialized instance of the constructor method's declaring class.

The Array Class

For the sake of completeness, we'll conclude our overview of the Core Reflection APIs with the `Array` class. The most important thing to realize about `Array` is that this class doesn't have any constructors: You don't create instances of class `Array`.

Rather, `Array` is a repository of static methods that let you create and operate on arrays with the same polymorphic convenience that you enjoy with other types of object. For example, the expression

```
newInstance(componentType, length)
```

has the same effect as

```
new componentType[length]
```

in that both return an instance of an array of the specified type of component and with the specified size. Supplying an array of integers as the length argument, instead of a single integer, will return an array of arrays with corresponding dimensions.

Other methods defined on `Array` get and set element values, with both wrapped and unwrapped treatment of primitive types—in the manner that we have seen above for other Core Reflection classes.

The JavaBeans APIs

With the Core Reflection APIs as a vital foundation, JavaBeans components can avoid the perils of jigsaw-puzzle modularity to become true inventories of reusable, adaptable, reliable code.

TIP: *JavaBeans are not inherently adaptable and reusable, in the way that browser-based Java applets are inherently safe. The potential, however, is there.*

To the extent that developers apply these capabilities correctly and effectively, a thriving marketplace in JavaBeans components can transform the business model and the end-user experiences of developing, selling, buying, and using software.

The rest of this chapter summarizes the JavaBeans APIs and makes some observations on why they matter to developers and users of JavaBeans components. Subsequent chapters will furnish more detailed explanations and many examples.

JavaBeans API Interfaces

The API interfaces give developers the tools they need to find out about a Bean and to invoke various types of tools that can tailor a Bean to a particular use. Beans can respond to changes in their environment through Java's notification mechanisms, without the design-time and runtime effort of writing crude polling loops. JavaBeans also looks ahead to the use of Java in a broad range of information appliances, which won't necessarily look anything like today's personal computers: For example, a Bean can be told that graphical interface facilities are not available in a given execution environment.

BeanInfo

Developers can let other components rely on the Core Reflection APIs to get the information that's needed to integrate a Bean into a larger system. They also have the option of providing a class that implements the interface `BeanInfo`.

The `BeanInfo` class can be named by adding "BeanInfo" to the fully qualified name of the class of the JavaBean, implying that the information class resides in the same directory as the Bean's .class file. It may be more convenient to place information classes in a particular set of directories, with a runtime environment providing a search path for these classes; in the latter case, all you'll need is the final class name component suffixed with "BeanInfo."

For example, if the class `YourBean` has the fully qualified name `host.yourPackage.YourBean`, its information class could be `host.yourPackage.YourBeanBeanInfo`. If a search path for information classes is defined to include the default path `host.beans.infos`, the information class could alternatively be `host.beans.infos.YourBeanBeanInfo`.

`BeanInfo` classes are examined by the JavaBeans API class `Introspector`. If a `BeanInfo` class is found, it's assumed to provide all of the information that the Bean developer meant to supply. Otherwise, an `Introspector` will use the Reflection APIs to analyze the target class directly, then continue its search for an explicit `BeanInfo` by moving up the chain of the Bean's superclasses. An `Introspector`'s search will continue until the `Introspector` either finds explicit information or reaches the top of the inheritance tree (see Figure 2.3).

`BeanInfo` classes can furnish icons for use in visual displays. They can use the method `getAdditionalBeanInfo()` to offer an arbitrary collection of other `BeanInfo` objects to a curious `Introspector`, without being constrained by naming conventions. And they can ease interactions with visual development tools by using `getDefaultEventIndex()` and `getDefaultPropertyIndex()` to provide shortcuts to the aspects of a component that are most often manipulated by development tools. Common examples might be the label on a button or the initial content of a text field.

Customizer

The `Customizer` interface is a very simple entry point to a potentially very complex piece of a JavaBeans component suite. It returns an instance of `java.AWT.Component` that can be instantiated within a graphical user interface. A `Component` can cover such a wide range of complexity that a developer can offer any desired degree of GUI-based support for customizing the facilities of a Bean.

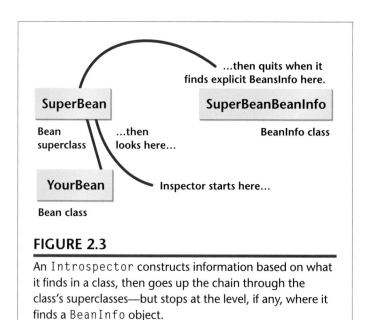

FIGURE 2.3

An `Introspector` constructs information based on what it finds in a class, then goes up the chain through the class's superclasses—but stops at the level, if any, where it finds a `BeanInfo` object.

PropertyChangeListener

Implementing the interface `PropertyChangeListener` requires supporting the method `propertyChange()`, letting an application register a listener object that will be notified of changes to properties of special interest. This avoids the inefficiency of repeatedly checking a value, for example, as part of a main event loop, by making the Java environment responsible for taking action on the specified `PropertyChange` event.

PropertyEditor

The `PropertyEditor` interface lets a component offer appropriate styles of user interface for editing the properties of that component, case by case, ranging from simple getting and setting of text to elaborate graphical presentations. The specification requires, logically enough, that any instance of `PropertyEditor` respond to calls on `setValue()` when that method is invoked on the corresponding type of property-representing object. If there is no custom editor supplied, it must support `setAsText()`.

This is consistent with the design philosophy that we described in Chapter 1: that any Bean, no matter how minimal its implementation, must be compatible with manipulation through visual tools—even if those tools can do no more with a minimal component than compose and display a table-type property sheet for inspection and editing of values.

VetoableChangeListener

Like `PropertyChangeListener`, the interface `VetoableChangeListener` offers a streamlined mechanism for notifying different parts of a system of particular changes elsewhere. As the name implies, however, `VetoableChangeListeners` can respond (by throwing a PropertyVetoException) if a change is in some way unacceptable and should be rolled back.

Visibility

The specification describes the `Visibility` interface as being meant for expert developers. It uses somewhat whimsical method names, rather than the more conventional "get" and "set" nomenclature, to emphasize that these methods will not normally be used by Beans that do their work in a typical graphical presentation environment.

The method `needsGui()` returns a Boolean `true` if the component simply has to have a GUI to do its job. A calling application might choose a less functional component if the alternative is one that won't work at all in a limited user interface context.

The method `avoidingGui()` returns a Boolean `true` if the component is currently in a non-GUI state. The most likely cause of an `avoidingGui()` "true" would be a component's having previously received a call to its method dontUseGui(). This state can be reversed by a call to the method okToUseGui().

JavaBeans API Classes

The API classes give the component-using developer a predefined collection of data structures and associated methods for creating, describing, and controlling components at both design time and runtime. Some of these API classes simplify development of basic components, while others are quite open-ended in the options that they offer to developers seeking competitive differentiation in the packaged component marketplace.

BeanDescriptor

An instance of BeanDescriptor is one of the types of information class returned by a BeanInfo object. The BeanDescriptor class's methods, getBeanClass() and getCustomizerClass(), return Class objects for (respectively) the class of the JavaBeans component and the class of its Customizer (discussed above under the interface of that name).

Beans

The simple name Beans identifies one of the core classes for providing methods to control and use JavaBeans components. The fundamental method of Beans is instantiate(), which in JavaBeans 1.0 first tries to create the component from a serialized object resource. If this fails, the method will then try to load the component from a conventional class.

> **TIP:** *Beans that are instances of* java.applet.Applet *are automatically given the necessary AppletStub and AppletContext, but there are subtleties in the initialization and startup requirements for applets that run in a browser versus those that are instantiated Beans. Examples later in the book will illustrate these points.*

For toolmakers, the method isDesignTime() will be important in determining whether a component should exhibit runtime or design-time behavior. Other methods of class Beans are less likely to arise in current projects; the methods isGuiAvailable() and setGuiAvailable(), for example, determine whether the executing code will assume that graphical user interface facilities can be used. The result of a call to isGuiAvailable() might determine, for example, whether a component pops up a dialog box for user interaction, as opposed to using some other mode of input/output (see Figure 2.4).

The methods getInstanceOf() and isInstanceOf(), which determine whether a JavaBeans component can furnish a particular view of some other object that can be manipulated in a particular way, are provided to support future evolution of the JavaBeans technology.

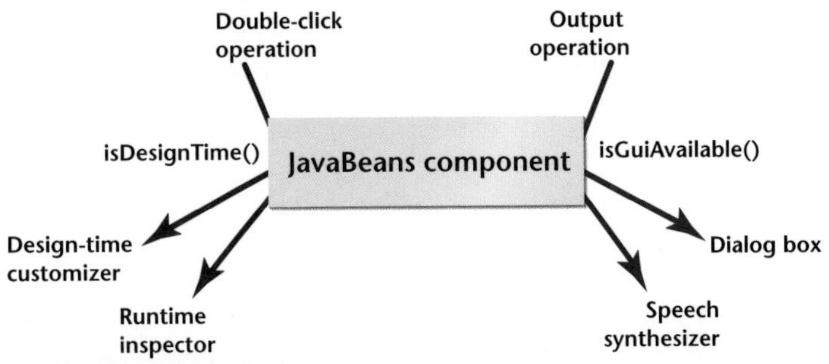

FIGURE 2.4

Runtime methods let a component tailor its behavior to its current situation.

EventSetDescriptor

An elaborate class called EventSetDescriptor provides the methods needed for determining the events that a given component may fire, and for finding out what listener methods may be invoked in response to those events.

FeatureDescriptor

One of the greatest strengths of JavaBeans is the fact that Beans can ask so many questions about each other, with the answers wrapped in classes such as BeanDescriptor, EventSetDescriptor, MethodDescriptor, ParameterDescriptor, and PropertyDescriptor, and the PropertyDescriptor subclass IndexedPropertyDescriptor. These classes have much in common, and the FeatureDescriptor class puts all those common traits in one place.

FeatureDescriptor provides a number of conveniences for this family of classes. The attributeNames() method returns an enumeration of the locale-independent names that are accessible through setValue() and getValue(). Informative displays for component-assembling developers and component-based applications' users are supported by set/getDisplayName() and set/getShortDescription(), which let a component offer localized information.

The methods setHidden()/isHidden() control indications that a feature is not meant for use by anything but the internal mechanisms of a tool, while setExpert()/isExpert() provide standard methods for differentiating between features that should be accessible to all users and features that should be, in some way, limited to more advanced users.

IndexedPropertyDescriptor

Some properties provide numerically indexed access, in the manner of an array. The `IndexedPropertyDescriptor` subclass of `PropertyDescriptor` handles these situations.

Introspector

The primary functions of the methods of the class `Introspector` were described above in connection with the `BeanInfo` interface. Variations on the `getBeanInfo()` method allow a developer to control the height to which the process of searching for information may climb along the inheritance tree, and to determine and/or control the path that will be followed as an `Introspector` searches for component information (see Figure 2.5).

MethodDescriptor and ParameterDescriptor

It's hard to whip up real enthusiasm for describing these classes. They encapsulate descriptive information about methods and the parameters to those methods, and they're chiefly of interest to developers who want to provide a richer class of information than what's inherently available through the basic Core Reflection APIs.

FIGURE 2.5

An `Introspector` seeks out a `BeanInfo` object and uses its contents to display appropriate tools during the design phase of application development.

PropertyChangeEvent, PropertyChangeSupport, and VetoableChangeSupport

The first of these classes was mentioned above in the context of the interface `PropertyChangeListener`. The latter two are more interesting.

`PropertyChangeSupport` and `VetoableChangeSupport` are utility classes that can be used in either of two ways: by inheriting from the class or by including an instance as a member field of some other class. The methods of `PropertyChangeSupport` are `addPropertyChangeListener()`, which adds a

PropertyChangeListener to the listener list; removePropertyChangeListener( ), which has the opposite effect; and firePropertyChange( ), which reports an update to the registered listeners. VetoableChangeSupport has similarly named methods with corresponding functions.

PropertyDescriptor

After the last few rather insipid classes, we finally come to something with a little zest. The class PropertyDescriptor has to answer some important questions to let a JavaBeans development tool meet the Java team's goals for intuitive operation.

The methods getPropertyEditorClass( ), getPropertyType( ), getReadMethod( ), and getWriteMethod( ) let other code determine the nature of a component's property and let the component say how it would like to have those properties changed. The methods isBound( ) and isConstrained( ) return Boolean values that indicate whether a change to a property will fire a PropertyChange event (for bound properties) or a VetoableChange event (for constrained properties). These characteristics are mutable through the methods setBound( ) and setConstrained( ).

PropertyEditorManager

Rather than wandering around asking individual properties how they want to be edited, it's more convenient to use the defined class PropertyEditorManager.

The PropertyEditorManager class has a registerEditor( ) method that lets the programmer register an editor for a given type. If this has not been done, PropertyEditorManager can fall back on a default-naming convention, looking for a class whose name is the fully qualified name of the target type with "Editor" appended—for example, host.yourPackage.YourBeanEditor. If this doesn't work, PropertyEditorManager can do the same thing that was done when searching for BeanInfo classes: It takes the simple class name, appends "Editor," and follows a designated search path to see if it can find a corresponding class.

The specification promises that a conforming implementation of JavaBeans 1.0 will have default property editors for the primitive types boolean, byte, short, int, long, float, and double, and for the API classes String, Color, and Font.

SimpleBeanInfo

Like the default SecurityManager that forbids everything, the minimal BeanInfo class, called SimpleBeanInfo, denies knowledge of everything. In effect, it also asserts that there is nothing that can be known: For example, it responds to a call on getAdditionalBeanInfo( ) with no other BeanInfo objects. It provides no information on class or customizer when queried with getBeanDescriptor( ). Likewise for default events, default properties, event sets, icons, methods, and properties.

As with the default `SecurityManager`, `SimpleBeanInfo` is not intended to be used without modification. Rather, the methods should be overridden as desired.

Summary

We've seen that JavaBeans components can be implemented in a minimal fashion, relying on the low-level facilities of the Core Reflection APIs to let other components or enclosing environments find out what they need to know. The classes `Field`, `Method`, and `Constructor` let objects inquire about each other's structure, content, and behavior in an object-oriented fashion and under the control of Java's security mechanisms. The designers have also introduced facilities that pave the way for high-performance execution of "trusted" code.

The JavaBeans APIs give component developers enormous freedom to enrich their work with graphical customization tools, with supplemental information classes, and with interactive conversations among a group of components where they can compare notes on each other's capabilities and requirements. API classes and methods let a Bean have different behaviors at design time and runtime, encouraging Bean creators to make Bean-based development convenient without creating unattractive runtime overheads. Beans can also be constrained at runtime to use appropriate user interface technologies, whether they're running on a mouse/window desktop or executing in some other kind of information appliance.

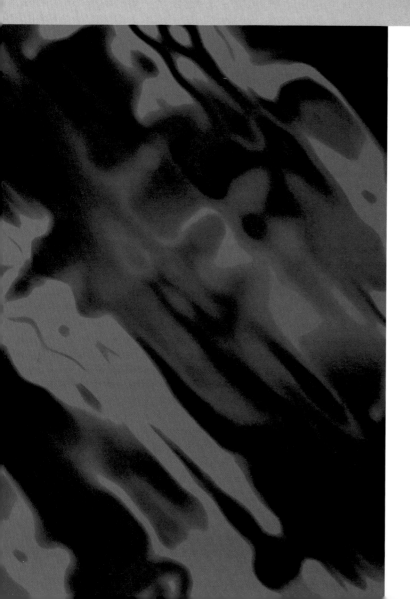

Chapter *3*

Beans in Action

- ▸ JavaBeans and Visual Tools

- ▸ JavaBeans the Old-Fashioned Way

Now that you understand most of the conceptual basics of JavaBeans, you're probably anxious to see the practical side of the technology. This chapter heads in a different direction from the first two by showing how JavaBeans components are used in practical development settings. More specifically, you'll see how Beans are used both in a visual development environment and in traditional Java code.

This chapter is geared toward showing you how Beans fit into the scheme of things at a practical level. However, it won't get into the specifics of how to build complete applications with Beans. Rather, the focus is on demonstrating how some of the conceptual aspects of JavaBeans translate to real-world scenarios. You won't leave this chapter with a thorough understanding of Java application development, but you will hopefully better appreciate the motivation behind, and importance of, the JavaBeans technology.

In this chapter, you'll learn

▶ How to use Beans in visual tools

▶ How to use Beans in straight Java code

▶ The three C's of Bean development: create, customize, and connect

JavaBeans and Visual Tools

Perhaps the most critical feature of the JavaBeans technology is its comprehensive support for visual application builder tools. In providing this support, JavaBeans not only defines the logical structure of Beans but also the way in which Beans are used. This creates a very interesting situation for Bean developers because it allows them to directly control how their Beans are integrated with, and manipulated through, development tools. The benefit for users is more intuitive design-time layout and editing capabilities.

Before you get to thinking JavaBeans is totally revolutionary, understand that the seamless integration of software components with development tools isn't anything new. However, most other software component technologies are complicated to work with on the development side, making it difficult for a wide range of developers to benefit from building their own components. JavaBeans ushers in a whole new era of component development by defining automatic support for development tools. It's possible for a Bean developer to build a normal Java class adhering to a minimal set of guidelines and have it automatically integrate intelligently with builder tools. Does that prospect sound exciting at all? If not, maybe you need to see an example of how JavaBeans and visual development tools are rapidly changing the face of Java.

Third-party development tool vendors are busily adding support for JavaBeans to their products. Unfortunately, precious few are available in any usable form as of this writing. One such tool is Powersoft's PowerJ (Figure 3.1), which as of this writing is available in beta form with a limited degree of JavaBeans support. The beta version of PowerJ supports the integration of JavaBeans components, but limits their usage and editing capabilities. Even so, it provides a good example of how visual Java development environments are using the JavaBeans technology.

The next few sections focus on PowerJ and how it supports JavaBeans. If you want to follow along, you can download an evaluation copy of PowerJ from Powersoft's Web site, which is located at `http://www.power-soft.com`. The beta version of PowerJ provides limited support for working with JavaBeans. It is fully expected that the final release will include more thorough support, but the beta version is sufficient for showing a glimpse of how JavaBeans will integrate into commercial third-party tools.

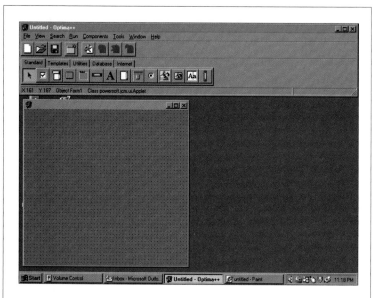

FIGURE 3.1

The Powersoft PowerJ visual Java development environment

Adding Beans to a Visual Tool

Perhaps the best place to start in regard to PowerJ's support for JavaBeans is the addition of Beans to the PowerJ environment. PowerJ provides a menu command for adding Beans which leads to a wizard-style interface for specifying the Bean to be added. Figure 3.2 shows this menu command, Add Java Component, being selected from the main PowerJ menu.

FIGURE 3.2

Adding a JavaBean to PowerJ using the Add Java Component menu item

NOTE: *PowerJ also supports the integration of ActiveX components. ActiveX is Microsoft's software component technology.*

After selecting the Add Java Component menu command, you are presented with a wizard-style interface for entering more information about the Bean to be added (Figure 3.3). From this interface, you can click the Browse button to find the Bean you want to add. When you click the Browse button you are presented with a file selection dialog box where you can browse to the Bean's class. For the purposes of this discussion, let's use a Bean developed later in the book: the Needle Gauge Bean. If you have already installed the CD-ROM for the book, you should be able to find the Bean in the Source\HTPJB\Chap12\NeedleGauge directory beneath the main installation directory (Figure 3.4).

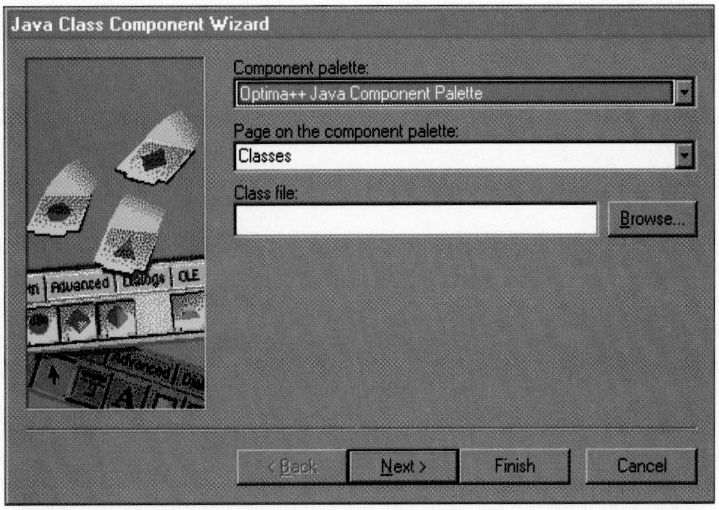

FIGURE 3.3

PowerJ's Java class component wizard

NOTE: *The Needle Gauge Bean is a graphical gauge with a needle that functions like the fuel gauge in an automobile. You'll learn how to build the Needle Gauge Bean from scratch in Chapter 12, "A Needle Gauge Bean."*

Once you've selected the Bean's class, you are presented with another page of the class component wizard (Figure 3.5). The default settings

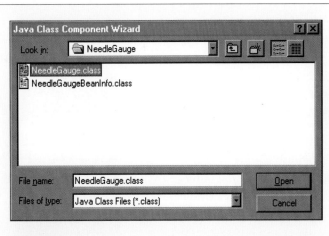

FIGURE 3.4

Selecting the Needle Gauge Bean class in PowerJ's Java class component wizard

are sufficient for this example, so just click the Next button to move on. You are then presented with a page that allows you to provide an icon for the Bean (Figure 3.6). This icon will be used by PowerJ for Bean selection purposes. PowerJ provides a large set of icons to choose from; there's even a gauge icon (Gauge.ico) that suits the Needle Gauge Bean very well (Figure 3.7). Figure 3.8 shows the icon page of the class component wizard after you've selected the gauge icon.

> **NOTE:** *JavaBeans includes built-in support for icons that application builder tools are supposed to use when representing a Bean in a toolbar or palette. Apparently PowerJ ignores this functionality in order to allow Java classes that aren't Beans to be integrated with the environment as well. This may change in the final release of PowerJ, since builder tools are strongly encouraged to use JavaBeans' built-in facilities.*

At this point, all you have to do to finish adding the Bean is click the Finish button. After doing so, you're shown a window that displays the status of the Bean's addition to the PowerJ environment (Figure 3.9). PowerJ performs some

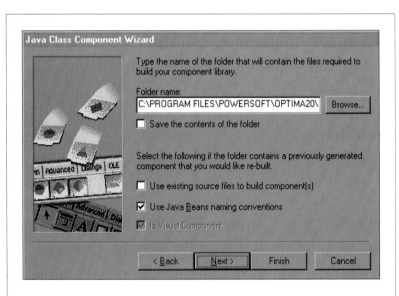

FIGURE 3.5

Configuring the Needle Gauge Bean class in PowerJ's Java class component wizard

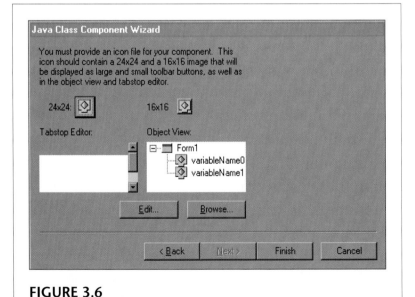

FIGURE 3.6

The icon page of PowerJ's Java class component wizard

processing and eventually finishes with the Bean successfully added.

Working with Beans in a Visual Tool

With the Needle Gauge Bean successfully added to PowerJ, you get a better idea of how Beans are used in the context of visual development environments. There are certain common issues all builder tools must address when supporting JavaBeans. One of these issues is allowing the user to select a Bean so it can be laid out and edited. Some tools use a toolbar approach, where Beans are arranged as an array of icons or names. Other tools use a floating palette approach, where the tools are arranged like a toolbar but the palette window is detached and can be moved around as desired.

PowerJ uses a hybrid approach to Bean selection that involves a tabbed set of toolbars. In PowerJ, Beans are added to a toolbox under a particular tab in a set of tabs that all contain different types of components. Figure 3.10 shows the newly added Needle Gauge Bean under the Classes tab of the PowerJ component toolbar. (The arrow icon to the left of the needle gauge icon represents the selection tool.)

I haven't really said anything about the empty window just

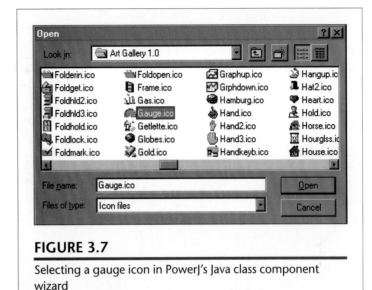

FIGURE 3.7

Selecting a gauge icon in PowerJ's Java class component wizard

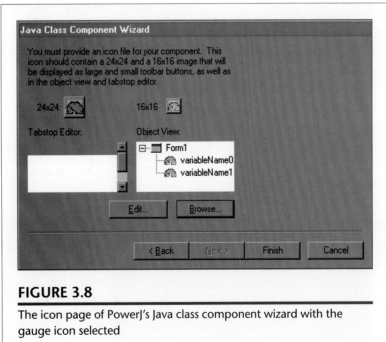

FIGURE 3.8

The icon page of PowerJ's Java class component wizard with the gauge icon selected

below the main PowerJ window. This window is a form window, which is typically used as a container for components (Beans). To add a Needle Gauge Bean to the form window, click on the Needle Gauge Bean icon in the toolbar (under the

Classes tab) and then click on the form window. Figure 3.11 gives you an idea of what the form window looks like after you've added the Bean.

The Bean has now been added to a form and is ready to be customized and put to work...sort of. Unfortunately, the PowerJ beta doesn't support JavaBeans fully enough to actually test a Bean's functionality. However, you can still drag the Bean around and resize it in the form window. You can also run the PowerJ Object Inspector to find out more information about the Bean by selecting Object Inspector from the View menu. Figure 3.12 shows what kind of information the Object Inspector displays for the Needle Gauge Bean.

Notice that the Object Inspector includes two tabs for viewing the properties and events for the Bean. Unfortunately, the

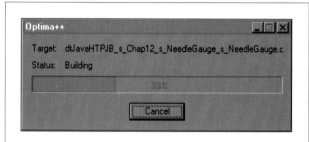

FIGURE 3.9

The PowerJ status window that is displayed while the Bean is being added

FIGURE 3.10

The Needle Gauge Bean displayed under PowerJ's Classes tab

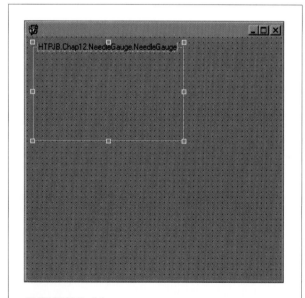

FIGURE 3.11

A Needle Gauge Bean laid out on a PowerJ form

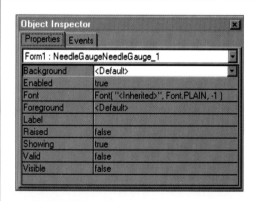

FIGURE 3.12

A view of the Bean's properties through PowerJ's Object Inspector

beta release of PowerJ isn't fully capable of determining properties and events for a Bean. However, the Object Inspector should still give you a good idea as to how Beans are interacted with in the forthcoming final release of PowerJ, as well as in visual tools in general.

JavaBeans the Old-Fashioned Way

One of the biggest benefits of the JavaBeans technology is its built-in support for visual layout and editing using application builder tools. Even though the beta release of Powersoft's PowerJ visual tool is limited in its JavaBeans support, it still manages to give you a good idea of the significance of the visual design aspect of JavaBeans. I now want to shift gears and look at a completely different scenario involving JavaBeans: the use of Beans in hand-coded Java programs.

You're about to see that laying out and editing Beans visually isn't the only approach available to developers. Granted, it's the approach being touted as "the" way to build applications with JavaBeans, but it may not be for everyone. There are plenty of developers who feel more at home hacking away at straight source code. I have to admit that even I like working solely at the code level at times because it ultimately gives you more insight into what's going on in your program. The bottom line is that everyone has their own ideas about what type of development environment works best for them. By supporting both types of development approaches, JavaBeans provides options for differing development styles.

Perhaps the most important thing to understand about using Beans directly in Java code is that Beans are not much different from any other Java classes. In fact, the only real difference is the additional overhead in Beans that supports component-related features such as exported properties, introspection, and application builder tool integration. Beans also support persistence and event processing, but these two services are useful in all Java classes, not just in Beans. In general, a Bean can be treated like a normal Java class with some extra overhead that can often be ignored when working at the source code level.

Even though using Beans directly in code is a more involved process than simply pointing and clicking in a visual tool, the task of building Java applications out of Beans at the code level is conceptually similar to using visual tools for the same purpose. Not surprisingly, the primary difference is that you have to do everything in code that the builder tools enable you to do visually. More specifically, the following steps are required to build applets or applications out of Beans in a non-visual environment:

1 Create the Beans

2 Customize the Beans

3 Connect the Beans

> NOTE: *This discussion focuses on using Beans directly in Java code to build stand-alone applications. Developing applets with Beans is an identical process, so the discussion applies equally to it.*

You can think of these steps as the three C's of JavaBeans development: create, customize, and connect. The last of these steps, "Connect the Beans," involves connecting Beans together using events. Since you haven't learned much about events and how they fit into JavaBeans at this point, we won't get into them in this chapter. Don't worry, events play a critical role in JavaBeans, so you'll learn plenty about them as the book unfolds.

Creating Beans by Hand

In a visual application builder tool, creating an instance of a Bean is as simple as selecting the Bean from a toolbox or palette and clicking in the editing (form) window for the application you are developing. Creating Beans directly in source code isn't much more difficult, but it definitely isn't as elegant or intuitive as pointing and clicking with the mouse. To create a Bean directly in code, you create an instance of the Bean class just as if it were any other Java class. In applications, the best place to perform this creation is inside the constructor for the application class. The following line of code creates a Needle Gauge Bean with default settings:

```
NeedleGauge gauge = new NeedleGauge();
```

If you want to use settings that are different than the default, you can use the second constructor for the Bean and pass in all the settings as arguments. The following line of code does this:

```
NeedleGauge gauge = new NeedleGauge(true, "Volume", 0.0, 10.0, 10, 5.0);
```

> NOTE: *Don't worry if the arguments to the needle gauge constructor don't make any sense to you. You'll learn all about the Needle Gauge Bean when you build it in Chapter 12.*

Once a Bean is created in code, you still have to add it to an application's window in order for it to be associated with the application. This is due to the fact that an application class is a container class, which is capable of holding graphical AWT elements such as Beans. To add a Bean to an application you just call the application's add() method, which is inherited from the Container class. The following is an example of adding the Needle Gauge Bean to an application using the `add()` method:

```
add(gauge);
```

As you can see, adding a Bean to an application in straight Java code is a very straightforward process. Keep in mind that this code is placed in the application class's constructor along with the Bean creation code. You typically will create all your Beans and then add them to an application in the application class's constructor.

Customizing Beans by Hand

Once you've created all of your Beans and added them to an application, you must customize them to fit the needs of the application. It's pretty rare that you would want to use a Bean with its default settings, so customization is a standard part of using Beans at the code level. Bean customization is really just as important as Bean creation because it determines how Beans will function and appear in an application. The one way you might avoid explicit customization is by using detail constructors to create your Beans, in which case you are effectively customizing them upon creation. However, you typically will need to customize at least a few Beans before you can use them.

Customizing a Bean is simply a matter of calling one or more of its public methods with the desired settings. Usually you will use a Bean's accessor methods to customize the Bean by setting its properties to different values. *Accessor methods* are public methods used to get and set the properties of a Bean. Bean customization usually occurs just after you add Beans to an application. The application class's constructor is a good place to handle this chore. The following piece of code shows how you might customize the Needle Gauge Bean after creating it and adding it to an application:

```
NeedleGauge gauge = new NeedleGauge();
add(gauge);
gauge.setRaised(true);
gauge.setLabel("Voltage");
```

This code creates and adds a Needle Gauge Bean, then customizes it by setting two of its properties. The raised property is first set to `true`, which results in the Bean having a raised 3D border. The label property, which determines the label text drawn below the needle gauge itself, is also set. You're probably thinking that you could have just as easily set these properties by using the detail constructor for the Needle Gauge Bean, like this:

```
NeedleGauge gauge = new NeedleGauge(true, "Voltage", 0.0, 5.0, 25,
    5.0);
add(gauge);
```

This would work for the properties modified here, but not for inherited properties, since they typically can't be altered through a constructor. For example, you can't alter the foreground color for the Needle Gauge Bean without customizing the Bean outside of the constructor, since the foreground color property is inherited by the Bean. The only way to modify inherited Bean properties is by setting them with an accessor method, like this:

```
NeedleGauge gauge = new NeedleGauge(true, "Voltage", 0.0, 5.0, 25,
   5.0);
add(gauge);
gauge.setForeground(Color.red);
```

This code sets the foreground color of the Needle Gauge Bean to red, which results in the label and division marks for the Bean being drawn in red. As you can see, Bean customization is a very straightforward process of calling the appropriate public methods to get the desired results. Granted, it's not as fancy as clicking and setting properties in a visual application builder tool, but it accomplishes the same task.

Summary

This chapter brought you closer to the practical side of JavaBeans by showing you how Beans are used in development environments. You learned about the kinds of support visual development tools provide for JavaBeans. You even got a glimpse of a commercial development environment centered around the use of JavaBeans components, Powersoft's PowerJ. Many more JavaBeans-compatible tools are in the works and will be available by the time you read this.

In addition to showing how Beans fit into visual tools, this chapter also discussed the use of Beans in straight Java code. Working with Beans at the source code level can be very useful in situations where you need to keep an eye on all the underlying details. You learned that using Beans in Java code is little different than using traditional Java classes. In learning how to use Beans in Java code, you found out about the three C's of developing applications with Beans: create, customize, and connect.

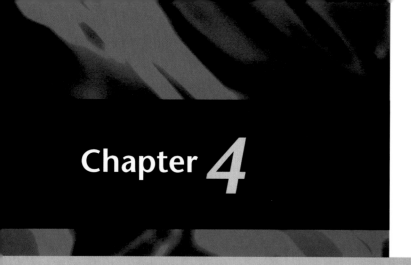

Chapter 4

Packaging Beans with JAR Files

- ▶ JAR Basics
- ▶ JAR Files and JavaBeans
- ▶ Manifest Files
- ▶ The JAR Utility

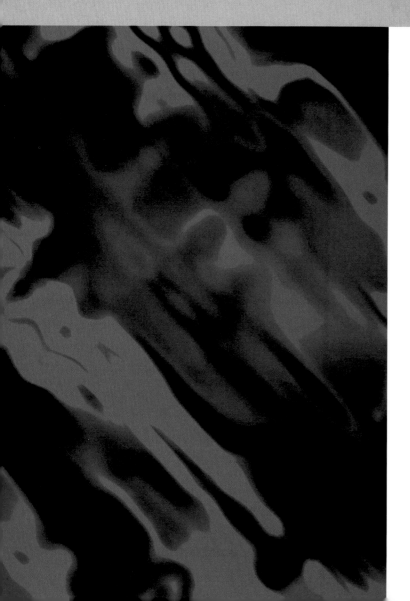

Although JavaBeans is a very powerful technology by itself, it relies heavily on the support of some other core areas of the Java system. One of these areas relates to how JavaBeans components are distributed to end-users. I'm referring to Java archives, which are compressed files designed to hold Java applets, applications, or Beans, along with any associated resources. Java archives are commonly referred to as JAR (Java ARchive) files.

JAR files are extremely important to JavaBeans because they provide the mechanism by which Beans are packaged and distributed to end-users. JAR files allow Beans to be shipped as individual entities that include all required support files. Furthermore, JAR files provide support for digitally signing Beans so they can operate under less restrictive security constraints in a Web environment. This chapter takes a look at JAR files and how they are used with JavaBeans. In the later parts of the chapter you'll learn how to use the JAR utility, which allows you to package JAR files for distribution.

In this chapter, you'll learn

▶   JAR fundamentals

▶   How JAR files relate to JavaBeans

▶   What a manifest file is

▶   How to use the JAR utility

JAR Basics

JAR files are a powerful means of compressing and storing multiple files into a single unit. JAR files are very much like other types of compression archives such as ZIP and TAR, except that JAR files additionally provide support for security authentication. JAR files are useful to Java developers in a variety of ways. For example, a Java applet can be compressed into a JAR file and given a digital security signature. You'll learn more about JAR security and digital signatures a little later in the chapter. The JAR file contains all of the classes and resources required by the applet. This applet can then execute in a distributed environment without the stringent constraints of Java's applet security model. Furthermore, if the applet is being executed within a Web page, its transfer time is greatly improved because only one HTTP file transaction occurs.

NOTE: *Prior to the invention of JAR files, each supporting file for an applet had to be transferred individually, incurring the overhead of an HTTP transaction (connection) for each. For applets with lots of classes or resources, this is costly overhead.*

Even without addressing the importance of JAR files to JavaBeans, it's clear that JAR files are a significant Java technology. Here is a list of some of the reasons why JAR files are so critical to Java:

▶ JAR files are cross-platform

▶ JAR files support audio, image, and class files

▶ JAR files are backward-compatible with existing applet code

▶ JAR files provide an open standard that is highly extensible

JAR Files Are Cross-Platform

JAR files are completely cross-platform because the standard is written entirely in Java. This has been a very important goal of the Java technology from the beginning, and is clearly still a major issue in newer Java technologies such as JavaBeans.

JAR Files Support Different Types of Files

JAR files are fully capable of handling many types of files including image, sound, and class files. This is critical, since Java will no doubt evolve to support other content types in the future. For now, it's nice to be able to bundle images, sounds, and classes into a single distributable JAR file.

JAR Files Are Backward-Compatible

JAR files are backward-compatible with prior releases of Java. This means that, for example, you can package applets written in Java 1.02 into JAR files. This seemingly inconsequential issue highlights an important point about JAR files: JAR is basically a standard for archiving files. Contrast this with other Java technologies, which are typically programming APIs in addition to being standards. There is no programming API for JAR except the underlying compression APIs it happens to use. Your sole interface to JAR files is the JAR utility, which you'll learn about a little later in the chapter.

Jar Files Provide an Open and Extensible Standard

The final point to be made about JAR files is that they define an open standard that is highly extensible. This means that the JAR standard can grow and evolve to support future enhancements to Java. Since the Java technology is in a constant state of evolution, this is an important requirement of JAR files.

That pretty much wraps up the basics surrounding JAR files and how they fit into Java. Let's move on to how they impact JavaBeans.

> **NOTE:** *JAR files use a compression scheme based on the one used in the very popular PKZip utility. Check out the* `java.util.zip` *package in the JDK 1.1 documentation for more information.*

JAR Files and JavaBeans

Although JAR files are useful to Java as a whole, this book is about JavaBeans, so you're probably ready to find out exactly what JAR files have to do with JavaBeans. From a design and development perspective, you'll be glad to know that JAR files have nothing to do with JavaBeans. In other words, you don't have to do anything special to a Bean at the coding level to support JAR files.

JAR files enter the picture with JavaBeans when it comes time to package up a Bean for distribution. The standard technique for compressing and packaging Beans for distribution is provided by JAR files. Using JAR files, you can group the classes and resources for a Bean into one compressed unit to organize them, conserve space, and in some cases provide a measure of security. Bean resources can include anything from images and sounds to custom resources such as Bean-specific data files. Grouping the classes and resources for a Bean cleans up the delivery of Beans a great deal because it eliminates the task of keeping up with lots of different support files. Additionally, for a Bean being delivered in the context of a Web page, having a single JAR file means that only one HTTP transaction is necessary, which is much faster than the multiple transactions required for individual files.

If bundling beans in JAR files doesn't sound like all that big a deal, consider the fact that there is a higher motive at work here. The benefits of better organization, faster Web file transfers, and security are important, but the primary reason to use JAR files with Beans is because application development tools require them. Application builder tools that support the integration of Beans fully expect to see Beans packaged as JAR files. This is due to the fact that JAR files act as the standard packaging scheme for Beans. The bottom line is that all Beans should be packaged in JAR files, unless there is some good reason why you don't want a Bean to be used in an application builder tool.

An example of a tool that requires Beans to be packaged in JAR files is the BeanBox test container, which ships with the Bean Developer's Kit. The BeanBox test container, which you'll learn about in the next chapter, is a demonstration implementation of an application builder tool. The BeanBox recognizes only JAR files when it assembles its toolbox of Beans. This brings up a good question about JAR files and Beans: How do application builder tools know what Beans are included in a JAR file? Since JAR files are ultimately just a bunch of files compressed together, potentially including multiple class files, it isn't readily apparent which class files are actually Beans. The answer to this question can be found in manifest files, which are text files that describe the Beans contained in a JAR file, along with security information, if necessary.

NOTE: *A JAR file is fully capable of storing multiple Beans. This allows you to package an entire library of related Beans together in one JAR file. Just as with individual Beans, the manifest file is responsible for formally listing all the Beans contained in a JAR file.*

Manifest Files

A *manifest file* is a text file placed in a JAR file that lists information about the files contained in the JAR file. More specifically to JavaBeans, manifest files are responsible for identifying the Beans within a JAR file. Manifest files also serve as the means by which classes are digitally signed for security purposes. It's important to understand that not all files in a JAR file need to be listed in the manifest file (for example, the manifest file is not itself listed). However, each JavaBeans class must be listed, along with any classes that are digitally signed. Figure 4.1 shows how a manifest file identifies the Bean classes in a JAR file.

The structure of manifest files is very simple. Every manifest file begins with a preliminary section that contains, at a minimum, the JAR version number. This version number corresponds to the version of the JAR standard used to create the JAR file. In Java 1.1, the JAR version is 1.0. The preliminary section of a manifest file looks like this:

```
Manifest-Version: 1.0
```

You can also specify the JAR version required for using the JAR file. If the actual version is higher than the required version, then JAR extensions may be used. This is an example of how a required version is specified:

```
Required-Version: 1.0
```

After the preliminary section come the entries for each individual file in the JAR file. Each entry corresponds to a single Bean in the archive. So, for a JAR file containing only one Bean, there is only one entry in the manifest file. Each Bean entry in the manifest file consists of two required pieces of information: the name of the Bean's class file and a flag in-

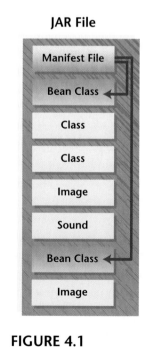

FIGURE 4.1

A manifest file identifying Bean classes in a JAR file

dicating that the class is in fact a Bean. The following is an example of how these two pieces of information are specified:

```
Name: MyBean.class
Java-Bean: True
```

Each Bean entry can also contain digital signature information for security purposes, but that's another topic altogether (see the sidebar on digital signatures). A complete manifest file including the MyBean entry looks like this:

```
Manifest-Version: 1.0

Name: MyBean.class
Java-Bean: True
```

NOTE: *For more information about JAR file security, please refer to the JDK 1.1 documentation.*

As you can see, the complete manifest file for a single Bean is very simple; you basically just provide the name of the Bean class and specify that it is in fact a Bean. If you want to include more Beans in an archive, you just add more entries to the manifest file. It's important to note that every JAR file contains a manifest file, regardless of whether you explicitly provide manifest information. You may then be wondering at this stage exactly how a manifest file of your own is associated with a JAR file. Hang on, because that answer is coming right up.

The JAR Utility

You're no doubt eager to get on with learning exactly how JAR files are created. JAR files are created and modified with the JAR utility (jar), which ships with the

---

Digital Signatures

The security features provided by JAR files are a significant part of the JAR technology. JAR security centers around the concept of a digital signature, which is analogous to a handwritten personal signature. Digital signatures are designed to give users confidence that a file within a JAR archive hasn't been tampered with. The creator of an archive attaches their digital signature to files that are to be secure; these files are considered signed. Users have the option of allowing signed files to access privileged resources or system functions. Of course, digital signatures say nothing about the original files themselves, so it becomes important for users to trust only signed files coming from a reputable vendor.

Java Developer's Kit 1.1. The JAR utility works very much like ZIP or TAR utilities in that it enables you to combine and compress multiple files into a single archive. However, the JAR utility is specifically geared toward creating archives that support JavaBeans. The syntax for jar is

```
jar Options Files
```

> NOTE: *The JAR utility also supports the digital signature security mechanism provided in Java 1.1.*

The Files argument specifies the files used when working with a JAR file, and varies according to the options in the Options argument. The Options argument specifies options related to how the JAR utility manipulates a JAR file. Here is a list of the jar options:

▶ c Specifies that a new archive is to be created.

▶ m Specifies that the manifest file for the archive is to be created using an external manifest file. The external manifest file is provided as the second file in the Files list following the options.

▶ t Lists the contents of an archive.

▶ x *File* Extracts all the files in an archive, or just the named files if additional files are specified.

▶ f Specifies the name of the archive to be accessed, where the name is provided as the first file in the Files list. The f option is used in conjunction with all the other options.

▶ v Causes the JAR utility to generate verbose output, which results in more information being displayed regarding the actions performed on an archive.

> NOTE: *Unlike most command line utilities, the* jar *utility doesn't require you to use a / or - when specifying options.*

Examining an Existing Archive

To get a better idea of how the JAR utility works, let's examine the JAR file for one of the Beans shipped with the BDK. The Juggler Bean is one of the demo Beans provided with the BDK and has a corresponding JAR file, Juggler.jar, located in the \BDK\JARS directory.

The following `jar` command lists all the files stored in the Juggler.jar archive:

```
Jar tf Juggler.jar
```

The results of executing this command are shown in Figure 4.2. As you can see in the figure, the Juggler Bean requires two classes and a variety of images.

The listing of the JAR file doesn't tell you exactly which class is the Bean class, though you can certainly guess. To find out for sure, you can extract the manifest file from the archive. To make things easier, you can just extract all the files in the archive with the following command:

```
jar xf Juggler.jar
```

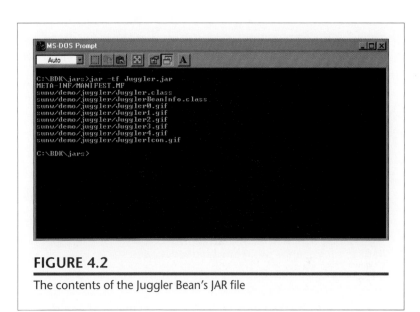

FIGURE 4.2

The contents of the Juggler Bean's JAR file

This command results in all of the Bean's files being extracted to the relative paths specified in the JAR file. In other words, the files are placed in subdirectories beneath the \BDK\JARS directory. Figure 4.3 shows what the \BDK\JARS directory looks like after you've executed the extraction command.

As you can see in the figure, there are two new directories: META-INF and SUNW. If you look back at Figure 4.2, you'll notice that these directories corre-

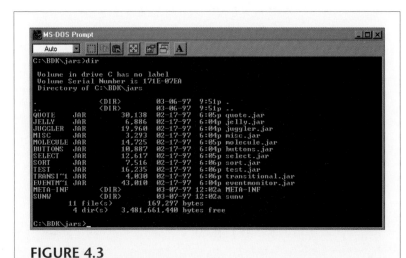

FIGURE 4.3

The listing of the \BDK\JARS directory after you've extracted the contents of the Juggler Bean's JAR file

spond to the relative paths for each file in the archive. To see the manifest file for the Bean, you have to change to the new \BDK\JARS\META-INF directory, where you'll find a file called MANIFEST.MF. This is the manifest file that was just extracted from the Juggler Bean's JAR file. It is shown in its entirety in Listing 4.1.

Wow, what a mess! And you thought manifest files were supposed to be simple and straightforward. In fact, they still are. If you look carefully at Listing 4.1, you'll find the familiar information discussed earlier in the chapter: a preliminary section with the JAR version number (1.0), the name of the Bean class (Juggler.class), and the flag stating that the class is a Bean. The rest of the information in the manifest file specifies digital signatures for all the files in the archive, which is a little beyond the scope of this discussion. Please refer to the JDK 1.1 documentation for more information about Java security.

This manifest file was associated with the Juggler Bean's JAR file using the m option to the JAR utility, which allows you to specify an external (user-defined) manifest file.

LISTING 4.1   The Juggler Bean's Manifest File

```
Manifest-Version: 1.0

Name: sunw/demo/juggler/Juggler.class
Java-Bean: True
Digest-Algorithms: SHA MD5
SHA-Digest: iak9FNHkNxIOHXKHtWE9aGkhboQ=
MD5-Digest: EShsa6mAycsDgBNNivEXRw==

Name: sunw/demo/juggler/JugglerBeanInfo.class
Digest-Algorithms: SHA MD5
SHA-Digest: aVi52xkXvbrqrBBkW4lmI9GJvSo=
MD5-Digest: cy2MF8RT8c8AncXB7ZKtVA==

Name: sunw/demo/juggler/Juggler0.gif
Digest-Algorithms: SHA MD5
SHA-Digest: BoXVBkl+aKR7/2+f80rqxYbltTc=
MD5-Digest: SOLrOrGbrm+3aJNgJgIwdQ==

Name: sunw/demo/juggler/Juggler1.gif
Digest-Algorithms: SHA MD5
```

CONTINUES

Creating a New Archive

You just saw how to examine an existing JAR file, but you haven't seen how to create a new archive. Creating new JAR files is surprisingly simple; you just use the c option in the JAR utility and specify the files you want to include. For example, if you had a directory of GIF images you wanted to package into a new JAR file named Images.jar, you would execute the following command in the directory containing the images:

```
jar cf Images.jar *.gif
```

The c and f options are used in this example to specify that a JAR file is to be created with the name Images.jar. The wildcard *.gif is used to add all the GIF files in the directory to the archive.

This approach works fine for creating generic JAR files, but it doesn't address the issue of the manifest files required for Beans. To create a JAR file for a Bean,

---

LISTING 4.1   The Juggler Bean's Manifest File (Continued)

```
SHA-Digest: BoXVBkl+aKR7/2+f8ØrqxYbltTc=
MD5-Digest: SOLrOrGbrm+3aJNgJgIwdQ==


Name: sunw/demo/juggler/Juggler2.gif
Digest-Algorithms: SHA MD5
SHA-Digest: vf+oWwJoCJXwdØFTwIAOqBwShc8=
MD5-Digest: ØUQOpDSyiy7ziKGuk8o2xQ==


Name: sunw/demo/juggler/Juggler3.gif
Digest-Algorithms: SHA MD5
SHA-Digest: 5ngCVC3l4zj4zefuY5VØzWjGKAM=
MD5-Digest: ØXIiV4Hs97ZLE6Vh5wYH3g==


Name: sunw/demo/juggler/Juggler4.gif
Digest-Algorithms: SHA MD5
SHA-Digest: 7/z73JtPbxHmsn61TQplq2cvuDs=
MD5-Digest: GY6JSNxiIabXhvoK2ZjjYQ==


Name: sunw/demo/juggler/JugglerIcon.gif
Digest-Algorithms: SHA MD5
SHA-Digest: Irqj25Pd5hgucribaj3QUIU3UAc=
MD5-Digest: BSØbØMJ3J+/tI4G/NFxVEw==
```

you have to use an additional option: the m option. This example creates a JAR file for a Bean called ImageViewer, whose manifest file is named ImageViewer.mf:

```
jar cfm ImageViewer.jar ImageViewer.mf *.class *.gif
```

As you can see, it takes three options (cfm) to create a JAR file for a Bean. The name of the new JAR file is identified by the first argument, while the name of the external manifest file is provided as the second argument. The remaining two arguments are wildcards used to add all the classes and images in the current directory to the archive.

That's all it takes to create a JAR file for a Bean. Once you've built a JAR file for a Bean, you can distribute the Bean however you choose. Then users of the Bean can incorporate it into their own applets and applications using application builder tools.

Summary

This chapter introduced you to JAR files, which are a powerful means of packaging Beans for distribution. JAR files are extremely important to JavaBeans because they define the standard format for distributing Beans. JAR files enable Bean developers to package all of the classes, resources, and support files for a Bean into a tight, secure unit. Visual development tools that support JavaBeans expect Beans to be installed in the form of JAR files.

Beyond their organizational value, you also learned in this chapter how JAR files provide compression and security features. Compression helps speed the transfer of JAR files in an online setting, such as when a Bean is being used on a Web page. JAR security is also important in the online world, where it becomes critical for users to trust the Beans they download and use.

Chapter 5

Testing Beans with the BeanBox

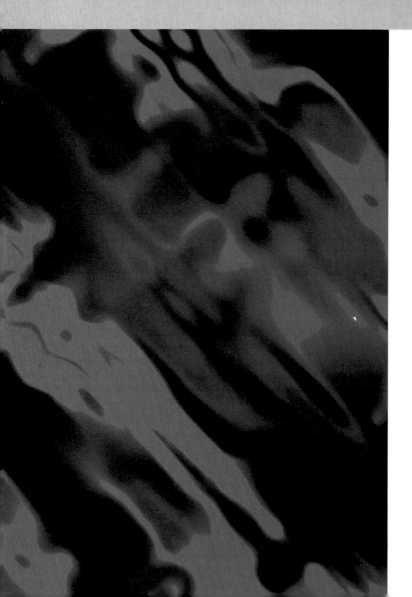

▶ **Introducing the BeanBox**

▶ **Working with Beans in the BeanBox**

In Chapter 3 you learned how Beans are used in a popular application builder tool, Powersoft's PowerJ. Application builder tools are a major area of interest for JavaBeans users since one of the key features of JavaBeans is its support for builder tool integration. In light of this, JavaSoft provides a test container in the Beans Development Kit that acts very much like an application builder tool. The idea is that Bean developers can use the test container to try out their Beans in the absence of real builder tools.

The test container I'm referring to is called the BeanBox, and it provides an example implementation of the kind of functionality required of a Bean-compliant application builder tool. This chapter explores the BeanBox and how you can use it to try out Beans in a visual development environment. I think you will find the BeanBox to be a neat utility that will play an important role in the Bean development process.

In this chapter, you'll learn:

▶ What the BeanBox is

▶ How the BeanBox works

▶ How to create, edit, and connect Beans in the BeanBox

5

Introducing the BeanBox

One of the enormous benefits of JavaBeans as a software component technology is its extensive support for the use of Beans in visual application builder tools. Although the builder tool support in JavaBeans ultimately results in better development tools, JavaSoft was faced with an initial problem caused by the technology being so young; it takes time for tool vendors to add full support for visual Bean interaction. Without builder tools to test their Beans in, Bean developers find themselves in the strange situation of having to guess whether their Beans will work correctly. And without Beans to test, builder tool developers have a difficult time testing their tools.

To help remedy this "chicken or the egg" dilemma, JavaSoft decided to build its own demonstration builder tool. It called the tool the BeanBox, and bundled it with the BDK. The BeanBox enables you to lay out, edit, and interconnect Beans visually, just as you would in a real application builder tool. I say "real" because the BeanBox isn't intended to be a fully functional development tool for creating applications with Beans. Rather, it is intended to provide a demonstration of how Beans might be used in a visual environment. In doing so, the BeanBox becomes an indispensable tool for Bean development because it provides a stable test bed for trying out Beans as they are being created.

> NOTE: *Although the BeanBox provides a means of visually editing and manip-*
> *ulating Beans, it in no way attempts to suggest a standard for real application*
> *builder tools to follow. In other words, it is fully expected that each builder tool*
> *will use its own approach to visual Bean editing; the only strict requirement for*
> *tools is that they conform to the JavaBeans API.*

Running the BeanBox

The BeanBox is provided as a stand-alone Java application that is executed using
the standard JDK interpreter. To execute properly, the BeanBox requires specific
settings in the CLASSPATH environment variable. Since manually setting CLASS-
PATH each time you want to run the BeanBox is a little cumbersome, a batch file is
included in the BDK that handles the details of setting the variable properly. This
batch file is called run.bat and is responsible for setting the CLASSPATH environment variable and then executing the BeanBox. You should always use this batch
file to run the BeanBox, since it automatically sets CLASSPATH to the values required by the BeanBox. If you are the type of person who simply must know how
everything works, I'll humor you by showing exactly what run.bat does; check
out the following listing of the run.bat batch file for Windows 95/NT:

```
if "%OS%" == "Windows_NT" setlocal
set CLASSPATH=classes
java sun.beanbox.BeanBoxFrame
```

The first line performs some initialization specific to Windows NT. The batch
file then sets CLASSPATH to the classes path (\BDK\beanbox\classes), which
contains support classes for the BeanBox. Finally, the last line executes the BeanBox
within the JDK interpreter. You really don't have to worry about any of these details to use the BeanBox; I just thought you might want to know why you run it
with a batch file as opposed to running it directly with the Java interpreter. In summary, to run the BeanBox, just execute the run.bat batch file. It's that simple!

When you run the batch file, the BeanBox initializes itself and looks for any
installed Beans to add to its ToolBox. An installed Bean is any Bean stored in the
\BDK\JARS directory. All Beans stored in this directory are automatically included
in the BeanBox's ToolBox. You can also manually add new Beans via a menu command once the BeanBox is up and running, but they aren't permanently kept in
the BeanBox across sessions. So the best way to add Beans to the BeanBox is to
copy them to the \BDK\JARS directory.

> NOTE: *This discussion assumes you have installed the BDK to the default*
> *\BDK directory. If you've installed it to a different directory, look for the JARS*
> *directory beneath that directory instead of the BDK directory.*

You may be a little curious about what exactly should be copied to the \BDK\JARS directory. If you recall from the previous chapter, application builder tools typically expect Beans to be stored in JAR files. The BeanBox is no different in this regard. So to add a Bean to the BeanBox you simply copy its JAR file to the \BDK\JARS directory. I think you're starting to get the picture about adding Beans to the BeanBox; let's move on!

Anatomy of the BeanBox

When the BeanBox is executed, it starts up by displaying three different windows. Each of these windows performs a different function within the scope of the BeanBox. Figure 5.1 shows the BeanBox in all its glory.

The window to the far left is the ToolBox window, which lists all the Beans registered for use with the BeanBox. This ToolBox should look vaguely familiar to you if you have any experience using visual development tools. Figure 5.2 shows the ToolBox window.

NOTE: *Some application builder tools refer to toolboxes as tool palettes.*

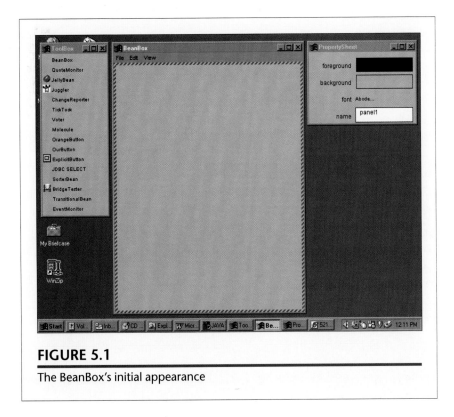

FIGURE 5.1

The BeanBox's initial appearance

FIGURE 5.2

The BeanBox
ToolBox window

As you can see, the ToolBox lists a variety of different Beans available to the BeanBox. These Beans are all demo Beans provided with the BDK to demonstrate the development and use of Beans. Notice that some of the Beans have graphical icons associated with them. These Beans use a special Bean information class to specify the icon to be displayed in visual development environments. This is a specific feature of JavaBeans geared toward making Beans integrate well with development tools. Beans that don't include icon information via a Bean information class are listed in the ToolBox by name only.

The second window associated with the BeanBox is the main container window, which is shown in Figure 5.3. The main container window is the heart of the BeanBox and serves as the area where Beans are visually placed and manipulated. The main container window is very similar in function to form windows in other form-based visual development environments such as Visual Basic. This window has three menu items, File, Edit, and View, which enable you to perform a wide range of functions on Beans in the BeanBox.

> NOTE: *Form-based application builder tools are built around the concept of a form, which is a window capable of containing graphical components such as Beans.*

The last window in the BeanBox is the PropertySheet window, which lists all the properties associated with the currently selected Bean. When the BeanBox first starts up, the Property-Sheet window lists properties associated with the BeanBox container itself. Figure 5.4 shows the PropertySheet window.

This PropertySheet window provides a means of editing the individual properties of a Bean. A property editor is displayed in the PropertySheet window for each editable property in a Bean. Property editors are compact, graphical editors for JavaBeans properties. The BDK includes built-in property editors for the following Java data types:

▶ Boolean

▶ Byte

▶ Color

▶ Double

▶ Float

▶ Font

FIGURE 5.3

The BeanBox main container window

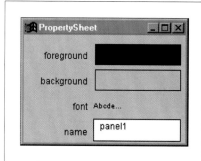

FIGURE 5.4

The BeanBox PropertySheet window

- ▶ Int

- ▶ Long

- ▶ Number

- ▶ Short

- ▶ String

NOTE: *In addition to a property sheet, a Bean can also have a customizer, which is a more advanced Bean-specific visual editor. For Beans that have an associated customizer, the Edit menu in the BeanBox provides a Customize command that runs the customizer on the Bean.*

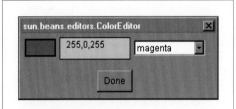

FIGURE 5.5

The property editor dialog box for the background color property

When you first run the BeanBox, the PropertySheet window displays the properties for the BeanBox container itself. You can easily edit these properties by clicking on them with the mouse. For example, click the background property to edit the background color for the container. Figure 5.5 shows the property editor dialog box allowing you to edit the background color.

The background color property editor dialog box enables you to easily change the background color for the container either by entering RGB (red, green, blue) colors or by selecting a standard color from a drop-down list. Try selecting a different color, such as magenta, to see how it affects the appearance of the container. Figure 5.6 shows what the BeanBox container window looks like after you've set the background color to magenta.

Working with Beans in the BeanBox

Now that you have some idea of what the BeanBox is, it's time to put it to the test and learn how to work with Beans in it. Using Beans in the BeanBox is very simple and straightforward, and is a good demonstration of the benefits of visual editing with JavaBeans. The first step in using Beans with the BeanBox is adding a Bean to the main container window. You do this by clicking on a Bean's name or icon in the

FIGURE 5.6

The BeanBox container window with the background color property set to magenta

ToolBox window, which turns the mouse pointer into a cross. You then simply click in the container window at the location where you want the Bean to be placed. A new Bean will appear, centered at the location you clicked with a default size and set of properties.

For the purposes of learning how Beans are laid out and manipulated in the BeanBox, let's work through an example. We'll use demo Beans that come standard with the BDK; these Beans are shown in the ToolBox window. Begin by selecting the ExplicitButton Bean in the ToolBox and adding it to the container window. Figure 5.7 shows what the container window looks like after you've added this Bean.

NOTE: *The ExplicitButton Bean is an example Bean provided with the BDK that functions much like the standard Java AWT* `Button` *class.*

You probably noticed that the new Bean is drawn with a hashed boundary, which indicates that it is the currently selected Bean. This means that the PropertySheet window reflects the properties for this specific Bean. Beans are selected by default when you first add them to the container window. To select a Bean that isn't already selected, just click the Bean.

The next step in this example BeanBox session is editing the properties of the ExplicitButton Bean you just created. More specifically, you need to change the Bean's label property to reflect the button's usage. You accomplish this through the PropertySheet window, where you need to change the Bean's label property value to "Start". Figure 5.8 shows what the property sheet for the Bean looks like after you've modified this property.

You're actually going to need two Button Beans for this example, so go ahead and add another ExplicitButton Bean next to the one you just edited. Once the second Bean is added, you need to edit its label property to set its value to "Stop". After you've done this, the container window should look similar to Figure 5.9.

Connecting Beans Together with Events

With the two Button Beans in place, you're ready to get down to business. You're going to wire the buttons to an-

FIGURE 5.7

The container window after you've added an ExplicitButton Bean to the BeanBox

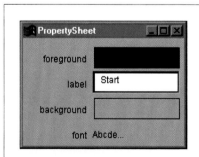

FIGURE 5.8

The PropertySheet window for the ExplicitButton Bean after you've edited the label property

other Bean that displays an animation. By doing so, you'll be able to stop and start the animation by pressing the buttons. This is where you really get a glimpse of the power of JavaBeans in a visual development setting: Visually creating, editing, and connecting Beans is an enormously powerful ability. But enough with talking about it, let's get on with doing it!

The Bean I'm referring to that displays an animation is called Juggler and is included in the ToolBox just like the ExplicitButton Bean. You need to add a Juggler Bean to the container window; just select the Juggler Bean from the ToolBox and click on the container just below the ExplicitButton Beans. After you've done this, the container window should look like Figure 5.10. Notice that the Juggler Bean starts juggling (animating) as soon as you add it to the container.

With the Juggler Bean in place, you are ready to wire the buttons to it and get some results. The wiring of Beans is handled through events. For instance, when a Bean fires an event in response to some change in its state, the event can result in a public method being called in another Bean. Fortunately, the BeanBox allows you to make this event/method connection visually, which makes the task very intuitive. The Edit menu in the BeanBox includes an Events menu item that contains all the events supported by the currently selected Bean. To connect an event to a method in another Bean, you first select the desired event from this menu.

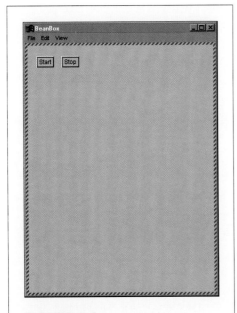

FIGURE 5.9

The main container window after you've added both ExplicitButton Beans to the BeanBox

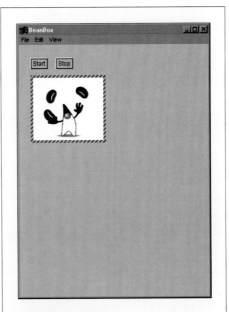

FIGURE 5.10

The main container window after you've added a Juggler Bean to the BeanBox

The goal in the example is to connect the Button Beans to the Juggler Bean so the juggling animation is stopped and started when you click the buttons. To connect the first button to the Juggler Bean, select the Button Bean and click the Edit menu in the BeanBox. You'll see an Events menu item that has a group of event types beneath it. Select the button push menu item and then the actionPerformed item beneath it (see Figure 5.11). You'll then see a line originating from the Button Bean that moves as you move the mouse around. This line shows graphically where the action event is to be connected to. Move the mouse over the Juggler Bean and click to connect the Button Bean's action event to the Juggler Bean. You'll be presented with a dialog box that shows the available target methods defined in the Juggler Bean. Figure 5.12 shows this dialog box.

Select the startJuggling() method from the dialog box to mark it as being associated with the Button Bean's event action. Once you do this, the Event Target dialog box displays information indicating that the BeanBox is performing the necessary steps behind the scenes to facilitate the connection (Figure 5.13). This takes a few seconds, after which the connection is established and the dialog box disappears. From then on, the startJuggling() method will be called on the Juggler Bean any time the first ExplicitButton Bean is pressed.

You're now halfway there! The next step is to repeat this procedure and connect the second ExplicitButton Bean to the stopJuggling() method of the Juggler Bean. After you do this, you can test the buttons by clicking them to start and stop the animating Juggler Bean.

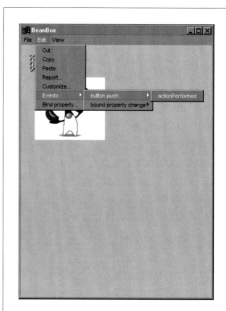

FIGURE 5.11

The Edit menu selections required to connect the ExplicitButton Bean's action event to the Juggler Bean

Moving and Resizing Beans

If your Beans aren't quite lined up the way the Beans are in Figure 5.10, feel free to move them around. You can do this by selecting one of the Beans and moving the mouse over the hashed border surrounding it until the mouse cursor changes to a cross with arrows. You then click and hold down the mouse button while you drag the mouse. This allows you to move the Bean around in the container.

You can also resize Beans that support resizing by moving the mouse over one of the corners of the hashed border until the mouse cursor changes to a diagonal line with arrows at each end. You then click and drag the mouse while holding down the mouse button to resize the Bean. Incidentally, there is no need to resize any of the Beans in the BeanBox example here because they automatically size themselves to fit their content.

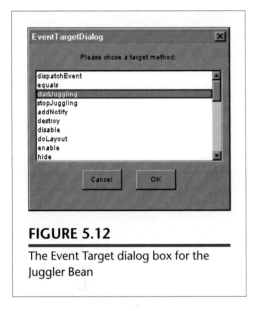

FIGURE 5.12

The Event Target dialog box for the Juggler Bean

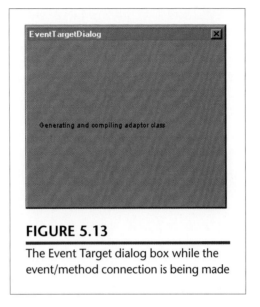

FIGURE 5.13

The Event Target dialog box while the event/method connection is being made

You may think it's kind of strange to have the Beans connected together and interacting with each other in an environment that is clearly development oriented. In other words, it's sort of awkward having the hashed border appear around the buttons as you click them, as if you were going to edit them. Fortunately, the BeanBox provides a means of testing out Beans in more of a runtime setting. You can switch the BeanBox out of design mode by selecting Disable Design Mode from the View menu. When you disable design mode, the ToolBox and PropertySheet windows disappear, and you aren't allowed to select, move, or resize Beans. This mode is useful for trying out Beans once you have them edited and connected together.

Saving and Loading Beans

The BeanBox fully supports the saving and loading of Beans, which is functionality you would expect from an application builder tool. To save the example you've just worked through, select the Save menu item from the File menu. You will be prompted to enter a file name to save the Beans to; you can enter any name you want. When you save the contents of the BeanBox, the persistence facilities in JavaBeans are used to store away the state of each Bean. You'll learn all about persistence in Chapter 8.

Now clear the BeanBox by selecting Clear from the File menu. All three of the Beans you created are cleared from the BeanBox. You can reload the Beans and the connections you made between them by selecting Load from the File menu. Select the file you saved the Beans to and the BeanBox will load the Beans back into the BeanBox with the exact settings they had when you saved them. The ability to save and load Beans is very powerful; I think you'll be surprised later in the book when you learn about how Beans automatically support the saving and loading of their internal states.

> **NOTE:** *The ability to save and load the state of a component is a very critical part of any component technology. JavaBeans is a step ahead of most component technologies in this regard because of its automatic support for the saving and loading of components. With JavaBeans, it's possible to build a Bean and have it fully support the saving and loading of its state entirely through automatic means.*

Summary

This chapter focused on the BeanBox, a very important tool that comes with the Beans Development Kit. You learned all about the BeanBox, including its importance as a test harness for Beans under development and how to use it to create, customize, and connect Beans.

This chapter explained that the BeanBox isn't meant to be a fully functioning Bean development tool, but instead a working example of how a Bean development tool might work. You can expect to see fancier, more interactive tools for Bean development and testing in the very near future, but the BeanBox will probably still hold its own as a simple yet highly effective way to test Beans. For this reason, I strongly suggest spending some more time trying out Beans in the BeanBox. It can help you gain more insight as to how your own Beans will function in a graphical development setting, and beyond that it's a pretty fun tool!

Part 2

Working with the JavaBeans API

Chapter 6

Bean Happenings:
The Event Handling APIs

- ▶ Tonight's Main Event

- ▶ The New versus the Old

- ▶ Something Happened? Tell Me More

- ▶ JavaBeans Events: They Come in Threes

- ▶ Applied Delegation

- ▶ Putting It All Together

- ▶ What About Event Sources?

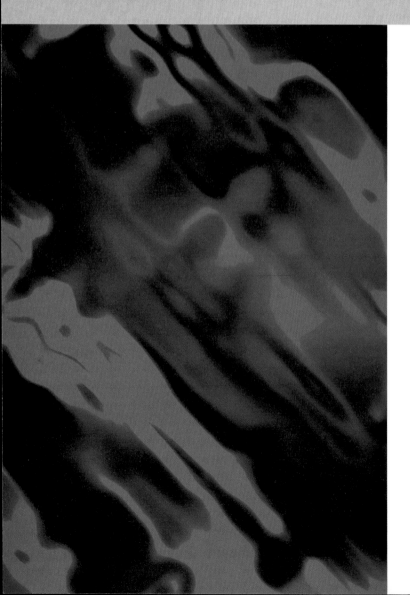

In this chapter, you'll learn what events are from the programmer's point of view and why they're so important. You'll also explore the three event models supported by Java, and learn when, why, and how each should be used. Very little of this chapter is specific to JavaBeans; most of it applies to the Java Development Kit v1.1 (referred to as the JDK 1.1 from here on) in general.

In this chapter, you will learn

▶ The importance of events and the event paradigm in component programming

▶ That Java and JavaBeans support three event models

▶ When to use each model

▶ Some guidelines for writing event sources

Tonight's Main Event

"In physics, the fundamental concept is event. The collision between one particle and another is an event, with its own location in spacetime. Another event is the emission of a flash of light from an atom. A third is the impact of the pebble that chips the windshield of a speeding car. A fourth event, likewise fixing in and by itself a location in spacetime, is the strike of a lightning bolt on the rudder of an airplane. An event marks a location in spacetime; it is like a steel stake driven into spacetime."[1]

Wait a minute; this is a book about programming JavaBeans, not spacetime physics. What's that previous paragraph doing here? Well, in modern programming under a GUI (Graphical User Interface), events are also one of the fundamental concepts. It's so fundamental that it really reaches beyond JavaBeans; much of what we'll talk about applies to programming (especially Java programming) in general. Since physicists have been dealing with the concept of events for years now, maybe we can learn something from their idea of events.

Physicists are nothing if not precise, yet surprisingly enough, their definition of an event is pretty simple: Something happened. Guess what? This will serve our purposes pretty well also, but programming extends the idea of "something" to a new level. An event can be concrete like the user clicking the mouse or something a little more abstract like a component gaining input focus.

---

1   Introductory quote on events: Taylor and Wheeler, *Spacetime Physics: Introduction to Special Relativity,* 2nd ed. (New York: W.H. Freeman and Company, 1992), 10.

The New versus the Old

Events are a fundamental concept of GUIs, object-oriented programming, and components. Events are so important that programming for a GUI (and, by extension, components like JavaBeans, whether graphical or not) is often referred to as **event-driven programming**. Event-driven programming is the new model. Procedural programming was the old model. Let's compare and contrast event-driven programming versus procedural programming.

Procedural Programming

A piece of software written using the procedural model might have a huge loop that, for example, constantly asked its environment if the user has supplied any input. When some input was received (like the user pressing a key), the code would jump out of the loop, do something based on the input (update the screen maybe), and eventually return to the loop. Note that this could be thought of as a linear, one-dimensional process. The simple numbered list, below, should convey the basic idea.

1 Check for key press

2 If key has been pressed, go to step 4

3 Go back to step 1

4 Examine the key

5 Update the screen based on key pressed

6 Go back to step 1

Event-Driven Programming

The event-driven model takes a more "hands-off" approach. Using the same example, the event-driven program would tell the environment, "Let me know when the user supplies some input." Control would then (eventually) be returned to the environment: the operating system or virtual machine (VM) in Java's case. Specifically *how* the program is notified when the user supplies input depends on the actual implementation of events. Java's VM would call a method on an object. This method would probably change the state of the object, and ultimately update the screen. This is a non-linear, two-dimensional idea that couldn't easily be represented by a numbered list; Figure 6.1, below, should do much better.

Something Happened? Tell Me More

We loosely defined an event earlier as "something happened." This is a good start, but we need something a little more concrete. Let's look at the physics analogy again for a moment: First, when talking about an event, physicists will want to know what happened; they need some way of *identifying* the type of the event. Second, and even more important, each event has some information associated with it that distinguishes it from other events of the same type. A physicist is always interested in two specific pieces of information: when the event occurred, and where. An example might be, "Two particles collided in this device on this table in my laboratory at 2:17 P.M."

In programming, things are almost identical, but the information associated with an event is much more open-ended. First, we need to know what type of event occurred (just as before). Second, depending on the type of the event, we often need some additional information about the event. It will hardly ever be when and where the event occurred. An example might be, "The user clicked the mouse button and at that time, the mouse pointer was at location x = 100 and y = 200 on the screen."

JavaBeans Events: They Come in Threes

Java supports three distinct event models. Why three? Could the designers at Sun not make up their minds? Actually, all three are justified: one for historical reasons of compatibility, and the other two for practical reasons. If this all sounds a bit more complicated than it should be, hang in there. To really get it all sorted out, we're going to have to roll up our sleeves, dig around in all three models, and understand why the different models are needed. If you'd prefer to simply know how to properly use events with JavaBeans and not worry about why there are three event models, you may want to skip forward to the section entitled Putting It All Together.

Inheritance-Based Event Handling

The first of the three is the old event model from Java 1.0. This event model is often referred to as an inheritance-based model because it uses an inheritance

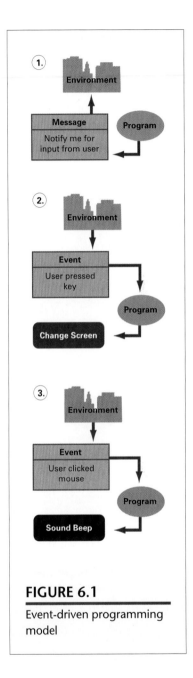

FIGURE 6.1

Event-driven programming model

6

mechanism (overriding a method inherited from a super-class) to work its magic. This event model is tightly coupled (more on this later) to the AWT (the Abstract Windowing Toolkit which is Java's class library for providing graphical user interfaces) and was mainly designed to handle events from the local GUI platform.

Event Representation

If you've programmed Java applets or applications that used the AWT, you're probably already familiar with the inheritance-based event model in Java 1.0. All events are described by a single class: `java.awt.Event`. This event class contains an integer member variable, id, which identifies which event happened. There are also several other member variables used to supply additional information about the event. The x and y member variables, for example, represent the position of the mouse pointer for mouse events.

Event Delivery and Processing

When the AWT needs to send an event to a component, it simply calls the component's `handleEvent()` method (`handleEvent()` is declared high-up in the AWT class hierarchy in `java.awt.Component`). To actually handle an event, we have to define our own class which inherits from one of the AWT components and override `handleEvent()`. Let's say we have an application that uses a `Frame` component from the AWT. If we wanted this component to watch for key-presses from the user and display the letter that was typed in its window area, we would have to define our own class that inherits from `Frame` and, at a minimum, overrides `handleEvent()` and `paint()`. Here's the complete source.

```java
// EchoKey Class event example using old event handling
// EchoKey.java
//
// event example using old event handling mechanism

import java.awt.*;

class EchoKey extends Frame {
  private char[] key;
  public EchoKey() {
    key = new char[1];
    key[0] =    ;
  }
  // handle events
  public boolean handleEvent(Event e) {
    switch (e.id) {
    case Event.WINDOW_DESTROY:
```

```
        System.exit(Ø);
        return false;
      case Event.KEY_PRESS:
        key[Ø] = (char)e.key;
        repaint();
        break;
      }
      return super.handleEvent(e);
    }
    public void paint(Graphics g) {
      // draw the most recently pressed key
      g.drawChars(key, Ø, 1, 1Ø, 4Ø);
    }
    // create an EchoKey object and display it
    public static void main(String args[]) {
      EchoKey  ek = new EchoKey();
      ek.setSize(255, 128);
      ek.show();
    }
  }
```

Note that `handleEvent()` also looks for `Event.WINDOW_DESTROY` events and shuts the application down. Compile this using `javac` (the Java compiler supplied with the JDK) and then execute it from the command line using `java EchoKey`.

As you press keys, they should appear in the window (see Figure 6.2).

Summary of Old Inheritance-Based Model

In short, this method works well enough when deriving from one of the components in the AWT (which is how things are generally done when writing a Java applet), but it's not without drawbacks. Notice in the above description of Java 1.0 style events, it's impossible to not talk about the AWT. That's because Java 1.0 events are intimately tied to the AWT; Java 1.0 events and the AWT are said to be *tightly coupled*. In some situations, tight coupling is appropriate, but this isn't one of those instances. Also, the switch-case statements in `handleEvent()` can often become complex and unmanageable. But we're not going to cover this method in

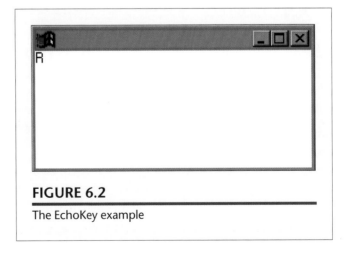

FIGURE 6.2

The EchoKey example

any more detail; this is a book about JavaBeans, and JavaBeans demand a new, more powerful event model.

Delegation-Based Event Handling

JavaBeans demanded a new, more powerful event model that allowed communication of events between Beans. This event model is known as a delegation-based event model.

Event Representation

One of the first differences you'll notice about this event model is how the events are represented. Rather than use a single event class with a numeric identifier, the new delegation-based model uses a hierarchy of event classes all deriving from `java.util.EventObject`. `EventObject` has no numeric identifier. Instead, the types of classes that derive from it determine the types of the events; different events are represented by different classes. This is a much more natural and powerful representation, especially in an object-oriented language like Java. Figure 6.3, below, shows the class hierarchy that ships with `JavaBeans` and the JDK 1.1. Sometimes an individual class, such as `java.beans.PropertyChangeEvent`, represents a single event. Often, however, it's useful to represent several related events in a single class and use a numeric identifier (like the old event model) to indicate the specific event. For example, `java.awt.KeyEvent` represents both key presses and key releases; a numeric identifier (which is actually declared in `AWTEvent`) specifies which of the two occurred.

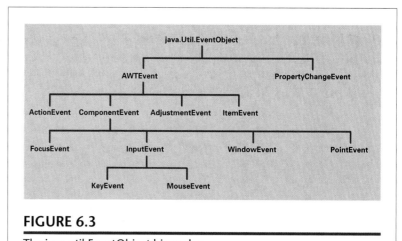

FIGURE 6.3

The java.util.EventObject hierarchy

Event Delivery and Processing

The new event representation is certainly powerful, but the real difference between the delegation-based model and the old inheritance-based model becomes apparent when we examine how events are delivered and processed. In fact, both models get their names from the way events are delivered and processed.

For delivery and processing of events, the delegation-based model introduces the concepts of event sources and event listeners. Let's look at event listeners first.

Conceptually, an event listener is any object that receives events from an event source. Java draws on a hierarchy again to represent listeners, a hierarchy of interfaces with `java.util.EventListener` at its root. Figure 6.4, below, shows the `EventListener` hierarchy shipped with the JDK 1.1 and `JavaBeans`. Notice that each event class from the EventObject hierarchy has a corresponding event listener interface. These event listener interfaces have one method for each individual event represented by their corresponding class (remember that an event object will often represent more that one event). For example, `KeyEvent` represents key-pressed, key-released, and key-typed (a key-press followed by a key-release) events. There is an associated `KeyListener` interface which declares the methods `keyTyped()`, `keyPressed()`, and `keyReleased()`. All three accept a `KeyEvent` as their argument.

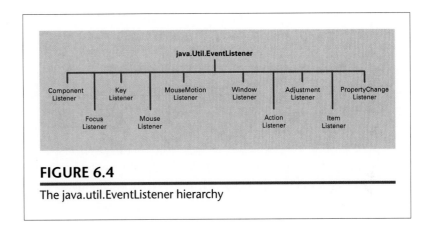

FIGURE 6.4

The java.util.EventListener hierarchy

```
public interface KeyListener extends EventListener {
    public void keyTyped(KeyEvent e);
    public void keyPressed(KeyEvent e);
    public void keyReleased(KeyEvent e);
}
```

So far, we've only described the listener *interfaces*. An actual event listener implements the appropriate interface. Let's use the same example from the previous section on the old inheritance model: a Frame component handling key events. We'll declare a class that `extends Frame` and `implements KeyListener`:

```
class EchoKey2 extends Frame implements KeyListener {
    // . . .
    public void keyTyped(KeyEvent e) { /* process keyTyped */ }
    public void keyPressed(KeyEvent e) { /* process keyPressed */ }
    public void keyReleased(KeyEvent e) { /* process keyReleased */ }
    // . . .
}
```

This is only half of the story though; we need to get the event source into the picture to make things actually start working. Conceptually, an event source is any component that needs to send events to event listeners. By convention, an Xxx event source provides a public method of the form:

```
addXxxListener(XxxListener)
```

Typically, an Xxx listener will "register" itself with the source by calling the addXxxListener() method and passing itself as the argument. The event source keeps a list of added listeners. When an Xxx event occurs, the source goes through its list and calls the appropriate method on each listener with the event as an argument.

For our EchoKey2 example, we're looking for an event source with addKeyListener(), but where is this event source? In this case, it's our own EchoKey2 object! More specifically, Component (which is a super-class of our EchoKey2 class) defines addKeyListener(). So an instance of our EchoKey2 class (an actual EchoKey2 object) is both a key event listener (because it implements the KeyEvent interface) and a key event source (because one of its super-classes defines the appropriate addKeyListener() method). Here's the complete EchoKey2 source code:

```
// EchoKey2 Class
// EchoKey2.java
//
// event example using the new delegation-based model

import java.awt.*;
import java.awt.event.*;

class EchoKey2 extends Frame implements KeyListener, WindowListener {
  private char[] key;
  public EchoKey2() {
    key = new char[1];
    key[0] =    ;
    addWindowListener(this);
    addKeyListener(this);
  }
  // these methods implement the KeyListener interface...
  public void keyTyped(KeyEvent e) { }
    // remember the key that was pressed
  public void keyPressed(KeyEvent e) {
    key[0] = (char)e.getKeyCode();
    repaint();
  }
}
```

```
public void keyReleased(KeyEvent e) { }
// these methods implement the WindowListener interface
public void windowClosed(WindowEvent e) { }
// exit when the user closes the window
public void windowClosing(WindowEvent e) {
  System.exit(0);
}
public void windowDeiconified(WindowEvent e) { }
public void windowIconified(WindowEvent e) { }
public void windowOpened(WindowEvent e) { }
public void windowActivated(WindowEvent e) { }
public void windowDeactivated(WindowEvent e) { }
public void paint(Graphics g) {
  // draw the most recently pressed key
  g.drawChars(key, 0, 1, 10, 40);
}
// create an EchoKey2 object and display it
public static void main(String args[]) {
  EchoKey2  ek = new EchoKey2();
  ek.setSize(255, 128);
  ek.show();
}
}
```

In addition to implementing the KeyListener interface, EchoKey2 also implements the WindowListener interface so we can watch for window closing events and shut the application down.

Summary of Delegation-Based Model

The delegation-based event model represents events using a hierarchy of EventObject classes and uses a source/listener paradigm for sending events. This is a more generic event model than the old inheritance model, but it can also be more cumbersome. If your first thought when looking at the EchoKey2 example is how much more complicated it looks than the old inheritance model in EchoKey, you're not alone. Wasn't this new event model supposed to be better, easier, faster? That's where the third event model comes in, but before we examine it, let's look at some examples that better demonstrate the strengths of the delegation-based event model.

Applied Delegation

The EchoKey2 example was a bit contrived; it duplicates the behavior of the EchoKey example. The delegation-based model is actually best used for communicating an event from one component to another. We're going to look at some better examples of using the delegation-based model in this section. We'll cover *adapters* which are event listeners that sit between the event source and the object that actually wants to act on the event. We'll see why they're needed and look at a powerful new extension to the Java language that makes using adapters much easier.

From One Bean to Another

The EchoKey2 example dealt with direct input from the user: key presses. These events are generated by the GUI in response to the user doing something. What about events that come from other sources, like other Beans? This is the situation the delegation-based model handles really well.

> NOTE: *The old inheritance model also had a technique for handling events from other objects via the* action *method. The action method goes hand-in-hand with the handleEvent() method. It's called when an object within a component generates an event. This technique is workable when a button, for example, needs to send an event to the component that contains it, but it's not a general solution like the delegation-based model.*

Our next example will listen for events from a button. CountUp, listed below, contains a button. When the user clicks on the button, an internal integer is incremented and the display is updated. It counts the number of button presses.

```java
// CountUp Class
// CountUp.java
//
// example of processing action events generated
// by a button using delegation-based model.

import java.awt.*;
import java.awt.event.*;

class CountUp extends Frame implements ActionListener, WindowListener {
  private int num;

  public CountUp() {
    Button  plusButton = new Button("Plus (+)");
```

```
    // initialize num
    num = 0;
    // FlowLayout will arrange buttons automatically for us
    setLayout(new FlowLayout());
    add(plusButton);
    addWindowListener(this);
    // register with the button
    plusButton.addActionListener(this);
  }
// Increment the count by one
public void incCount() {
    num++;
    repaint();
}
// implement the ActionListener interface
public void actionPerformed(ActionEvent e)
{
    incCount();
}
// these methods implement the WindowListener interface
public void windowClosed(WindowEvent e) { }
// exit when the user closes the window
public void windowClosing(WindowEvent e) {
    System.exit(0);
}
public void windowDeiconified(WindowEvent e) { }
public void windowIconified(WindowEvent e) { }
public void windowOpened(WindowEvent e) { }
public void windowActivated(WindowEvent e) { }
public void windowDeactivated(WindowEvent e) { }
public void paint(Graphics g) {
    // display the current count
    g.drawString(String.valueOf(num), 0, 10);
}
// create a CountUp object and display it
public static void main(String args[]) {
    CountUp   c = new CountUp();
    c.setSsize(255, 128);
    c.show();
  }
}
```

6

The constructor for `CountUp` creates a button, adds it to the display (by simply calling `add`), and registers itself as an `ActionEvent` listener by calling the button's `addActionListener()` method.

This isn't much different from the EchoKey2 example. Plus, the old inheritance-based model would be even easier; you could simply override the `action()` method and not even worry about registering yourself with the button (the action event would automatically go to the component that contained it). Things start to get a little more interesting when we add a second button.

Let's add a button that decrements the count. We could simply create another button in the constructor, add it, and register with it:

```
public CountUp() {
    Button  plusButton = new Button("Plus (+)"),
            minusButton = new Button("Minus (-)");

    // initialize num
    num = 0;
    // FlowLayout will arrange buttons automatically for us
    setLayout(new FlowLayout());
    add(plusButton);
    add(minusButton);
    addWindowListener(this);
    // register with the buttons
    plusButton.addActionListener(this);
    minusButton.addActionListener(this);
}
```

This would work, but the same method, `actionPerformed()`, would be called both when the user presses the plus button and the minus button; `actionPerformed()` would have to examine the `ActionEvent` it was passed, determine which button sent it, and act accordingly. This is very similar to how things would have been done using the old technique of overriding the `action()` method. Ideally, we would like for the `plusButton` to call one method when it's pressed, and the `minusButton` to call a different method. This isn't directly possible with the old override-action technique.

TIP: *You could just have* `action()` *determine which button was pressed and then call the appropriate method, but that can turn into a lot of work when there are several similar components.*

The delegation gives us an extra lever however: addActionListener().
Using this in combination with adapters, we can get very close to the desired
result.

Adapters: Making Life Easier

Adapters are event listeners that sit between the event source and the object that
actually wants to respond to events. Adapters have many uses, such as:

▶ Wiring events from a source to methods on a listener

▶ Filtering events

▶ Demultiplexing multiple event sources to a single listener

▶ Providing default behavior for event listener methods

▶ Controlling the order that an event is delivered to multiple listeners

We're interested in a demultiplexing adapter for our example (the default behavior for listener methods that adapters provide is an added bonus). Instead of
directly implementing the ActionListener interface in our class, we'll create an
adapter for each button that implements the ActionListener interface. Each
adapter will then call the appropriate methods on our class. Here's the complete
example...

```java
// CountUD Class
// CountUD.java
//
// example of processing action events generated
// by two buttons using delegation-based model
// and adapters.import java.awt.*;

import java.awt.event.*;

// this class handles events generated by the
// plus button
class PlusAdapter implements ActionListener {
  // keep a reference to a CountUD object
  // so we can call one of its methods when
  // processing the event
  CountUD count;

  PlusAdapter(CountUD c) {
    count = c;
  }
```

6

```
  public void actionPerformed(ActionEvent e) {
    // process the event by calling the appropriate
    // method on count
    count.incCount();
  }
}


// this class handles events generated by the
// minus button
class MinusAdapter implements ActionListener {
  // keep a reference to a CountUD object
  // so we can call one of its methods when
  // processing the event
  CountUD count;

  MinusAdapter(CountUD c) {
    count = c;
  }
  public void actionPerformed(ActionEvent e) {
    // process the event by calling the appropriate
    // method on count
    count.decCount();
  }
}


class CountUD extends Frame implements WindowListener {
  private int num;

  public CountUD() {
    Button  plusButton = new Button("Plus (+)"),
            minusButton = new Button("Minus (-)");

    // initialize num
    num = 0;
    // FlowLayout will arrange buttons automatically for us
    setLayout(new FlowLayout());
    add(plusButton);
    add(minusButton);
    addWindowListener(this);
    // register our adapters with the buttons
    plusButton.addActionListener(new PlusAdapter(this));
```

```
      minusButton.addActionListener(new MinusAdapter(this));
    }
    // Increment the count by one
    public void incCount() {
      num++;
      repaint();
    }
    // Decrement the count by one
    public void decCount() {
      num-;
      repaint();
    }
    // these methods implement the WindowListener interface
    public void windowClosed(WindowEvent e) { }
    // exit when the user closes the window
    public void windowClosing(WindowEvent e) {
      System.exit(0);
    }
    public void windowDeiconified(WindowEvent e) { }
    public void windowIconified(WindowEvent e) { }
    public void windowOpened(WindowEvent e) { }
    public void paint(Graphics g) {
      // display the current count
      g.drawString(String.valueOf(num), 10, 40);
    }
    // create a CountUD object and display it
    public static void main(String args[]) {
      CountUD  c = new CountUD();

      c.setSize(255, 128);
      c.show();
    }
  }
```

This is much cleaner from a purist, object-oriented point of view; much of the complexity that was in the CountUp class has moved to the adapters. However, it's still quite a bit of work to write the adapters, keep a reference to the CountUD object, and then call the appropriate method on the CountUD object when processing the event. If we step back and look at the relationships between classes here, we note that the adapters can only be used in conjunction with a CountUD object; it almost seems as though they should be part of the CountUD class. Java has one more new trick up its sleeve to solidify this idea and help simplify things even more: inner classes.

Inner Classes: Easier Still

A new feature has been added to the Java language itself that supports the idea of a class specifically intended for use with another class: inner classes. All the classes we've seen so far are known as top-level classes. Java 1.1 now allows us to declare a class inside of another class. This "inner-class" has access to the methods and member variables of the containing class. Look at this example:

```
class TopLevel {
  private int num;

  class Inner {
    public void incNum() {
      num++;
    }
  }
}
```

Notice that class Inner is declared inside of class TopLevel. Also notice that the incNum() method in class Inner increments num directly. But num is a member of class TopLevel. Now this may not seem so earth-shattering; from the syntax, that looks pretty natural. The compiler is having to perform a little magic to pull this off, though. We won't go into the details here, but basically, the compiler is automatically doing what we did in our adapter classes.

This sounds perfect for using adapter classes with our own components. In fact, inner classes were added to the language for exactly this situation (although there will certainly be other uses also). Let's rewrite CountUD (we'll call it CountIC for Count Inner Classes) to use inner classes.

```
// CountIC Class
// CountIC.java
//
// example of processing action events generated
// by two buttons using delegation-based model
// and inner-classes.

import java.awt.*;
import java.awt.event.*;

class CountIC extends Frame {
```

```
private int num;

public CountIC() {
  Button  plusButton = new Button("Plus (+)"),
          minusButton = new Button("Minus (-)");

  // initialize num
  num = 0;
  // FlowLayout will arrange buttons automatically for us
  setLayout(new FlowLayout());
  add(plusButton);
  add(minusButton);
  // register our WindowListener inner class as a WindowListener
  addWindowListener(new ProcessWindow());
  // register our inner adapters with the buttons
  plusButton.addActionListener(new PlusAdapter());
  minusButton.addActionListener(new MinusAdapter());
}
// Increment the count by one
public void incCount() {
  num++;
  repaint();
}
// Decrement the count by one
public void decCount() {
  num--;
  repaint();
}
// this inner adapter class processes events
// generated by the plus button
class PlusAdapter implements ActionListener {
  public void actionPerformed(ActionEvent e) {
    incCount();
  }
}
// this inner adapter class processes events
// generated by the minus button
class MinusAdapter implements ActionListener {
  public void actionPerformed(ActionEvent e) {
    decCount();
  }
```

6

```
      }
      // this inner adapter class process Window events
      class ProcessWindow extends WindowAdapter {
        public void windowClosing(WindowEvent e) {
          System.exit(0);
        }
      }
      public void paint(Graphics g) {
        // display the current count
        g.drawString(String.valueOf(num), 10, 40);
      }
      // create a CountIC object and display it
      public static void main(String args[]) {
        CountIC  c = new CountIC();

        c.setSize(255, 128);
        c.show();
      }
    }
```

This example uses three adapters: one for each button and one for the
WindowListener.

Let's look at the WindowListener adapter first. Since we're using an adapter
for WindowListener, class CountIC doesn't implement the WindowListener
interface. Instead, we define an inner-class called ProcessWindow that extends
WindowAdapter. WindowAdapter is an adapter provided with the JDK 1.1 that
implements the WindowListener interface and provides default behavior ("do-
nothing") for all the methods in the WindowListener interface. Since
WindowAdapter provides default behavior for all the methods, we only have to
implement the one method we're interested in: windowClosing(). Remember,
before, we had to implement all the other methods in the WindowListener interface and provide blank methods for the ones we weren't interested in. Inner
classes as adapters are already starting to pay off! Note in the constructor for
CountIC, we call addWindowListener() like this:

```
      addWindowListener(new ProcessWindow());
```

The button adapters are much simpler now. They implement
ActionListener and directly call the appropriate method on CountIC from their
actionPerformed() method. Notice that the way the adapters are registered
with the buttons (via addActionListener()) has changed slightly: We no longer
pass this to the adapter when we create it. Don't be fooled, though; the compiler
is just passing this to the adapter automatically.

The new delegation-based model works well for sending an event from one Bean to another. In the previous examples, events were sent from buttons to our Frame class. Throw in adapters and inner classes, and it's also pretty easy to use. The delegation-based model isn't so natural for handling the window events, however. We used adapters and inner classes to implement the `WindowListener` interface, but the old inheritance model was still easier to use in some ways. The simple fact is, sometimes the inheritance model is more appropriate. This is a situation that arises often in programming; a hammer is designed for nails. It may work with screws, but it's not the best tool to use in that situation. The delegation-based model may work when sending an event to a sub-class from a super-class (when receiving that window closing event for example), but it's not the best tool to use in that situation. A sub-class inherits from a super-class, so you really need a model based on inheritance.

Inheritance-Based Event Handling Revisited

The AWT in the JDK 1.1 provides yet another event model: a new inheritance-based event model. This model is similar to the original inheritance model, but it's completely compatible with the new delegation-based model. Strictly speaking, this model is specific to the AWT and not JavaBeans in general. The AWT could be thought of as an ambitious use of JavaBeans (although that's not how things actually happened historically). In other words, we can certainly learn something from the AWT's new inheritance model. As well see later, using a model identical to the AWT's new inheritance model is an excellent way to actually implement a JavaBean.

Event Representation

Most importantly, the new inheritance model uses the same event objects that the delegation-based model does. Everything you've learned about the `EventObject` hierarchy under the delegation-based model applies here.

Event Delivery and Processing

Events are delivered and processed through the method `processEvent()`.

```
protected void processEvent(AWTEvent e) { /* . . . */ }
```

The `processEvent()` method is directly analogous to `handleEvent()` under the old model. It accepts an `AWTEvent` (which extends `EventObject`) object as an argument, but unlike `handleEvent()`, it returns nothing. An `AWTEvent` object has a numeric identifier that's used to determine the actual event.

Also note that `processEvent()` is declared as protected, so a sub-class can override it. The `processEvent()` methods defined in many of the AWT components make life easier for programmers by splitting the events out into groups identical to the classes of events used in the delegation-based model. For handling key events, for example, the processKeyEvent() method is provided:

```
protected void processKeyEvent(KeyEvent e) { /* . . . */ }
```

The processEvent() method provided in the AWT provided another bit of functionality that was missing from the old inheritance model: event filtering. The appropriate processXxxEvent() method will be called only if Xxx events are enabled. There are two ways to enable an event: Call addXxxListener() with a valid listener (this is what we did with the delegation-based model) or call enableEvent() with the appropriate event mask defined in AWTEvent. Let's revisit the EchoKey example one more time and use the ProcessXxxEvent() method.

```
import java.awt.*;
import java.awt.event.*;

class EchoKey3 extends Frame {
  private char[] key;
  public EchoKey3() {
    key = new char[1];
    key[0] =    ;
    // enable the events we're interested in
    enableEvents(AWTEvent.KEY_EVENT_MASK |
                 AWTEvent.WINDOW_EVENT_MASK);
  }
  // process key events
  protected void processKeyEvent(KeyEvent e) {
    switch (e.getID()) {
      case KeyEvent.KEY_PRESSED:
        key[0] = (char)e.getKeyCode();
        repaint();
        break;
    }
    super.processKeyEvent(e);
  }
  // process window events
  protected void processWindowEvent(WindowEvent e) {
    switch (e.getID()) {
      case WindowEvent.WINDOW_CLOSING:
        System.exit(0);
        break;
```

```
      }
      super.processWindowEvent(e);
   }
   public void paint(Graphics g) {
      // draw the most recently pressed key
      g.drawChars(key, 0, 1, 10, 40);
   }
   // create an EchoKey3 object and display it
   public static void main(String args[]) {
      EchoKey3  ek = new EchoKey3();
      ek.setSize(255, 128);
      ek.show();
   }
}
```

The constructor for `EchoKey3` calls `enableEvent()` with a mask that enables key and window events. Then, it's simply a matter of overriding `processKeyEvent()` and `processWindowEvent()`. Don't forget to pass the event on to your super-class. For example, `processWindowEvent()` calls `super.processWindowEvent(e)` after it's done its processing.

Summary of New Inheritance-Based Model
The new inheritance model works a lot like the original inheritance model, but, unlike the original, it's completely compatible with the delegation-based model. Use the new inheritance model when processing events generated by a component you're extending through inheritance.

6

Putting It All Together
We've examined three event models in some detail. Let's look back and see how these methods relate to one another and talk about when each should be used (Figure 6.5).

We're stuck with the old inheritance model for historical reasons. It shouldn't be used in new code. You'll probably see it a lot in example Java 1.0 code, however, so it helps to be familiar with it. Here's a recap of the old inheritance model:

▶ Uses a single event class to represent objects

▶ Events are delivered through the handleEvent() method

▶ Replaced by new models

▶ Should not be used in new code

The delegation-based model is new to the JDK 1.1 and JavaBeans. It's most useful when communicating events between components such as from a button to the frame containing it. Here are some points to remember regarding the delegation-based model:

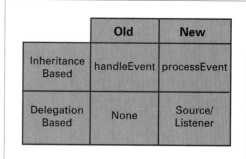

FIGURE 6.5

Event models: the big picture

- Uses a hierarchy of classes to represent events

- Uses a source-listener paradigm to deliver events

- Works well for sending events between components

- Uses adapters to act as go-between from source to listener

- Uses inner classes to make adapters easier to use

- Should be used in new code

The event objects used by the delegation model

- Represent one or more events

- Identify events or groups of events by a hierarchy of classes

- Identify individual events within a group by a numeric identifier

An event listener

- Implements an `EventListener` interface

- Registers itself with an event source

- Receives events from an event source

An event source

- Provides addXxxListener() methods

- Maintains a list of listeners

- Sends events to registered listeners by calling an individual method on each listener

The new inheritance-based model is similar in use to the original inheritance model, but it's compatible with the new delegation-based model. The new inheritance model

- Uses the same hierarchy of classes as the delegation-based model to represent events

- Delivers events through the `processEvent()` method

- Is useful when extending an AWT component

- Should be used in new code instead of `handleEvent()`

What about Event Sources?

In this chapter, we've mostly concentrated on processing events. What if you're writing your own Bean that needs to generate events (in other words, it's an event source). We'll look at this in more detail in Part 3: Building Your Own Beans (Chapters 11 through 15), but in general your Bean must provide the appropriate addXxxListener() method for each event it's generating.

It must also maintain a list of listeners for each event; you'll probably want to use a simple vector object for this. In addition, try to follow a pattern similar to the AWT components. If you wrote a complex timer Bean, for example, that generates a `TimerEvent`, put the code that sends the events to the listeners in a protected method named `processTimerEvent()`. By providing this method and making it protected, you make life easier for someone who wants to extend your Bean and use the new inheritance-based model to process your timer events.

Summary

In this chapter, you learned the importance of events and the event paradigm in component programming. You also examined the three event models supported by Java and JavaBeans and when to use each model. Finally, you looked at some guidelines for writing event sources.

6

Chapter 7

What's in a Bean: The Properties APIs

▶ **Changing States**

▶ **Using Properties in Your Own Beans**

▶ **The PropertyEditor Interface: A Closer Look**

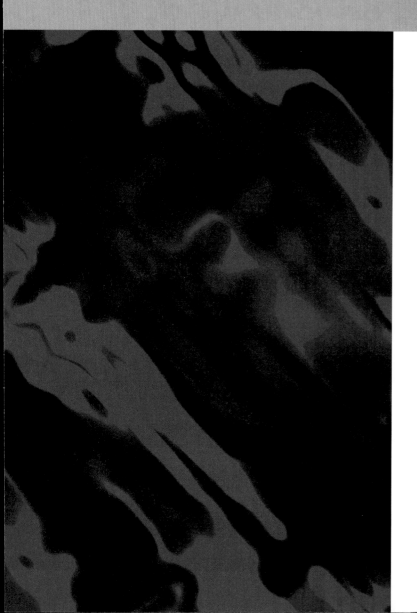

In this chapter, you'll learn to control the behavior and appearance of Beans using *properties*. We'll examine how properties are manipulated using the demonstration design tool, the BeanBox, included with Sun's Bean Development Kit (the BDK). We'll also create a simple Bean to demonstrate how properties are exposed to a design tool. Finally, we'll delve into techniques that allow a Bean you design to watch and reject the changes to properties on another Bean.

What is a software component, and what distinguishes it from an "ordinary" object? Components are objects, but they're objects that are self-contained and highly reusable; design a component once and drop it into any application that needs that kind of functionality. Components are supposed to be the ultimate in code reuse.

Note that reuse and self-containment are contradictory in a certain sense. To actually use (or reuse) a component, you need to be able to manipulate it. A completely self-contained component would be isolated from everything else; there would be no way of manipulating it. A compromise between usability and isolation is needed; we need a controlled mechanism for manipulating a component. Properties provide one of these mechanisms.

In this chapter, you will learn

▶ That properties control the internal state of a Bean

▶ How to manipulate a Bean's properties from a design tool like the BeanBox

▶ About the various property types supported by Java and how they differ

▶ How to expose a Bean's properties to design tools

▶ How to use custom editors for properties

7

Changing States

JavaBean components are objects, and like all objects, they have an internal state; they have member variables. Many of these member variables need to be manipulated by the designer using the Bean. Other member variables, however, are for internal use only, and allowing the designer access to these could be disastrous. In addition, the way that the aspects of a component are represented by its member variables may not be the most natural representation for the designer using the Bean. This is where properties come in. Properties provide controlled, user-friendly manipulation of the internal state of a Bean. Properties also provide a clear separation between the interface to a Bean and the implementation of the Bean. We can change the way a Bean works internally without causing problems as long as we don't change the interface (including the properties).

NOTE: *In programming, the terms interface and implementation have very specific meanings that differ somewhat from their conversational meaning. The interface to an object is its set of accessible methods and data members. A programmer uses an object via its interface. The implementation of an object, on the other hand, involves the internal workings of the object. This includes the methods and data members that may only be accessed by the object itself and the actual code in the methods. When you hear the term interface, think "What does the object do?" When you hear the term implementation, think "How does it do it?" Well-designed objects have a clear distinction between implementation and interface. Keeping the two separate allows the implementation (the internal workings) of an object to change without affecting the interface, and not changing an object's interface is very important. If an object's interface changes, it makes life difficult for everyone who was using the previous version. The ability to change an object's implementation is equally important. It's often useful to get an object out there that works. You can always come back later and make it better, faster, and smarter if you've kept the object's interface and implementation well separated.*

Let's get a little more familiar with properties by actually using some Beans and manipulating their properties. The BDK ships with a demonstration Bean manipulation tool called the BeanBox. The BeanBox is a container for other Beans and is itself a Bean (so you can drop a BeanBox inside of another BeanBox). It allows the manipulation of Beans, including their properties. Look in the directory in which you installed the BDK, and you should find a `beanbox` directory. This directory provides both an MS-DOS batch file (run.bat) and a Unix shell script (run.sh) for running the BeanBox. To execute the BeanBox from a command shell, change to the beanbox directory and just type "run" under Windows 95/NT or "run.sh" under Unix.

TIP: *As with all Java tools, you'll need to have the "bin" directory of the JDK 1.1 in your path to use the BeanBox.*

Figure 7.1, below, shows the BeanBox running with one of the simpler Beans dropped into it. The center window is the BeanBox itself. The window on the left is the toolbox of available Beans. Click on the JellyBean in the toolbox for example, and your cursor should change to cross-hairs. Click somewhere inside of the BeanBox window to drop an instance of the JellyBean component in the BeanBox.

We're mainly interested in the window on the right: the PropertySheet window. This window displays the properties and their current values for the selected

Bean. You may change a property by clicking on it. Click on the color property for example, and a standard color editor dialog should appear (`sun.beans.editors.ColorEditor`). This dialog allows the color to be specified by typing in its RGB value or by picking from a list of common colors.

> **NOTE:** *This is a good example of the disparity between how a property is represented internally (as a* `Color` *object which ultimately represents the color by packing the red, green, and blue values into a single integer) versus how the user would like to choose the property (as a simple color name).*

As new colors are chosen, the value of the internal variable used by the JellyBean to store the color is updated; the internal state of the JellyBean changes, but the more obvious effect is that the color of the JellyBean changes. This demonstrates one of the other characteristics a property can have: Inspecting or changing a property can have side-effects. In this case, changing the color property caused the Bean to repaint with the new color.

Calling the repainting of the Bean with the new color a side-effect may seem a bit backwards. After all, from the user's viewpoint the ultimate goal in changing the color property is to change the displayed color of the Bean. From a programmer's point of view, however, changing a property generally means changing a member variable of the Bean. Reading the current value of a property usually means reading the current value of a member variable. If this were all there were to properties, there'd be no difference between member variables and properties. Properties strive to be more than simple member variables, however. They're like super-variables. Change a property, and the underlying member variable changes, but other effects (side-effects) can result. In the end, everyone's satisfied. The programmer's satisfied because the member variable was changed, and the user is satisfied because the desired goal (changing the displayed color of the Bean in our example) was accomplished.

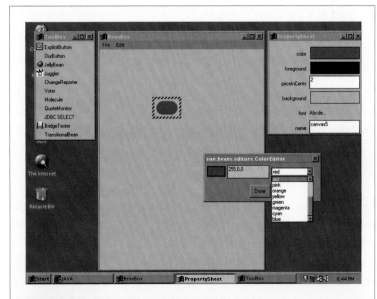

FIGURE 7.1

Manipulating properties from the BeanBox

Experiment with some of the JellyBean's other properties. The foreground property changes the foreground color (and uses the same color editor as the color property). The priceInCents property is a simple property that can have numeric values. When you click on it, the PropertySheet doesn't bring up an editor. Instead, the PropertySheet displays the current value of the priceInCents property using a text edit field. You change the property by simply typing the new value into the edit field. Also note that changing the priceInCents property has no visible effect on the JellyBean. It does change the internal state of the JellyBean, however. Rest assured that the JellyBean remembers the value that you type in for the priceInCents property, and if some other Bean were to ask the JellyBean for the value of this property, it would report back the value you entered.

Using Properties in Your Own Beans

The previous section examined using the properties of a Bean in a tool like the BeanBox. What if you're writing your own Bean that needs to provide properties for manipulation by the user? How does a design tool know which properties a Bean supports and how they're changed? That's what we're going to examine in this section. Fortunately, Java makes exposing simple member variables (member variables that are either data types built into the Java language or common objects provided with the JDK) as properties very easy for the Bean writer as long as some simple naming conventions are followed. Things get a bit more complicated when the type of the member variable is more complex, but Java provides a mechanism for "telling" the environment how to handle these complex types.

What's in a Name?

The simplest way to get a Bean up and running with properties is to allow Java to automatically figure out the properties for your Bean using *introspection*. We'll examine introspection in more detail in Chapter 9. For now, we'll just point out that introspection allows a tool to examine a Bean at run-time and determine the methods that a Bean provides.

The properties of a Bean are always accessed using public methods provided by the Bean. Specifically, a property will have a *getter* and a *setter* method. The primary purpose of the getter method is to return the current value of the property, but it may have other side-effects. Similarly, the primary purpose of the setter method is to accept a new value as an argument and update the internal state of the Bean, but it also may have other side-effects, such as repainting the Bean or notifying other Beans that the property has changed. If we name the getter and setter methods properly, the design tool can use introspection, see these methods, and know that these are the methods to access a property.

Simple Properties

Suppose we have a simple Bean that has a background color property. The declaration of the getter and setter methods for our Bean with the background color property might look like this:

```
public Color getBackground();
public void setBackground(Color newBackgroundColor);
```

The JDK adopts a naming convention for automatically detecting properties. Using our background example, let's see how the BeanBox automatically detects the background property. The BeanBox uses introspection and sees that our Bean has a method named "getBackground" that accepts no arguments and that returns a `Color` value. It also finds a matching method named "setBackground" that returns nothing and that accepts a `Color` value. So "background" is assumed to be a property of type `Color`. The BeanBox (which serves as a container for Beans) has a built-in editor for properties of type `Color`, so it adds "background" to the property sheet automatically.

Boolean Properties

Boolean properties use Java's built-in `boolean` data type. They can have one of two values: `true` or `false`. One example might be a Boolean property named "enabled" which allows the Bean to be manipulated by the user when set to `true` but blocks user interaction when set to `false`. In this case, it's more natural to ask the question, "is the Bean enabled?" rather than stating "get the value of the enabled property." As a result, it's become customary in many programming circles to use "is" when naming a method for retrieving the value of a Boolean property or variable rather than "get". The JDK 1.1 supports this idea for Boolean properties by allowing a different name for the getter method. If our Bean had a Boolean property named "enabled", we could declare the getter and setter methods like this:

```
public boolean isEnabled();
public void setEnabled();
```

Using getEnabled() would still be legal (or you could provide both), but generally it's more consistent to just stick with "is" for Boolean properties.

Indexed Properties

Indexed properties act like an array of properties, all of the same type. Suppose we had a CDPlayer Bean that allowed naming the track list on a CD. We could use an indexed property of strings to store the track names:

```
public String getTrackName(int i);
public void setTrackName(int i, String newTrackName);
```

7

The getter and setter methods both take an additional integer argument that specifies the index of the property we want to get or set. If you call the getter or setter with an index that's out of the current array bounds, they may throw a java.lang.ArrayIndexOutOfBoundsException runtime exception. You may also optionally provide getter and setter methods that accept and return the entire array.

```
public String [] getTrackName();
public void setTrackName(String [] newTrackName);
```

You might be tempted to rename these methods to something more appropriate like "getTrackList" and "setTrackList" since you're dealing with the entire list of tracks, but don't do it. This doesn't fit in with the naming convention established for Beans. These methods must be named the same as their counterparts which accept an integer argument. Otherwise, the JDK's introspection mechanism won't recognize them as referring to the same indexed property.

Constrained and Bound Properties

Some Beans may want to watch the property changes that are occurring on another Bean, validate the change, and possibly reject it in some cases. Other Beans may want to simply watch the property changes that are occurring on another Bean without validating the change. *Constrained properties* are properties that may be validated by another Bean before any changes are made. JavaBeans supports simple watching of property changes through *bound properties*. Note that a property may both be constrained and bound.

Constrained Properties

The setter method for a constrained property must support PropertyVetoException. When the setter method is called, an event is generated and sent to all registered Beans that may want to veto the change. Note that the new JDK 1.1 style events are being used here, so you may want to review Chapter 6, "Bean Happenings: The Event Handling APIs," to become familiar with these new events. The listening Bean implements the VetoableChangeListener interface and can reject a change by throwing a PropertyVetoException. The (abbreviated) declaration for the VetoableChangeListener interface looks like this:

```
public interface VetoableChangeListener extends
  java.util.EventListener {
  void vetoableChange(PropertyChangeEvent evt)
    throws PropertyVetoException;
}
```

The Bean with the setter method should provide the standard methods for adding and removing listeners (addVetoableChangeListener() and removeVetoableChangeListener()).

```
public void addVetoableChangeListener(VetoableChangeListener l);
public void removeVetoableChangeListener(VetoableChangeListener l);
```

Finally, in the setter method for the property, a PropertyChange event is created and vetoableChange() is called on each registered listener. The BDK provides a support class, VetoableChangeSupport, that simplifies all the dirty work by implementing the add and remove listener methods for you. One way to use VetoableChangeSupport is to simply extend it, but this usually isn't feasible; most Beans will inherit from (extend) one of the AWT components (non-GUI Beans might be an exception), and Java doesn't allow you to extend from more than one class (thank goodness). The alternative is to contain a VetoableChangeSupport object as a member variable.

Here's the abbreviated declaration for VetoableChangeSupport.

```
public class VetoableChangeSupport implements java.io.Serializable {
  public VetoableChangeSupport(Object sourceBean);
  public void addVetoableChangeListener(VetoableChangeListener l);
  public void removeVetoableChangeListener(VetoableChangeListener l);
  public void fireVetoableChange(String propertyName,
                        Object oldValue, Object newValue)
                        throws PropertyVetoException;
}
```

The constructor takes a single source object as an argument. This argument is stored away and, as we'll see in a moment, used by the fireVetoableChange() method. The first two methods are the standard methods for adding and removing listeners. The fireVetoableChange() method is called with the name of the property, the old value, and the new value as arguments. It then creates a new PropertyChangeEvent.

```
public class PropertyChangeEvent extends java.util.EventObject {
  public PropertyChangeEvent(Object source, String propertyName,
                        Object oldValue, Object newValue);

  public String getPropertyName();
  public Object getNewValue();
  public Object getOldValue();
  public void setPropagationId(Object propagationId);
  public Object getPropagationId();
}
```

Notice that the constructor for a `PropertyChangeEvent` wants the source of the event in addition to the name of the property, the old value and the new value. Rather than pass itself as the source (which would only be correct if you had extended from `PropertyChangeSupport`), `fireVetoableChange()` uses the source parameter that was passed to its constructor. Here's a code snippet demonstrating how a Bean might use `PropertyChangeSupport`.

TIP: `PropertyChangeEvent` *accepts* `Objects` *for the old and new values, so any properties of the built-in types (*`int`*,* `boolean`*, and so on) must be wrapped in their corresponding object derived class (Integer, Boolean, and so on).*

```java
// VetoablePropertyExample
// VetoablePropertyExample.java

import java.beans.*;
class VetoablePropertyExample {
  public int getNumber() {
    return num;
  }
  public void setNumber(int newNum) throws PropertyVetoException {
    vetos.fireVetoableChange(/* property name */"number",
                             /* old value */ new Integer(num),
                             /* new value */ new Integer(newNum));
    // no-veto exception was thrown, so make the change
    num = newNum;
  }
  public void addVetoableChangeListener(VetoableChangeListener l) {
    vetos.addVetoableChangeListener(l);
  }
  public void removeVetoableChangeListener(VetoableChangeListener l) {
    vetos.removeVetoableChangeListener(l);
  }

  private VetoableChangeSupport
    vetos = new VetoableChangeSupport(this);
  private int num = 0;
}
```

Bound Properties

The mechanism for handling bound properties is very similar to the mechanism used for constrained properties. A listener implements the PropertyChangeListener interface. The Bean with the bound properties provides the standard methods for adding and removing listeners:

```
public void addPropertyChangeListener(PropertyChangeListener l);
public void removePropertyChangeListener(PropertyChangeListener l);
```

When the setter method for a bound property is called, it should first compare the old value with the new value. If they're the same, it should just silently return without doing anything (no registered listeners should be notified). This is more efficient than always notifying and, more importantly, can prevent infinite loops from occurring when one Bean notifies another Bean which ultimately ends up calling the setter method again, which notifies the Bean again, and so on. If the value is different, a property change event is created and sent to each registered PropertyChangeListener. After everyone's been notified, the property is actually updated.

The BDK provides a support class, PropertyChangeSupport, that makes registering listeners, removing listeners, and sending the events easier. This class is virtually identical to the VetoableChangeSupport class discussed above, so we won't go over it in detail here. Instead, here's a code snippet that demonstrates how it might typically be used.

```java
// PropertyChangeExample
// PropertyChangeExample.java

import java.beans.*;
class PropertyChangeExample {
  public int getNumber() {
    return num;
  }
  public void setNumber(int newNum) {
    if (getNumber() == newNum)
      return;
    changes.firePropertyChange(/* property name*/ "number",
                               /* old value */ new Integer(num),
                               /* new value */ new Integer(newNum));
    // make the change
    num = newNum;
  }
  public void addPropertyChangeListener(PropertyChangeListener l) {
```

```
        changes.addPropertyChangeListener(l);
    }
    public void removePropertyChangeListener(PropertyChangeListener l) {
        changes.removePropertyChangeListener(l);
    }

    private PropertyChangeSupport changes =
            new PropertyChangeSupport(this);
    private int num = 0;
}
```

Bringing It All Together

Rather than provide an example Bean with both bound and constrained properties
and an associated listener Bean, we'll defer to the example Beans included with
the BDK. The JellyBean is a good example of a Bean with a constrained and bound
property. Its priceInCents property is both constrained and bound.

The ChangeReporter Bean allows you to watch bound properties. To try this
out, drop a JellyBean and a ChangeReporter Bean into
the BeanBox. Next, select the JellyBean and choose
Edit, Events, propertyChange, propertyChange from
the menu. Notice that a red line is now drawn from
the JellyBean to your mouse pointer as you move it
around. Move your mouse pointer to the edge of the
ChangeReporter Bean and click. See Figure 7.2.

An EventTargetDialog should appear, as shown
in Figure 7.3.

Choose the reportChange() method and click
OK. This hooks all property changes events from the
JellyBean up to the reportChange() method of the
ChangeReporter Bean. In other words, it registers
the ChangeReporter Bean as a property change
event listener with JellyBean. As you change the
priceInCents property, the ChangeReporter Bean
will display your changes; it reports the property
change events generated by the bound property,
priceInCents.

The Voter Bean supports vetoing properties.
Drop one in the BeanBox and note that one of its
properties is vetoAll. When this is set to true (the
default), the Voter Bean will veto any property change
events it receives via its vetoableChange() method.

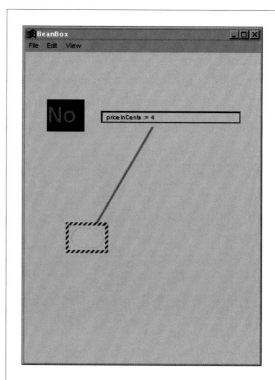

FIGURE 7.2

Connecting the propertyChange event from a
JellyBean to a ChangeReporter Bean

Set vetoAll to `false`, and Voter will allow not veto
PropertyChange events. To try this out, hook the
JellyBean we just used to the Voter Bean as we did before; select the JellyBean, choose Edit, Events,
vetoableChange, vetoableChange from the menu,
and click on the edge of the Voter Bean. Finally,
Choose `vetoableChange` for the target method.
Now as you try to change the priceInCents property,
an error dialog will appear. See Figure 7.4.

Refer to the code for JellyBean, ChangeReporter,
and Voter to see how everything comes together for
constrained and bound properties.

Custom Property Editors

So far, we've only used the built-in property editors supplied with the JDK. The JDK provides property editors
for all of the intrinsic data types supported by the Java
language: `boolean`, `byte`, `short`, `int`,
`float`, and `double`. The JDK also supplies property editors for the classes
`java.lang.String`, `java.awt.Color`,
and `java.awt.Font`. If your property is
one of these types, and you want the
built-in editor to be used, you're all set.
Just provide the appropriate getter and setter methods, and the PropertySheet will
use the built-in editor by default.

Beyond the built-in editors, the JDK
supports custom editors through the
`PropertyEditor` interface. There are (at least) two basic reasons for creating a
custom editor.

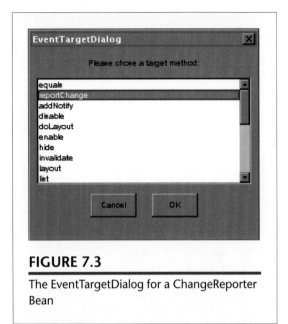

FIGURE 7.3

The EventTargetDialog for a ChangeReporter
Bean

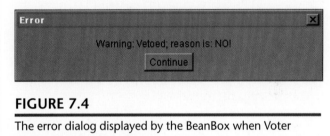

FIGURE 7.4

The error dialog displayed by the BeanBox when Voter
vetoes a property change

1   You need specialized editing of one of the supported types not provided
by the built-in editor

2   Your property isn't one of the supported types (so there is no built-in
editor)

The second one is pretty obvious, but when would a built-in editor not suffice? Let's say we have a "direction" property that's of type `String`. Here's a simple

demo Bean named "Arrow" that uses a "direction" property to decide which way to point.

```java
// Arrow Bean Class
// Arrow.java

package HTPJB.Chap7.Arrow;

import java.io.Serializable;
import java.awt.*;

public class Arrow extends Canvas implements Serializable {
  private String dir;
  public Arrow() {
    super();
    setDirection("North");
    setBackground(Color.lightGray);
    setSize(20, 20);
  }
  public String getDirection() {
    return dir;
  }
  public void setDirection(String newDir) {
    dir = newDir;
    repaint();
  }
  public synchronized void paint(Graphics g) {
    int width = getSize().width;
    int height = getSize().height;
    Point tail = new Point(),
          head = new Point(),
          leg1 = new Point(),
          leg2 = new Point();

    tail.setLocation(width - 1, height / 2);
    head.setLocation(0, height / 2);
    leg1.setLocation(width / 2, 0);
    leg2.setLocation(width / 2, height - 1);
    if (getDirection().startsWith("N")) {
      tail.setLocation(width / 2, height - 1);
      head.setLocation(width / 2, 0);
```

7

```
        leg1.setLocation(0, height / 2);
        leg2.setLocation(width - 1, height / 2);
    } else if (getDirection().startsWith("S")) {
        tail.setLocation(width / 2, 0);
        head.setLocation(width / 2, height - 1);
        leg1.setLocation(0, height / 2);
        leg2.setLocation(width - 1, height / 2);
    } else if (getDirection().startsWith("E")) {
        tail.setLocation(0, height / 2);
        head.setLocation(width - 1, height / 2);
    }

    g.setColor(getBackground());
    g.fillRect(0, 0, width - 1, height - 1);
    g.setColor(Color.black);
    g.drawLine(tail.x, tail.y, head.x, head.y);
    g.drawLine(head.x, head.y, leg1.x, leg1.y);
    g.drawLine(head.x, head.y, leg2.x, leg2.y);
  }
}
```

TIP: *To use this Bean, first compile it using javac (the Java compiler supplied with the JDK). You'll need to add the source directory for the examples to your CLASSPATH to compile successfully. Next, create a JAR file containing the resulting class file, and put it in the jars directory under the directory in which the BDK is installed. Refer to Chapter 4, "Packaging Beans with JAR Files," for more details. Note that you don't need a manifest file for this example. You can tell the JAR tool not to add a manifest file with the "-M" switch. Also you need to execute the jar command from the source directory for the examples (the same directory you added to your classpath). On my machine, the source code for all the examples is under the c:\Source directory. This example is in the c:\Source\HTPJB\Source\Chap7\Arrow directory. So I've added c:\Source to my CLASSPATH, and from this same directory, I execute the following command from the command line to create the JAR file:*

```
c:\Source>jar cfM Arrow.jar HTPJB\Chap7\Arrow\Arrow.class
```

After you've created the JAR file and placed it in the JARs directory, run the BeanBox. The Arrow Bean should now appear in the ToolBox.

To change the arrow's direction, type "North," "South," "East," or "West" into the edit field for the "direction" property. Figure 7.5 shows how this would look in the BeanBox.

Custom Editors for Built-In Types

Typing the direction into the edit field works, but it's not a very user friendly way of specifying the direction. First, the users can type anything they want into the edit field. Arrow actually only looks for "N," "S," or "E" as the first character and assumes "W" otherwise. If the user types in "Left," or "South," or even "Hello," the arrow will point west, which is probably not what was expected. We'd like to restrict the

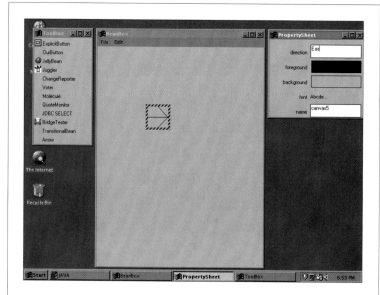

FIGURE 7.5

The Arrow Bean without a custom DirectionEditor

legal values for direction to "North," "South," "East," and "West." We could enforce the legal values by making direction be a constrained property. If the user types in something other than "North," "South," "East," or "'West," it would simply be rejected.

This really isn't much better, though. We'd be much better off if the property editor were simply an AWT Choice control (also known as a drop-down combo box) with the legal values rather than a plain old edit field. The user could just click on the Choice control and a list of the four legal values would be displayed. The user could then just pick the desired value. A support class is provided with the JDK that makes this particular example very easy. PropertyManagerSupport implements the PropertyEditor interface. We can derive from it and override the getTags() method like this:

```java
// DirectionEditor Class
// DirectionEditor.java

package HTPJB.Chap7.Arrow;

public class DirectionEditor extends java.beans.PropertyEditorSupport {
  public String[] getTags() {
    String result[] = { "North", "South", "East", "West" };
    return result;
```

```
    }
  }
```

Thanks to all the functionality provided by the `PropertyEditorSupport` class, this is all our `DirectionEditor` needs to provide. Unfortunately, this, by itself, won't cause our editor to be used instead of the built-in String editor. The environment has no idea that this editor is supposed to be used instead of the built-in String editor; we need to tell it to use our editor. To do that, we need to step back for a moment and take a closer look at the automatic property detection mechanism upon which we've been relying so heavily. We'll examine all of this in more detail in Chapter 9, "Knowing Beans: The Introspection APIs," but here's the dime tour. Every Bean has a `BeanInfo` object associated with it that describes the properties, methods, events, and so on supported by the Bean. If we don't explicitly provide a `BeanInfo` object, the system effectively generates one for us by examining the methods in our Bean and looking for interface patterns (such as methods starting with "get" and "set" for properties).

To tell the environment to use our editor rather than the standard `String` editor, we need to provide our own `BeanInfo` object that describes the "direction" property. Our description will just specify the name of the property (which must be supplied) and the editor to use: `DirectionEditor`. We'll allow everything else (like the getter and setter methods) to take on default values. The thoughtful designers at Sun provided a class, `SimpleBeanInfo`, that implements `BeanInfo` with default behavior and makes life much easier. We'll extend this class and override the `getPropertyDescriptors()` method.

```java
// ArrowBeanInfo Class
// ArrowBeanInfo.java

package HTPJB.Chap7.Arrow;

public class ArrowBeanInfo extends SimpleBeanInfo {
  public PropertyDescriptor[] getPropertyDescriptors() {
    try {
      PropertyDescriptor pd = new PropertyDescriptor("direction",
                                                 Arrow.class);
      pd.setPropertyEditorClass(DirectionEditor.class);
      PropertyDescriptor result[] = { pd };
      return result;
    } catch (Exception ex) {
      System.err.println("ArrowBeanInfo: unexpected exeption: " + ex);
      return null;
    }
  }
}
```

The environment will use this class automatically, due, again, to a naming convention. When it sees the `ArrowBean`, it looks for a class named `ArrowBeanInfo`. Until now, we haven't provided this class, so the environment has been generating a `BeanInfo` object for us. Add this class (and the `DirectionEditor` class) to the JAR file, and your BeanBox should appear similar to Figure 7.6.

TIP: *The previous JAR file we created only contained a single class, so we were able to get by with no manifest file (see Chapter 4 for a discussion of JAR files and manifest files in general). This one will have three classes: Arrow.class, DirectionEditor.class, and ArrowBeanInfo.class. Of these three, only Arrow.class is a Bean. The other two are support classes. We'll need to use a manifest file in this case to indicate that Arrow.class is the only one that is a Bean. The source code supplied with this book provides the appropriate manifest file. When creating the JAR file, use the -m switch (rather than -M) to indicate that you're supplying a manifest file. On my machine, the source code is in the c:\Source directory, so I use this command:*

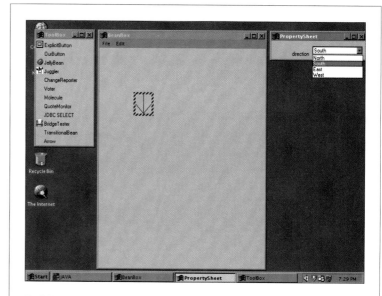

FIGURE 7.6

The Arrow Bean with a custom `DirectionEditor`

```
c:\Source>jar cfm Arrow.jar HTPJB\Chap7\Arrow\Arrow.mf
HTPJB\Chap7\Arrow\*.class.
```

After you've created the JAR file, copy it to the jars directory as before. The new Arrow Bean, with the new direction editor, should appear the next time you run the BeanBox.

Note that the other properties which were showing up (such as background) before we provided `ArrowBeanInfo` are gone now. Our getPropertyDescriptors() method in ArrowBeanInfo only returns the "direction" property, so that's all we get. To also get the "background" property, for example, simply add a new PropertyDescriptor entry for the "background" property to the getPropertyDescriptors() method.

Custom Editors for Custom Types

Let's return to the second reason for using a custom editor: Your property isn't one of the supported types (so there is no built-in editor). Things are actually a bit easier in this case. Editors are still implemented the same way we implemented the custom String editor above: by implementing the PropertyEditor interface (possibly by extending PropertyEditorSupport). It's simpler because you don't have to tell the environment to use your editor. If you define a class named Xyz, and you have a Bean with a property of type Xyz, the environment will look for a class named XyzEditor. If found, that class will be used as the editor (unless you explicitly tell it to use another class via a BeanInfo object).

From the point of view of the design tool you're using (the BeanBox, for example), whether the property is a built-in type or your own type really makes no difference, it just wants a properly named class for the editor. For the built-in types, those classes are provided for you in the JDK. You have to supply them yourself for custom types.

The PropertyEditor Interface: A Closer Look

We stated above that a custom property editor must implement the PropertyEditor interface, and left it at that. If you examine the documentation for PropertyEditor, you'll realize this is much easier said than done. For very simple cases, such as our example above, you can just extend PropertyEditorSupport and override a method or two. For more complex cases, we need to look at the PropertyEditor interface in more detail.

The PropertyEditor interface has a range of provisions for editing properties. On one end of the spectrum, many of the simpler properties can be treated as strings for editing purposes. For more complex data types, the PropertyEditor interface allows you to specify your own component for editing.

Taking Responsibility

A class implementing the PropertyEditor interface has two main responsibilities: displaying the value of the property to the user and receiving changes to the property from the user. The `PropertyEditor` interface provides three basic ways of handling both of these tasks. The three techniques are:

1   Display and edit using an AWT `TextField` control

2   Display and edit using an AWT `Choice` control

3   Display by painting a representation of the current value to a `Graphics` object and edit using your own component designed for just that purpose.

Which display/edit technique is used is controlled by the values returned from a handful of methods in the `PropertyEditor` interface: `getTags()`, `getAsText()`, `setAsText()`, `isPaintable()`, and `supportsCustomEditor()`. You may want to refer to the BDK's documentation for the `PropertyEditor` interface for a general description of these methods. Here are their prototypes in the `PropertyEditor` interface.

```
public abstract String[] getTags( );
public abstract String getAsText();
public abstract void setAsText(String text);
public abstract boolean isPaintable();
public abstract boolean supportsCustomEditor();
```

Using the TextField Control Technique

The first technique, display and edit using an AWT `TextField` control, is often the simplest to do. If your property can be sensibly represented as text, but it's not limited to a fixed set of values (which would be better handled using a Choice control), this is probably the method to use.

To enable this technique, your `PropertyEditor` must return `false` from both `isPaintable()` and `supportsCustomEditor()`, return `null` from `getTags()`, and return the current value of the property as a string from `getAsText()`. In addition, you'll want to have `setAsText()` update the property from the supplied String.

The `PropertyEditorSupport` class comes in especially handy here; it provides a rudimentary implementation of `getValue()`, `setValue()`, and `getAsText()`. The `getAsText()` provided in `PropertyEditorSupport` simply calls `getValue()` and tries to convert the returned object to a `String`. As long as your class does the right thing in its `toString()` method, this should be all you need. You'll have to implement `setAsText()` yourself; however, `PropertyEditorSupport` has no way of changing the value of a generic object using a string (maybe object should have a corresponding `setFromString()` method), so `setAsText()` should just use the supplied string to create an object of the appropriate type and call `setValue()` with this new object.

Many of the built-in types use this technique. Refer to the IntEditor and NumberEditor classes provided in the BDK for examples.

Using the Choice Control Technique

The second technique, display and edit using an AWT Choice control, is nearly as easy as the first. It's the technique to use if your property can be represented as text and is limited to a fixed set of values, such as the direction property in our example above which could only take on the values "North," "South," "East," and "West."

To enable this technique, your PropertyEditor must return false from both isPaintable() and supportsCustomEditor(), return a String[] from getTags() representing the legal values of the property as strings, and return the current value of the property as a string from getAsText(). Notice that the only difference between this technique and the first is that you're not returning null from getTags(). The same rules apply for setAsText() here as before. Just extend PropertyEditorSupport and override the getTags() and setAsText() methods.

The DirectionEditor we used above is a very simple example of this technique. We were able to cheat a little and not provide the setAsText() method because the property was already a string. If your property is anything other than a string (which will usually be the case), the default setAsText() provided by PropertyEditorSupport won't suffice; you'll have to provide it yourself.

Using the Fully Custom Control Technique

The third technique, display by painting a representation of the current value to a Graphics object and edit using your own component designed for just that purpose, is the most powerful and the most difficult to implement. It should be used when the property can't sensibly be represented as a string. Even if a property can be represented as a string, it may make sense to provide a fully custom editor to make life easier for the user. An object of type Color provided by the JDK can be represented as text using a comma-separated list of three values for the red, green, and blue components. But forcing the user to type in "128,128,128" for medium gray isn't very user-friendly, so the BDK provides a more powerful editor.

To enable this technique, your PropertyEditor must return true from both isPaintable() and supportsCustomEditor(). In addition, you should return null from getTags(). If your property truly can't be represented as text, getAsText() should return null and setAsText() should probably throw an IllegalArgumentException. If it can be represented as text, go ahead and provide the appropriate functionality in getAsText() and setAsText().

When implementing this technique, it's generally best not to extend PropertyEditorSupport. Rather, you'll extend one of the components in the AWT (probably Frame; we'll see why in a moment) and implement

`PropertyEditor`. This doesn't mean you can't use the functionality in `PropertyEditorSupport`, however. There's no point in reinventing the wheel for all the `PropertyChangeListener` code (as an example), so the `PropertyChangeSupport` class, which we looked at earlier when discussing bound properties, is provided. It includes some of the same code provided by `PropertyEditorSupport`. You can leverage this code by containing a `PropertyChangeSupport` object in your `PropertyEditor` rather than inheriting from `PropertyEditorSupport`. Your class might contain a `PropertyChangeSupport` member variable like this:

```
private PropertyChangeSupport support = new PropertyChangeSupport(this)
```

Then you can pass calls to `addPropertyChangeListener()` and `removePropertyChangeListener()` on to your `PropertyChangeSupport` object.

Your editor must also provide the `paintValue()` and `getCustomEditor()` methods; when you return `true` from the `isPaintable()` and `supportsCustomEditor()` methods, you're telling the environment to use these methods to display and edit your property. Here's the prototype for `paintValue()` in the `PropertyEditor` interface:

```
public abstract void paintValue(Graphics gfx, Rectangle box)
```

This method is similar to the paint method in a standard component, except you're given a rectangle within the graphics object within which you should paint. This method should paint a representation of the current value of the property into the rectangle on the graphics object.

The `getCustomEditor()` method is used for actually editing the value of the property. Its prototype in the `PropertyEditor` interface is shown below:

```
public abstract Component getCustomEditor()
```

As we stated above, most custom editors will extend `Frame`. This allows our implementation of `getCustomEditor()` to simply return itself.

```
public java.awt.Component getCustomEditor() {
  return this;
}
```

To understand how this component is used, let's look at what the BeanBox does with a `PropertyEditor` that returns `true` from `supportsCustomEditor()` (and `true` from `isPaintable()`). When the user clicks on the property, a dialog box is created with a "Done" button at the bottom portion. The top portion of the dialog box is occupied by the component returned from `getCustomEditor()`. This component will need to create any controls for changing the value of the property. It's completely open-ended and left up to the designer. Figure 7.7 shows how this looks for the JDK's built-in `ColorEditor`.

We've talked about the `ColorEditor` provided with the BDK before. It's an excellent example of using a custom editor for a property. Study the code provided in `ColorEditor.java` for lots of useful techniques.

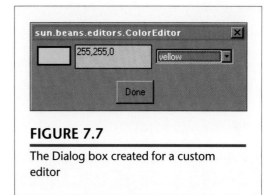

FIGURE 7.7

The Dialog box created for a custom editor

Summary

In this chapter, you learned that properties control the internal state of a Bean. We examined how to manipulate a Bean's properties from a design tool like the BeanBox, and we explored the various property types supported by Java and how they differ. We also discovered how to expose a Bean's properties to design tools and how to use custom editors for properties.

7

Chapter 8

Beans on Ice: The Persistence and Serialization APIs

▸ **A Real Bean Saver**

▸ **The Serializable Interface**

▸ **Object Versioning**

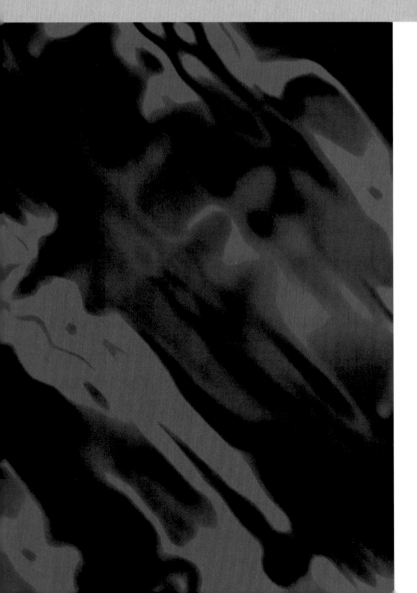

In this chapter, you'll learn how JavaBeans are saved to and restored from media that are more permanent than your computer's internal memory.

JavaBeans, like all objects, are transient in nature; when you turn your computer off, they're gone. To make a JavaBean have a longer lifetime, you have to save it to a medium that doesn't "forget" when the power to your computer is turned off. The process of saving an object is known as *serialization*. When your computer is restarted, your Beans can be reloaded (or de-serialized) from the permanent media. You'll often see the word "persistence" associated with the word "serialization" (take the title of this chapter, for example). *Persistence* refers to making an object permanent, generally by saving and restoring it. Objects that may be saved and restored are often referred to as *persistent objects*. Internal objects that aren't saved and restored are sometimes called *transient objects*.

In this chapter, you learn

▶ That a Bean must be serialized to save its state

▶ About the `Serializable` interface for serializing a Bean

▶ How to use the `readObject()` and `writeObject()` methods to control serialization

▶ About the `Externalizable` interface

▶ How to handle changes in versions of a Bean

A Real Bean Saver

So what's involved in saving an object to a permanent medium? There are two main pieces of information that need to be stored: the identity of the object and its internal state. The description of the methods and member variables for the object along with the code for the methods must also be available; in Java, this is the purpose of the .class file for the object.

Saving the identity of the object in effect records which class of objects an object belongs to. Under Java, this ultimately specifies the .class file that should be used when reloading this object.

The internal state of an object is what distinguishes it from all other objects of its class. The internal state consists of the values of all the member variables of an object. This usually constitutes the bulk of the information stored about an object.

Java provides several classes and interfaces in the `java.io` package that support object serialization.

8

The Serializable Interface

The Serializable interface in the java.io package is the quickest way to get up and running with persistent objects. It makes serializing an object incredibly simple compared to what was available in Java 1.0. To become persistent, an object must simply implement the Serializable interface (with a few caveats). If you're looking forward to a complex interface with lots of convoluted methods, prepare to be disappointed; here's the Serializable interface in its entirety.

```
public interface Serializable {
}
```

The Serializable interface has no methods or fields; it serves as a sort of tag that marks an object as being serializable. In most cases, a class that's not already serializable may be made so simply by adding "implements Serializable" to its class declaration. For example, the Arrow Bean we discussed in the previous chapter had the following class declaration:

```
public class Arrow extends Canvas implements Serializable {
    // . . .
}
```

Virtually every JavaBean should be persistent, and this in most cases means implementing java.io.Serializable. So you've made your class implement Serializable, now what? How is an instance of your class (an object) actually saved? This is where the DataOutput and ObjectOutput interfaces in the java.io package come into play. The DataOutput interface provides methods for writing primitive data types, like int, float, and String, to a data stream. ObjectOutput extends DataOutput and adds support for objects. Figure 8.1 depicts how the ObjectOutput interface might be used.

We've only talked about the input and output interfaces so far; the java.io package also provides several classes, such as ObjectOutputStream and

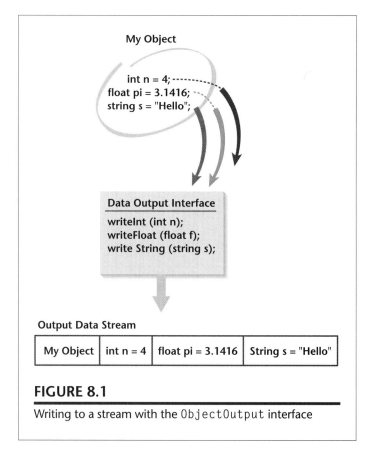

FIGURE 8.1

Writing to a stream with the ObjectOutput interface

ObjectInputStream, that implement the input and output interfaces. Here's how ObjectOutputStream might be used to write an int and an Arrow Bean to a file stream.

```
FileOutputStream fos = new FileOutputStream("test");
ObjectOutputStream oos = new ObjectOutputStream(fos);
Arrow arrow = (Arrow)Beans.instantiate(null,
  "HTPJB.Chap7.Arrow.Arrow");

arrow.setDirection("East");
oos.writeInt(4);
oos.writeObject(arrow);
```

The Complete Source

The complete source for this example is contained on the CD accompanying this book in the file ObjectOutputTest.java. To compile this, you will need to have the source installed on your machine and have your CLASSPATH set to point to this directory. On my machine, the source for this example is in the c:\Source\HTPJB\Chap8 directory, so I have

c:\Source in my CLASSPATH. I compiled ObjectOutputTest.java using javac (Sun's Java 1.1 compiler included with the JDK 1.1). To run it, I use Sun's Java interpreter from the command line like this:

```
c:\Source\HTPJB\Chap8>java
HTPJB.Chap8.ObjectOutputTest
```

Note that Beans.instantiate() is used to create an Arrow object rather than new. This is the "Bean-friendly" way of creating a Bean; we'll touch on this again in a moment. The above code sets the direction property of the arrow to "East," writes the integer 4 to the stream, and then writes the arrow to the stream. Here's the corresponding code snippet that would read this data back in:

```
FileInputStream fis = new FileInputStream("test");
ObjectInputStream ois = new ObjectInputStream(fis);
int n = ois.readInt();
Arrow arrow = (Arrow)ois.readObject();

System.out.println("read " + n);
System.out.println("read " + arrow.getDirection() +
  " pointing arrow.");
```

This basically just reverses the serialization process. The file is opened for reading and then an int and an Arrow object are read.

8

So what good is this? What have we accomplished and why? Well, suppose you write a Java application which uses some objects (a pretty good bet in Java) to hold data provided by the user. Odds are, the user would like to close your application at some point without losing all the data that's been entered. You could write the objects in your applications so that they know how to write the important data out to a file when your application is shut down and read the data back in when your application is started again. You could do this, but it would be a lot of work. Java's serialization mechanism does almost all the work for you. In the example above, the `Arrow` object didn't have to know how to write itself to a file; by simply implementing the Serializable interface, we got Java to handle all the messy details of writing the `Arrow` Bean's identity and state (data members) for us.

What did the above example accomplish? It wrote an integer and an Arrow Bean to a file and then read them back in. Why? Because that simple process (writing and reading objects) is very useful in real-world applications.

Beans.instantiate()

In the serialization code snippet above, we mentioned that `Beans.instantiate()` was used. There are two reasons why `Beans.instantiate()` should always be used to create a Bean rather than `new`: to ensure compatibility with future Bean technology and to automatically load a serialized Bean. `Beans.instantiate()` accepts a `ClassLoader` object and a `String` as arguments. Class loaders are used by Java to control how and from where objects are loaded. We won't go into class loaders in any more detail here; the built-in system class loader will serve our purposes just fine, and we'll always use the system class loader in our examples by passing in `null` for the `ClassLoader`. The String argument is the one in which we're interested; it specifies either the name (probably a file name) of a serialized Bean or the class name of a Bean. The code snippet above which serialized an `int` and an `Arrow` object used the second technique: The `String` specifies the class name of a Bean to create a fresh `Arrow` object. But the first technique, where the `String` specifies the name of a serialized Bean, is the one that `Beans.instantiate` tries first; it appends ".ser" to the `String` and tries to load the Bean from a resource. The term "resource" is used rather than "file" because the serialized Bean might, for example, be inside of a JAR file. `Beans.instantiate()` expects this ".ser" resource to contain a single serialized Bean. If `Beans.instantiate()` is unable to load the object from the resource (probably because the resource doesn't exist), it then tries to treat the `String` as a class name and create a fresh Bean using the Bean's no-arg constructor (a constructor that accepts no arguments). This points out something that we haven't explicitly stated before: Every Bean should have a no-arg constructor (because this is what `Beans.instantiate()` uses to create a new instance of a Bean).

Let's try using `Beans.instantiate()` to load a serialized Bean. Here's a (slightly) modified version of the code snippet we presented above that only serializes an Arrow object:

```
FileOutputStream fos = new FileOutputStream("arrow.ser");
ObjectOutputStream oos = new ObjectOutputStream(fos);
Arrow arrow = (Arrow)Beans.instantiate(null,
  "HTPJB.Chap7.Arrow.Arrow");

arrow.setDirection("East");
oos.writeObject(arrow);
```

This will save an east-pointing Arrow object to a file named "arrow.ser". Reading this object back in using `Beans.instantiate` is very simple:

```
Arrow arrow = (Arrow)Beans.instantiate(null, "arrow");
```

These examples are provided on the CD accompanying this book. The serialized Arrow Bean (arrow.ser) will need to be in your CLASSPATH for `Beans.instantiate` to properly deserialize it. On my machine, the source for the arrow serialization and deserialization code is in the c:\Source\HTPJB\Chap8 directory. I execute the serialization code like this:

```
c:\Source>java HTPJB.Chap8.ArrowSerialize
```

This creates the arrow.ser file in the c:\Source directory. I can then execute the deserialization code like this:

```
c:\Source>java HTPJB.Chap8.ArrowDeserialize
```

Object Handles

We've noted before that calling the `writeObject()` method of the `ObjectOutput` interface results in an object being written (serialized) to an output stream. But what actually happens? What is saved? Basically, `writeObject()` stores information that identifies the object and then each data field of the object is serialized. If an object contained a field of type `int`, for example, the `writeInt()` method of the `DataOutput` interface would be called for that field.

For fields that are not primitive types—for example, object references—things can get a bit more complicated. In Java, when an object has another object as a data field, it doesn't actually contain that object; it contains a reference to the object. The object itself exists in a different part of memory, separate from the object it's being referenced by. When serializing an object reference field, we can't just write the reference itself. First of all, the reference ultimately just identifies the section of memory that an object occupies. Save the reference itself, and it'll mean

8

nothing to a program that tries to load the object later; this program probably won't have any object at that section of memory, much less the proper one for the reference. Second, all the interesting information is not in the reference but rather in the object that's being referenced. The object itself needs to be written, not the reference.

For an object reference field, `writeObject()` needs to be called (again) on the object that's being referenced, but what happens if object A references object B and object B references object A? This is one of the simpler examples of a *circular reference* (an object referencing itself would be the simplest), and if you're not careful, you'll get caught in a loop writing object A, then object B, then object A, and so on. Even if there are no circular references, just blindly writing out an object often isn't very efficient; if object A references object C, causing it to be written, then later object B also references object C, there's really no need to write object C again.

The `writeObject()` method, fortunately, doesn't take this naïve approach. Each time it writes an object it in effect records a *handle* for the object. In this context, a handle can be thought of as a general-purpose reference to an object that *can* be written to a stream. Once an object has been written and the handle assigned, it's not written again; any later objects that reference it simply write the handle.

In a nutshell, the `writeObject()` method of the `ObjectOutput` interface writes the identity for an object and then all the information associated with the object, both direct data like a field of type `int` and indirect data contained in other objects referenced by the object.

The Transient Keyword

At the beginning of this chapter, we mentioned transient objects: internal objects that aren't serialized. A practical example might be the event listeners registered with an event source Bean. The event source Bean remembers the listeners using data fields, but the listeners aren't really part of the source. They're created externally to the source Bean and supplied to it at runtime. The same Bean running in a different context would likely have different event listeners registered. From the point of view of the source Bean, the listeners are transient (although they may not be transient from the point of view of whatever is hooking the listeners up with the source Bean); the event listeners don't need to be saved when the source Bean is serialized.

As we saw in the previous section, all the information associated with an object is written when the object is serialized. So how do we keep the transient fields from being written? The thoughtful designer of the Java language reserved the `transient` keyword for just this purpose. Prior to the JDK 1.1, the `transient` keyword was simply reserved and had no actual effect. In version 1.1, any field tagged with the `transient` keyword isn't written when an object is serialized. A transient `Component` field would be specified like this:

```
transient Component myComponent;
```

So when should a field be marked as transient? Unless the field contains data that is explicitly needed by the object to control its behavior (like a property), it should probably be transient. For example, suppose an object always creates a helper object in its constructor and assigns it to a field. If that field can always be re-created from the other information present, it should probably be transient.

The Other readObject and writeObject Methods

Java's technique of automatically serializing all fields not marked as transient is very powerful and makes life much easier for the programmer, but sometimes you need more control over how an object is written. The `ObjectInputStream` implementation of `ObjectInput` looks for a method named `readObject()` on the object it's reading, and the `ObjectOutputStream` implementation of `ObjectOutput` looks for a method named `writeObject()` on the object it's writing. These methods may be used to explicitly control how an object is read and written. Here's the signature for the `readObject()` and `writeObject()` methods.

```
private void readObject(java.io.ObjectInputStream stream)
   throws IOException, ClassNotFoundException;
private void writeObject(java.io.ObjectOutputStream stream)
   throws IOException;
```

> **NOTE:** *These are not the same methods defined in the* `ObjectInput` *and* `ObjectOutput` *interfaces. The* `readObject()` *and* `writeObject()` *methods in the* `ObjectInput` *and* `ObjectOutput` *interfaces are provided for you by these interfaces and are used by you for reading and writing an arbitrary object. The above* `readObject()` *and* `writeObject()` *methods, on the other hand, are provided by you and are used by Java's serialization mechanism to control the process.*

The `writeObject()` method is only responsible for writing the fields for its own class; the super-class and any sub-classes are responsible for writing their own fields. One common use for `writeObject()` might be to write some additional data to the stream beyond the data fields. In this case, the `defaultWriteObject()` method provided by `ObjectOutputStream` may be used to cause all the fields to be written automatically. The `writeObject()` method could then write any additional information. The `readObject()` method would have to reverse the process by calling `defaultReadObject()` to read in the fields. Then, `readObject()` would read the extra information.

The Externalizable Interface

The `Serializable` interface is convenient, but sometimes we need explicit control over how an object is written. The `Externalizable` interface may be used in this instance.

```
public interface Externalizable extends Serializable
{
    public void writeExternal(ObjectOutput out) throws IOException;
    public void readExternal(ObjectInput in)
                 throws IOException, java.lang.ClassNotFoundException;
}
```

Like the `Serializable` interface, the `Externalizable` interface serves as a tag to indicate that an object may be serialized. In addition, it declares the `writeExternal()` and `readExternal()` methods for saving the data fields. Unlike the `writeObject()` and `readObject()` methods that may optionally be provided when implementing the `Serializable` interface, the `writeExternal()` and `readExternal()` methods must be provided when implementing the `Externalizable` interface.

The `writeExternal()` and `readExternal()` methods are responsible for writing and reading the data fields of the object. Note that, unlike the `readObject()` and `writeObject()` methods, these are also responsible for writing any fields for the super-type of the object (i.e. data fields inherited by extending another class). If the super-type also implements the `Externalizable` interface, this would probably be done by calling `super.writeExternal()`. If the super-type doesn't implement the `Externalizable` interface, the fields of the super-type to which access is available would be written directly.

Object Versioning

The implementation of software in general, and objects in particular, isn't static; a programmer designs and implements an object, but that's seldom the end of the story. As the object is used, new requirements and uses arise. Often the implementation and interface (the data fields and public methods) of the object evolve over time.

A well-designed interface will usually isolate someone using the object from changes to its implementation. Indeed, this is one of the prime selling points of object-oriented programming. However, changes in the implementation of an object can often wreak havoc with serialization.

Suppose you design a serializable object that has a private data field of type String. Later you decide that it doesn't really need to be a String; maybe an int would fit the bill much better. So you change it to an int and modify the internals of your methods accordingly, but you're able to keep the signature of the public methods of your class unchanged (in other words, the interface to the class doesn't change). You distribute the new version of the class to everyone, confident that they'll never even know that the internal representation has changed since you've been really nice and kept the interface the same. The birds are chirping outside your window, everyone loves the new version of your class, and all is well with the world.

But what about any serialized objects of the old version of the class? When an attempt is made to read one of these serialized objects into the new classes, a String is found when an int is expected. Everyone is screaming at you because your class is throwing exceptions every time they try to load a serialized object, all is definitely not well with the world, and those chirping birds outside your window are really starting to get on your nerves.

Java's solution to this dilemma involves marking new versions of a class with an ID that tells the serialization mechanism that the new version is compatible with the original. The only thing left then is to identify what constitutes a compatible change.

When an object is serialized, its identity is saved first; that is, information about the type of object is written. But simply writing the name of the class, for example, isn't enough. Two classes could accidentally end up with the same name, or a new, incompatible version of the class might exist. So when an object is serialized, a unique 64-bit identifier, known as a *stream unique identifier (SUID)*, is written. This SUID is calculated using, among other things, the class name, fields, and methods. Nearly any change to the class will result in a different SUID. A primary use of this SUID is identifying different versions of a class.

A new version of a class that is compatible with an earlier version may identify itself as compatible by providing a static long data member named SerialVersionUID that contains the SUID of the earlier version of the class.

The SUID for the Arrow Bean used in the previous chapter is 7543306545722649166. If we made a new version of the Arrow Bean that was compatible with the original, we could mark it as compatible by adding this line to the class:

```
static final long serialVersionUID = 7543306545722649166L;
```

How did I determine the SUID? The JDK 1.1 provides a small command-line utility, `serialver`, which calculates the SUID for a class. I typed "serialver HTPJB.Chap7.Arrow.Arrow" from the command line to find the above SUID.

What constitutes a compatible change? The documentation for the JDK provides a detailed discussion of compatible and incompatible changes; here's a quick summary of incompatible changes:

▶ Deleting fields

▶ Moving classes up or down in the hierarchy

▶ Changing a non-static field to static (this is equivalent to deleting a field)

▶ Changing a non-transient field to transient (this is equivalent to deleting a field)

▶ Changing the type of a primitive field

▶ Changing the `writeObject()` or `readObject()` method so it no longer writes or reads the default field data, or changing it so it attempts to write or read the default field data when the previous version did not

▶ Changing a class from `Serializable` to `Externalizable` or vice versa

Here's a quick list of compatible changes:

▶ Adding fields

▶ Adding classes to the hierarchy

▶ Removing classes

▶ Adding `writeObject()` and `readObject()` methods

▶ Removing `writeObject()` and `readObject()` methods

▶ Adding `implements Serializable`

▶ Removing `implements Serializable`

▶ Changing the access to a field (`public`, `private`, and so on)

▶ Changing a field from static to non-static (this is equivalent to adding a new field)

▶ Changing a field from transient to non-transient (this is equivalent to adding a new field)

Summary

In this chapter, you learned that a Bean must be serialized to save its state. You also learned about the `Serializable` interface for serializing a Bean, and how to use the `readObject()` and `writeObject()` methods to control serialization. For more precise control, we discovered the `Externalizable` interface. Lastly, we examined how to handle changes in versions of a Bean.

8

Chapter 9

Knowing Beans:
The Introspection APIs

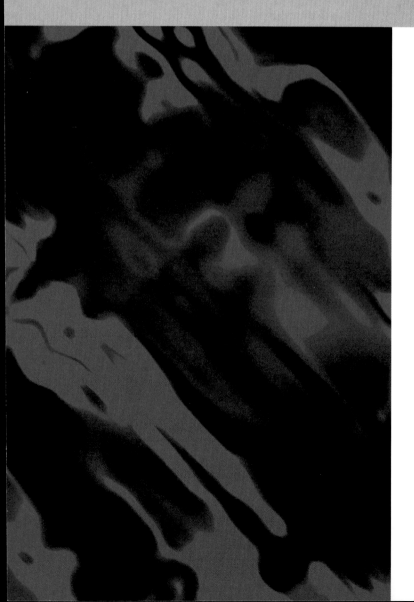

▸ **Let's Reflect on This**

▸ **Featuring in This Corner**

▸ **The BeanInfo Interface**

Introspection is one of the key technologies that makes a component architecture such as JavaBeans actually usable. *Introspection* is the ability of one object to examine another arbitrary object, about which it knows nothing, and discover its *features*. The features of an object are its methods, properties, events, and so on. Not all component technologies support introspection. Microsoft's ActiveX, for example, uses a registration and interface querying mechanism rather than introspection. Certainly, a great deal can be accomplished in a component technology without introspection, but adding introspection opens up whole new worlds of possibilities. Perhaps most importantly, it makes Beans easier to use with design tools.

In this chapter, you'll learn

▶ About the Java core reflection APIs

▶ About features and feature descriptor objects

▶ How to provide a `BeanInfo` object for a Bean

Let's Reflect on This

We'd be remiss in this chapter if we didn't talk about the *reflection* APIs added to the Java Development Kit v1.1 (JDK 1.1). The introspection APIs (and the serialization APIs discussed in the previous chapter) are largely built on top of the reflection APIs. Reflection could easily be the subject of an entire chapter. We'll just touch briefly on some of the more important points in this section, so you may want to refer to a book specifically on Java v1.1 for more details.

Reflection in the JDK 1.1 is somewhat like a lower-level version of introspection. At their most basic level, the reflection APIs allow us to examine the data fields, methods, and constructors of an object. The `java.lang.reflect` package defines five classes for describing the members of an object:

▶ Array

▶ Constructor

▶ Field

▶ Method

▶ Modifier

Of these five, the first four, `Array`, `Constructor`, `Field`, and `Method`, implement a common interface, the `Member` interface, which is also defined in the `java.lang.reflect` package. The `Field` class provides information about a field of an object, the `Method` class provides information about a method of an object, and so on. You never create an instance of one of these classes yourself;

9

the reflection APIs return these objects to you via methods in the java.lang.Class class. The Modifier class provides information about the modifiers (public, private, final, and so on) for a member.

Use a Little Class

The java.lang.Class class provides information about the class of an object. Given a Class object, you can ask for its name, its superclass, and so on. As before, you never create a Class object yourself; the system returns them to you from methods that you call. Given an arbitrary object, you can obtain its class using the getClass() method. The getClass() method is defined in java.lang.Object, so it's available for any object, since all classes ultimately have java.lang.Object as a superclass (in other words, all classes inherit getClass() from java.lang.Object). For example, suppose you've written a Bean that has a data member named target of type Object. You could obtain and print out the class of the target like this:

```
Class targetClass = target.getClass();
System.out.println(targetClass);
```

 ON THE CD: *A trivial (but complete) example that demonstrates obtaining the Class object from an object is included on the CD accompanying this book in a file named GetClass.java. This file may be compiled with your favorite Java 1.1 compiler such as Sun's* javac *included with the JDK 1.1 and run from the command line using a Java 1.1 interpreter such as Sun's* java *also included with the JDK 1.1.*

The JDK 1.1 adds several methods to java.lang.Class to support reflection. Most of these methods return instances of the java.lang.reflect classes mentioned above. For example, getMethods() returns an array of Method objects which represent all the public methods of the class.

Featuring in This Corner

We've already mentioned a few of the items that a Bean might need to describe: properties, methods, events, and so on. The JavaBeans introspection technology refers to all of these items collectively as *features*. As you might expect, JavaBeans uses objects (descriptor objects) to describe these features. Classes are provided for describing the following features:

▶ Methods

▶ Parameters of a method

▶ Events

▶ Properties

▶ The Bean itself

For example, the `PropertyDescriptor` class is provided for describing properties, and the `MethodDescriptor` class is provided for describing methods. Separate classes are needed for describing properties and methods because the description needs to provide different information for each. The description of a property might need to indicate whether or not a property is bound (see Chapter 7), but this bit of information isn't needed for methods because there's no such thing as a bound method in Java. As this example indicates, the description of a method is different from the description of a property, but they also have many elements in common; for instance, a property has a name and so does a method.

This looks like a job for inheritance. *Inheritance* is one of the central concepts in object-oriented programming; using inheritance, those elements common to all feature descriptors can be expressed in a base class. The specific feature descriptors, such as `PropertyDescriptor` and `MethodDescriptor`, extend (inherit from) this base class and add their own elements. Figure 9.1 shows the hierarchy of classes the JDK 1.1 provides for describing features. Note that the `FeatureDescriptor` class is at the root (top) of the tree, and all other classes ultimately inherit from it.

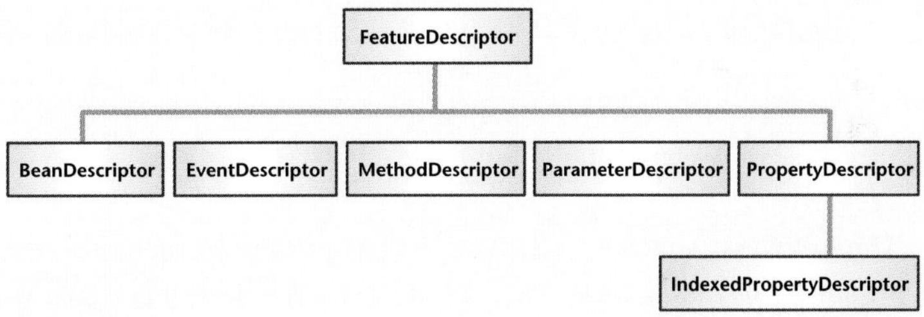

FIGURE 9.1

The feature descriptors class hierarchy

General Features

In JavaBeans, the common base class for all feature descriptors is `java.beans.FeatureDescriptor`. The `FeatureDescriptor` class captures quite a bit of functionality that's common to the descriptions of all Bean features. Specifically, `FeatureDescriptor` provides methods for setting and retrieving

▶ The names of a feature (two are provided: the programmatic name, which is used by the programmer working with the feature, and the display name, which is a more descriptive and user-friendly name)

▶ A short textual description of the feature

▶ Whether or not a feature is an expert feature that's intended for expert users rather than normal users

▶ Whether or not a feature is only intended for use by a design tool and should be hidden from users

In addition, `FeatureDescriptor` makes features extensible by providing methods for attaching and retrieving arbitrary attribute/value pairs. In a nutshell, each feature descriptor contains a *dictionary*. Dictionaries show up often in programming, especially object-oriented programming. A real-world dictionary is a collection of words associated with their definitions; a dictionary in programming is a collection of *associations*. An association is a pairing of two objects. Typically, the associations contained in a dictionary will pair a string, called the key, with an arbitrary object, called the value. A dictionary effectively gives us the ability to add data fields to an object at runtime. We'll look at how this might be used near the end of this section.

Name That Feature

The `FeatureDescriptor` class has four methods for naming a feature:

```
public String getName();
public void setName(String name);
public String getDisplayName();
public void setDisplayName(String displayName);
```

The `getName()` and `setName()` methods retrieve and set the *programmatic name* of a feature. The programmatic name is the internal name used to uniquely identify a feature.

The `getDisplayName()` and `setDisplayName()` methods retrieve and set the *display name* of a feature. This is the name that would actually be displayed to someone using the Bean. In most cases, the display name and the programmatic name will be the same; this is the default behavior. Sometimes, however, the display name may be *localized*. That is, it may be displayed in the appropriate local language and style depending on the location and settings (the *locale*) of the host machine.

Describe It to Me in Words

`FeatureDescriptor` supports short textual descriptions of a feature through two methods:

```
public String getShortDescription();
public void setShortDescription(String text);
```

This description is only for informational purposes; for example, a design tool might retrieve the short description when the user requests help for a feature.

The Experts Only Club

`FeatureDescriptor` supports expert features through two methods:

```
public boolean isExpert();
public void setExpert(boolean expert);
```

Marking features as expert eases the complexity of configuring a Bean. Many design tools may offer two (or more) views of a Bean. The expert view would show all human-readable methods, properties, and so on, but this view could be a bit overwhelming for some of the more complex Beans. The non-expert view would only display the more essential features of the Bean: the features which weren't marked as expert.

No Humans Allowed

Hidden features are also supported through two methods:

```
public boolean isHidden();
public void setHidden(boolean hidden);
```

Hidden features are for internal use by the Bean and the design tool that's manipulating it (or by other Beans). They are never intended to be directly manipulated by the user. The design tool being used might access a hidden property, for example, as a result of something the user has done.

The Component class provided with the JDK 1.1 for example provides a visible property. If visible is set to true, the component is displayed, but if visible is set to false, the component doesn't draw itself and effectively disappears. Making a component invisible can often be quite useful in a program, but you can get into trouble if you allow the user to change a component's visible property from a design tool; as soon as the user sets the component's visible property to `false` it disappears and there's no way to select it anymore. There's no way to set the component back to being visible.

The BeanInfo for `Component` (`ComponentBeanInfo`) therefore sets the visible property to be hidden. It doesn't show up in the property sheet of the BeanBox, but the property itself is still accessible from your code using the `isVisible()` and `setVisible()` methods.

The Sky's the Limit

What if a Bean needed to attach some sort of attribute to a feature of another Bean? To use a contrived example, let's say you've written a `MrSpock` Bean which you would like to examine (introspect) other Beans and attach a flag, similar to the hidden and expert flags, that marks a feature as interesting. `FeatureDescriptor` has a pair of methods that are well suited for just this purpose:

```
public void setValue(String attributeName, Object value);
public Object getValue(String attributeName);
```

Let's say that our MrSpock Bean initially assumes that everything is uninteresting. As it examines (introspects) other Beans, it might mark certain features as interesting. The MrSpock Bean might initially mark a feature as uninteresting like this:

```
feature.setValue("isInteresting", Boolean.FALSE);
```

Then, if it later discovers that a feature is one which should be looked at more closely, the "isInteresting" flag could be updated like this:

```
feature.setValue("isInteresting", Boolean.TRUE);
```

This piece of code could be used to determine if a feature is interesting:

```
if (((Boolean)feature.getValue("isInteresting")).booleanValue()) {
  // fascinating…
}
```

Describing Methods and Parameters

Methods are described using the `MethodDescriptor` class. `MethodDescriptor` extends `FeatureDescriptor`, keeping all of its methods and adding a few new ones. Specifically, `MethodDescriptor` adds methods for retrieving

▶ The method being described

▶ The descriptions of the parameters (arguments) to the method

What's Your Method?

The reflection APIs discussed at the beginning of this chapter define the `Method` class. This class provides information about a method, such as its name and the types of its parameters. `MethodDescriptor` can return a `Method` object for the method it's describing.

```
public Method getMethod();
```

So, `MethodDescriptor` effectively defers to the `Method` class to provide most of its information.

You're My Type, but What's Your Name?

The `Method` object returned by `getMethod` gives you access to just about all the information you'd want about a method. The only extra information you might want is the names of the parameters to a method (the types of the parameters are available from the `Method` object). Suppose a Bean has the following method:

```
public void someMethod(String text, int number, Object anObject) { //…
}
```

The `Method` object for this method will provide quite a bit of information about the method such as the name of the method ("someMethod"), the type of the returned value (`void`), and the types of the parameters (`String`, `int`, and `Object`). What if you'd like to obtain the names of the parameters (text, number, and anObject)? The Method object has no provision for this, so `MethodDescriptor` adds a method for the parameter names.

```
public ParameterDescriptor[] getParameterDescriptors();
```

This method returns an array of `ParameterDescriptor` objects, one for each parameter. `ParameterDescriptor` is another class that extends `FeatureDescriptor`. It currently does not add any new methods, however; it gets all of its functionality from `FeatureDescriptor`. The `getName()` or `getDisplayName()` method would be the main one to call when using a `ParameterDescriptor` object.

Describing Events

Recall that the JDK 1.1 uses a source/listener paradigm. An event source must implement a method for adding listeners for the event. Each event has an associated event listener interface. This listener interface contains one or more methods: one for each individual event that might occur. When an event occurs, the appropriate method in the listener interface is called for each registered listener. You may want to review Chapter 6 for more details about events.

The events supported by a Bean are described using the `EventSetDescriptor` class. It's called `EventSetDescriptor` rather than `EventDescriptor` because an event listener might provide methods for more than one event. The `KeyListener` interface, for example, has methods for both a key press and a key release. Thus, in general the `EventSetDescriptor` class may be describing a group of events rather than an individual event. `EventSetDescriptor` extends `FeatureDescriptor` and adds methods for

▶ Retrieving the methods used to add and remove listeners for the event.

▶ Retrieving the type of the listener interface.

▶ Retrieving descriptions of the methods in the associated listener interface for the event.

▶ Retrieving the methods in the associated interface for the event.

▶ Setting and determining if the event is in the default event set; Java allows a Bean to have a default event which is the event that would be most commonly used by someone.

▶ Setting and determining if the event is unicast. Events are normally multicast (meaning they can be sent to multiple listeners). Some events may be unicast: sent to only one listener.

You Can Know Who's Listening

Suppose we have a Bean which is an `Action` event source. The Bean will typically have a pair of methods of the form:

```
void addActionListener(XyzListener l);
void removeActionListener(XyzListener l);
```

These add and remove methods could be named differently (although it's not recommended because it might cause problems with some design tools that are expecting the naming conventions to be followed). Whatever they're named, an `EventSetDescriptor` object allows you to specify the add and remove methods when it's created. Two of its constructors accept the add and remove methods as arguments, as shown in Listing 9.1. Notice the `addListenerMethod` and `removeListenerMethod` arguments in these two constructors. After an `EventSetDescriptor` object has been created, you can query it for the set and remove methods that were specified when it was created using these two methods:

```
public Method getAddListenerMethod();
public Method getRemoveListenerMethod();
```

LISTING 9.1   Two of an EventSetDescriptor Object's Constructors

```
public EventSetDescriptor(String eventSetName,
          Class listenerType,
          Method listenerMethods[],
          Method addListenerMethod,
          Method removeListenerMethod)
          throws IntrospectionException;

public EventSetDescriptor(String eventSetName,
          Class listenerType,
          MethodDescriptor listenerMethodDescriptors[],
          Method addListenerMethod,
          Method removeListenerMethod)
          throws IntrospectionException;
```

The Listener Interface and Its Methods

Recall that each event listener interface may have multiple methods: one for each individual event. EventSetDescriptor provides a method for retrieving the type of the listener interface, the methods in an event listener interface, and the descriptors for the methods.

```
public Class getListenerType();
public Method[] getListenerMethods();
public MethodDescriptor[] getListenerMethodDescriptors();
```

Default Events

A Bean may define a *default event set*. This is the event set that's most commonly used by someone using the Bean. EventSetDescriptor provides methods for setting and determining whether an event set is in the default set.

```
public void setInDefaultEventSet(boolean inDefaultEventSet);
public boolean isInDefaultEventSet();
```

By default, all the event sets in a Bean are in the default event set; Java assumes all events are commonly used. Let's look at how these two methods might be used. The DefaultEvent class (Listing 9.2) uses both of these methods.

This class first defines the required no-arg constructor (a constructor that accepts no arguments); every Bean should provide a no-arg constructor because Beans.instantiate is the proper way to create a new Bean, and it creates a new Bean using the Bean's no-arg constructor.

The DefaultEvent class then defines the add and remove listener methods for Action events and PropertyChange events: addActionListener(), removeActionListener(), addPropertyChangeListener(), and removePropertyChangeListener(). This Bean doesn't actually fire any Action events or a PropertyChange events, but the introspection APIs don't know that. By providing these methods, we make the introspection mechanism think it might fire these events; we provide these methods so that when we request the EventSetDescriptors for this Bean a little later, we'll actually get something interesting back to work with.

The actual use of the setInDefaultEventSet() and isInDefaultEventSet() methods occurs in the main() method of DefaultEvent. The main() method has two parts. The first part uses the setInDefaultEventSet() method to set the "action" event to not be in the default set for a DefaultEvent Bean. The second part displays the names of all the event sets for a DefaultEvent Bean and uses the getInDefaultEventSet() method to determine whether each event set is in the default event set.

9

LISTING 9.2   The DefaultEvent Class

```
// DefaultEvent class
// DefaultEvent.java

package HTPJB.Chap9;

import java.awt.event.*;
import java.beans.*;
import java.util.Vector;

public class DefaultEvent {
  public DefaultEvent() {
  }
  public synchronized void addActionListener(ActionListener l) {
    pushListeners.addElement(l);
  }
  public synchronized void removeActionListener(ActionListener l) {
    pushListeners.removeElement(l);
  }
  public void addPropertyChangeListener(PropertyChangeListener l) {
    changes.addPropertyChangeListener(l);
  }
  public void removePropertyChangeListener(PropertyChangeListener l) {
    changes.removePropertyChangeListener(l);
  }

  public static void main(String args[]) {
    try {
      // create a DefaultEvent Bean
      DefaultEvent bean = (DefaultEvent)Beans.instantiate(null,
                "HTPJB.Chap9.DefaultEvent");
      // get its BeanInfo and EventSetDescriptors
      BeanInfo bi = Introspector.getBeanInfo(bean.getClass());
      EventSetDescriptor esd[] = bi.getEventSetDescriptors();

      // loop over all of them and set the "action"
      // event set to not be in the default set
```

CONTINUES

LISTING 9.2 The DefaultEvent Class (Continued)

```
      for (int i = 0; i < esd.length; i++) {
        String eventName = esd[i].getName();
        if (eventName.equals("action"))
          esd[i].setInDefaultEventSet(false);
      }
    } catch(Exception ex) {
      System.out.println("Exception " + ex);
    }
    try {
      // now create another DefaultEvent bean and get its
      // BeanInfo and EventSetDescriptors
      DefaultEvent bean = (DefaultEvent)Beans.instantiate(null,
                  "HTPJB.Chap9.DefaultEvent");
      BeanInfo bi = Introspector.getBeanInfo(bean.getClass());
      EventSetDescriptor esd[] = bi.getEventSetDescriptors();

      // loop over each event set descriptor, printing
      // whether its in the default event set
      for (int i = 0; i < esd.length; i++) {
        String eventName = esd[i].getName();
        if (esd[i].isInDefaultEventSet())
          System.out.println(eventName +
            " is in the default event set.");
        else
          System.out.println(eventName +
            " is not in the default event set.");
      }
    } catch(Exception ex) {
      System.out.println("Exception " + ex);
    }
  }
  private PropertyChangeSupport changes =
    new PropertyChangeSupport(this);
  private Vector pushListeners = new Vector();
}
```

9

Starting with part one, the main() method first creates a DefaultEvent Bean using Beans.instantiate. It then obtains the BeanInfo for this Bean using the system Introspector object. Next, the EventSetDescriptors are obtained from the BeanInfo using the getEventSetDescriptors() method. In this example, we'll get back two event set descriptors: one for the Action event set and one for the PropertyChange event set. We loop over all the event set descriptors, and when we find one named "action," we use the setInDefaultEventSet() method to mark it as not being in the default event set.

The main() method then repeats the entire process with a new DefaultEvent Bean, but this time it outputs the event set's name and uses the isInDefaultEventSet() method to print either "is in the default event set" or "is not in the default event set." Figure 9.2 shows the generated output.

 ON THE CD: *This example is provided with the CD accompanying this book in the DefaultEvent.java file. You will need to have the directory for the book's source code in your CLASSPATH to compile and run this example. On my machine, the source code for this chapter is in the c:\Source\HTPJB\Chap9 directory, so I've added c:\Source to my CLASSPATH. You can compile this example using your favorite Java 1.1 compiler such as Sun's javac, and you can run it using your favorite Java 1.1 interpreter such as Sun's java. To run this example using Sun's interpreter for example, I used this command line:*

FIGURE 9.2

The output from the DefaultEvent class

```
c:\Source\HTPJB\Chap9>java HTPJB.Chap9.DefaultEvent
```

Multicast or Unicast?

Events are normally multicast in Java. This means they may be sent to multiple listeners. Some events, however, are unicast: they may be sent to only one listener.

`EventSetDescriptor` provides methods for setting and determining whether an event is unicast.

```
public void setUnicast(boolean unicast);
public boolean isUnicast();
```

Describing Properties

The properties supported by a Bean are described using the `PropertyDescriptor` class. `PropertyDescriptor` extends `FeatureDescriptor` and adds methods for

- ▶ Setting and retrieving the editor for the property

- ▶ Obtaining the type of the property

- ▶ Retrieving the read and write (getter and setter) methods for the property

- ▶ Setting and determining whether a property is bound

- ▶ Setting and determining whether a property is constrained

You may want to review Chapter 7 for more about properties.

Property Editors

A property editor is used, naturally, to edit a property. Normally, we allow the JavaBeans APIs to automatically determine the appropriate editor. Sometimes, however, it's useful to explicitly specify the editor. We did this for the Arrow Bean example in Chapter 7. `PropertyDescriptor` provides methods for setting and retrieving the property editor.

```
public void setPropertyEditorClass(Class propertyEditorClass);
public Class getPropertyEditorClass();
```

What's Your Type

It's often useful to know the type of a property. `PropertyDescriptor` supplies a method which returns the type of the property.

```
public Class getPropertyType();
```

In the current implementation, the type is determined by looking at the type returned from the getter method and passed to the setter method.

The Getter and Setter Methods

`PropertyDescriptor` has three constructors and, correspondingly, there are three ways to specify the getter and setter methods via these constructors.

```
public PropertyDescriptor(String propertyName, Class beanClass);
public PropertyDescriptor(String propertyName, Class beanClass,
```

```
         String getterName, String setterName);
   public PropertyDescriptor(String propertyName, Method getter,
      Method setter)
```

The first constructor accepts the name of the property and the class of the Bean that the property resides in. The getter and setter methods are assumed to be of the standard form (getXyz and setXyz for a property named Xyz). Introspection is then used to find the getter and setter methods in the Bean class.

The second constructor accepts the name, the class of the Bean, and the names of the methods. Introspection is then used to find the getter and setter methods in the Bean class.

The third constructor accepts the name and the getter and setter methods explicitly. Introspection isn't needed in this case.

Finally, PropertyDescriptor provides a pair of methods for retrieving the getter and setter methods.

```
   public Method getWriteMethod();
   public Method getReadMethod();
```

Bound and Constrained Properties

A property may be bound, constrained, or both. Refer to Chapter 7 for more information on bound and constrained properties. PropertyDescriptor provides methods for setting and determining whether a property is bound and/or constrained.

```
   public boolean isBound();
   public void setBound(boolean bound);
   public boolean isConstrained();
   public void setConstrained(boolean constrained);
```

Describing the Bean Itself

Additional information about a Bean beyond its methods, properties, and events is described using the BeanDescriptor class. BeanDescriptor extends FeatureDescriptor and adds methods for

▶   Retrieving the class of the Bean.

▶   Retrieving the customizer for the Bean; customizers can be thought of as advanced property editors. They provide a very high-level, user-friendly means of configuring a Bean (setting its properties).

BeanDescriptor provides two constructors:

```
   public BeanDescriptor(Class beanClass);
   public BeanDescriptor(Class beanClass, Class customizerClass);
```

The first accepts only the class of the Bean and sets the customizer to null (none). The second accepts both the class of the Bean and the class of the customizer. We'll cover customizers in more detail in Chapter 10.

Finally, methods are provided for retrieving the Bean class and the customizer class.

```
public Class getBeanClass();
public Class getCustomizerClass();
```

The BeanInfo Interface

The BeanInfo interface is the central means of informing interested parties about your Bean. All of the descriptor objects described in the previous section come together in the BeanInfo interface. It allows you to provide information about the

- ▶ Description of a Bean
- ▶ Icons for representing a Bean in design tools, toolbars, and so on
- ▶ Properties of a Bean
- ▶ Events fired by a Bean
- ▶ Methods supported by a Bean

The abbreviated BeanInfo interface appears in Listing 9.3.

LISTING 9.3 The Abbreviated BeanInfo Interface

```
public interface BeanInfo {
    BeanDescriptor getBeanDescriptor();
    EventSetDescriptor[] getEventSetDescriptors();
    int getDefaultEventIndex();
    PropertyDescriptor[] getPropertyDescriptors();
    int getDefaultPropertyIndex();
    MethodDescriptor[] getMethodDescriptors();
    BeanInfo[] getAdditionalBeanInfo();
    java.awt.Image getIcon(int iconKind);

    final static int ICON_COLOR_16x16 = 1;
    final static int ICON_COLOR_32x32 = 2;
    final static int ICON_MONO_16x16 = 3;
    final static int ICON_MONO_32x32 = 4;
}
```

9

The getBeanDescriptor() method returns a single BeanDescriptor object which provides information about the class of the associated Bean and the customizer (if any) for the Bean. The getEventSetDescriptors(), getPropertyDescriptors(), and getMethodDescriptors() methods all return an array of the appropriate descriptor objects.

The getDefaultEventIndex method returns the index into the array returned by getEventSetDescriptors method of the default event. If there is no default event, it returns -1. Similarly, getDefaultPropertyIndex() returns the index into the array returned by the getPropertyDescriptors() method of the default property, or -1 is there is no default.

This leaves us with the getIcon() method. Beans may have up to four different icons: 16-by-16 pixels and 32-by-32 pixels in both monochrome and color. A design tool requests the icon for a Bean by calling getIcon() with one of the icon identifiers declared in the BeanInfoInterface: ICON_COLOR_16x16, ICON_COLOR_32x32, ICON_MONO_16x16, or ICON_MONO_32x32. If a Bean supports the specified icon, it should return an Image object of the correct size and number of colors. If it doesn't support the specified icon, it should return null. Ideally, Beans should support all four size and color combinations for icons. Alternatively, they may support only the two color icons. If only one icon size and color is supported, Sun recommends supporting the 16-by-16 pixel color icon.

Name That BeanInfo

Suppose that we have a Bean class named MyBean. When a BeanInfo object is requested for this Bean, Java will first try to create it by looking for a class named MyBeanBeanInfo which implements the BeanInfo interface. If the appropriate class isn't found, Java uses introspection and reflection to create a generic BeanInfo object for MyBean. This default BeanInfo works great for quick-and-dirty testing, but as soon as you want to add something as simple as an icon to your Bean, you'll need to supply your own class which implements the BeanInfo interface. This doesn't mean that you must provide full functionality for all the methods in the interface, however. If you would like to just add an icon, and not worry about the properties, events, and such, you may simply return null from all the get descriptor methods (getPropertyDescriptors(), getMethodDescriptors(), and so on).

The Beans Development Kit helps out by providing a class, SimpleBeanInfo, which implements all the methods in the BeanInfo interface with do-nothing behavior. You'll generally extend SimpleBeanInfo and override only the methods you want to customize. Listing 9.4 shows how a MyBeanBeanInfo class that supports 16-by-16 pixel and 32-by-32 pixel color icons might be implemented.

This class overrides the getIcon() method. The getIcon() method attempts to load the image object from a GIF file (GIF files are the standard graphic

LISTING 9.4 A MyBeanBeanInfo Class that Supports 16-by-16 Pixel and 32-by-32 Pixel Color Icons

```
// MyBeanInfo class
// MyBeanInfo.java

package HTPJB.Chap9;

import java.beans.*;

public class MyBeanBeanInfo extends SimpleBeanInfo {
  // Get the appropriate icon
  public java.awt.Image getIcon(int iconKind) {
    java.awt.Image img = null;

    switch(iconKind) {
      case BeanInfo.ICON_COLOR_16x16:
        img = loadImage("MyBean16.gif");
        break;
      case BeanInfo.ICON_COLOR_32x32:
        img = loadImage("MyBeanIcon32.gif");
        break;
    }
    return img;
  }
}
```

file type used in Java) when a 16-by-16 pixel or 32-by-32 pixel color icon is requested. Package this class along with the MyBean class and the two GIF files in a JAR file, and MyBean should magically have icons. See Chapter 5 ("Packaging Beans with JAR Files") for more information on JAR files.

The Arrow Bean presented in Chapter 7 provides another example of a BeanInfo object. It extends SimpleBeanInfo and overrides the getPropertyDescriptors() method (see Listing 9.5). This class installs a custom editor for the direction property rather than relying on the built-in String editor. One thing to note here is that since we're explicitly supplying a list of properties (we're only supplying one in this case), the other properties this Bean might have won't appear to the user. They would have appeared if we had allowed Java to use introspection to find the properties.

LISTING 9.5   The Arrow Bean's BeanInfo Object

```
public class ArrowBeanInfo extends SimpleBeanInfo {
  public PropertyDescriptor[] getPropertyDescriptors() {
    try {
      PropertyDescriptor pd = new PropertyDescriptor("direction",
                                                Arrow.class);
      pd.setPropertyEditorClass(DirectionEditor.class);
      PropertyDescriptor result[] = { pd };
      return result;
    } catch (Exception ex) {
      System.err.println("ArrowBeanInfo: unexpected exeption: " + ex);
      return null;
    }
  }
}
```

Summary

In this chapter, we learned how Beans can inform others about themselves. We also saw how the properties, events, methods, and other features of a Bean are described using feature descriptor objects. Lastly, we looked at how a BeanInfo object is used to inform others about the features of a Bean.

9

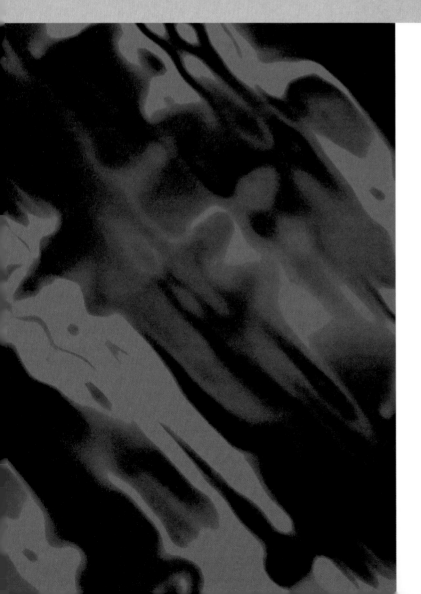

Chapter *10*

Beans As Tools:
The Application Builder APIs

▶ **Where Am I?**

▶ **Using Bean Customizers**

In this chapter, you'll learn how a Bean can obtain information about the environment it's being used in, such as whether there's a graphical user interface (GUI) available or whether the current user is an end-user or a program designer. You'll also examine customizers, which allow complex Beans to be manipulated and configured in a very high-level, user-friendly manner.

In this chapter, you'll learn

▶ How to get information about the environment in which a Bean is running

▶ How to use Bean customizers and how they compare with custom property editors

▶ How to provide a customizer for a Bean

Where Am I?

A Bean you write may be used in many different settings, and sometimes your Bean may need to find out information about the current environment in which it's running. The `java.beans.Beans` class provides a couple of methods for informing Beans about the environment:

```
public static boolean isGuiAvailable();
public static boolean isDesignTime();
```

A Bean may not always run in a graphical environment, especially if it's an invisible Bean such as the Timer Bean presented in Chapter 15. If your Bean needs to change its behavior based on whether a graphical user interface is available, use `isGuiAvailable()` to determine this.

> **NOTE:** *Invisible Beans are Beans that have no graphical representation. These Beans typically are used to provide some sort of functionality that's not graphical. A Bean that wires other Beans together might be one example.*

The BeanBox provided with the BDK (Beans Development Kit) is one common environment for testing a Bean, and it provides two different modes. The BeanBox starts up in Design mode. This mode draws a selection box around the currently selected Bean and displays the Bean ToolBox and property sheet. The View menu allows you to turn Design mode off and try out your Beans in an environment more similar to an actual application or applet. You can use the `isDesignTime()` method in `java.beans.Beans` to determine whether or not the current mode is

10

Design mode (whether you're using the BeanBox or a third-party design tool that supports JavaBeans and the JDK 1.1).

Using Bean Customizers

We examined custom property editors in Chapter 7. One of the custom editor techniques (the third) we examined involved a fully custom property editor. In this scenario, you, the programmer, are responsible both for displaying the current value of a property and for providing a component for editing the property. The color editor provided with the BDK's BeanBox provides an example of this technique.

A Bean *customizer* is very similar to a fully custom property editor. Instead of editing a single property of a Bean, however, a Bean customizer edits an entire group of properties. A customizer can be thought of as a custom property sheet for a Bean.

TIP: *The property sheet in the BDK's BeanBox is the panel on the right side of the screen which displays all the properties for the currently selected Bean. All JavaBeans design tools will provide something similar. A Bean customizer, in effect, provides an alternative property sheet that's specifically tailored for a Bean.*

When you're working with a design tool, the standard generic property sheet will most likely still be present and available for editing properties. If a Bean provides a customizer, however, you can invoke the customizer to set up the Bean's properties.

So how do you invoke the customizer for a Bean? This ultimately depends on the design tool you're using; the BeanBox provided with the BDK adds a "Customize..." item to the Edit menu when the currently selected Bean provides a customizer.

NOTE: *Notice the ellipses (...) in the "Customize..." item. This is a convention followed in most graphical user interfaces that indicates that a dialog box will appear when this item is selected. Keep this convention in mind when writing your own applets and applications (whether they're Java programs or not); your users will appreciate the thoughtfulness.*

The ExplicitButton demo Bean included with the BDK provides a customizer. Figure 10.1 shows the Edit menu that the BeanBox displays when an

ExplicitButton Bean is selected. Figure 10.2 shows the customizer for the ExplicitButton Bean. It's a pretty trivial customizer; the Caption is the only property that can be edited, and that could be more easily edited directly from the property sheet. This customizer's purpose is to provide an example of a simple customizer, not to provide a better way of configuring a button.

> **NOTE:** *If you think this customizer looks a lot like a custom property editor, such as the property editor for a color property, you're right. The BeanBox displays both in basically the same manner: It creates a dialog box and places a Done button at the bottom. For a custom property editor, the top portion of the dialog box is filled with an AWT Component object which allows the property to be edited. As we saw in Chapter 7, this component is provided by the Bean. For a customizer, the top portion of the dialog box is also filled with an AWT Component object. This component, however, allows the entire Bean to be configured rather than a single property. As we'll see a little later, this customizer component is once again provided by the Bean.*

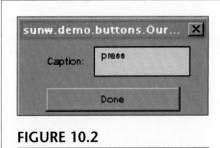

FIGURE 10.1

The Edit Menu displayed in the BeanBox when a Bean with a customizer is selected

A Customized Arrow Bean

Now let's get our hands dirty and create a customizer for a Bean. In this section, we'll resurrect the Arrow Bean we used in Chapter 7 and add a customizer to it. As an added bonus, we'll end up with another example of using the new JDK 1.1-style events and inner-classes (both of which were covered in Chapter 6, "Bean Happenings: The Event Handling APIs").

FIGURE 10.2

The customizer for the ExplicitButton Bean

Adding a customizer involves two basic steps:

1 Create a customizer class which ultimately inherits from `Component` and implements the `Customizer` interface (we'll cover the `Customizer` interface in a moment). This step actually involves a decent amount of work. This class must provide graphical fields and controls for editing the properties. The sky is basically the limit; you can get as fancy as you like.

2 Modify (or add) the `BeanInfo` for the Bean to tell others about our customizer.

10

The Customizer Interface

The BDK provides a `Customizer` interface that every Bean customizer must implement:

```
public interface Customizer {
  void setObject(Object bean);
  void addPropertyChangeListener(PropertyChangeListener listener);
  void removePropertyChangeListener(PropertyChangeListener listener);
}
```

The `addPropertyChangeListener()` and `removePropertyChangeListener()` methods are the same as the ones for a Bean which fires property change events. They should simply register and remove property change event listeners. This effectively means that every Bean customizer must be a property change event source. See Chapter 6 for discussions of events, event sources, and event listeners in general. Every time the user changes a property with the customizer, it should send a `PropertyChange` event to all registered listeners. We can take advantage of one of the support classes provided with the BDK, `PropertyChangeSupport`, for all of this functionality.

After our customizer is created by the design tool, the `setObject()` method will be called once to inform our customizer of the target Bean that should be manipulated. Listing 10.1 shows the customizer for the Arrow Bean.

LISTING 10.1 The Customizer for the Arrow Bean

```
// Arrow Bean Customizer Class
// ArrowCustomizer.java

package HTPJB.Chap10.Arrow;

import java.awt.*;
import java.beans.*;
import java.awt.event.*;

public class ArrowCustomizer extends Panel implements Customizer {
  public ArrowCustomizer() {
    setLayout(null);
  }

  public void setObject(Object obj) {
    target = (Arrow)obj;
```

CONTINUES

LISTING 10.1 The Customizer for the Arrow Bean (Continued)

```java
    // create the buttons
    Button  buttonNorth = new Button("North");
    Button  buttonSouth = new Button("South");
    Button  buttonEast = new Button("East");
    Button  buttonWest = new Button("West");
    // position them
    buttonNorth.setBounds(60, 5, 40, 20);
    buttonSouth.setBounds(60, 75, 40, 20);
    buttonEast.setBounds(110, 40, 40, 20);
    buttonWest.setBounds(10, 40, 40, 20);
    // register with them to listen for button presses
    buttonNorth.addActionListener(new NorthActionListener());
    buttonSouth.addActionListener(new SouthActionListener());
    buttonEast.addActionListener(new EastActionListener());
    buttonWest.addActionListener(new WestActionListener());
    // add them
    add(buttonNorth);
    add(buttonSouth);
    add(buttonEast);
    add(buttonWest);
    // create an arrow bean to show the user the direction
    try {
      view = (Arrow)target.getClass().newInstance();
      view.setDirection(target.getDirection());
      view.setBounds(60, 30, 40, 40);
      add(view);
    } catch (Exception ex) {
      System.err.println("Couldn't create Arrow bean");
    }
  }

public Dimension preferredSize() {
  return new Dimension(160, 100);
}

protected void setDirection(String newDir) {
  target.setDirection(newDir);
  view.setDirection(newDir);
```

CONTINUES

10

LISTING 10.1 The Customizer for the Arrow Bean (Continued)

```java
    support.firePropertyChange("", null, null);
  }

  class NorthActionListener implements ActionListener {
    public void actionPerformed(ActionEvent e) {
      setDirection("North");
    }
  }

  class SouthActionListener implements ActionListener {
    public void actionPerformed(ActionEvent e) {
      setDirection("South");
    }
  }

  class EastActionListener implements ActionListener {
    public void actionPerformed(ActionEvent e) {
      setDirection("East");
    }
  }

  class WestActionListener implements ActionListener {
    public void actionPerformed(ActionEvent e) {
      setDirection("West");
    }
  }

  public void addPropertyChangeListener(PropertyChangeListener l) {
    support.addPropertyChangeListener(l);
  }

  public void removePropertyChangeListener(PropertyChangeListener l) {
    support.removePropertyChangeListener(l);
  }

  private PropertyChangeSupport
    support = new PropertyChangeSupport(this);
  private Arrow target;
  private Arrow view;
}
```

10

Our step 1 above identified two requirements for a Bean customizer. To recap, a Bean customizer must ultimately inherit from `Component` as well as implement the `Customizer` interface. `ArrowCustomizer` fulfills these two requirements because it extends `Panel` and implements `Customizer`.

```
public class ArrowCustomizer extends Panel implements Customizer {
  // …
}
```

The constructor for `ArrowCustomizer` is very simple:

```
public ArrowCustomizer() {
    setLayout(null);
  }
```

It simply disables automatic layout by calling `setLayout` with a `null` argument. We'll explicitly control the positions of the components we add to the panel rather than relying on a layout manager.

TIP: *The AWT's* `Panel` *component extends* `Container`, *which, as its name implies, is designed to contain (hold) other components.* `Container` *provides support for using a layout manager to arrange the layout of the components that are contained. By default,* `Panel` *uses the flow layout manager, which tries to arrange components top-to-bottom and left-to-right. The flow layout manager would just get in the way and rearrange the positions of the components in our customizer, so we select no layout manager by calling* `setLayout()` *with* `null` *as the argument.*

The `setObject()` method is where most of the real setup work happens. This method will be called once after the BeanBox has created an instance of our Bean customizer. It tells our customizer which Bean to customize. In our case, the `Object` we're passed should always be an `Arrow` object (this is an `ArrowCustomizer`, after all). `ArrowCustomizer` contains a field named `target` of type `Arrow`. The first thing we do in `setObject()` is cast the `Object` we're passed to type `Arrow` and assign it to `target`:

```
target = (Arrow)obj;
```

Next, `setObject()` creates four buttons for the four directions used by an Arrow Bean. Each button is created with the appropriate label: "North," "South," "East," and "West." We then arrange them in a diamond pattern (with the "North" button at the northernmost point and so on) by adjusting their sizes and positions with `setBounds()`, as shown in Listing 10.2.

10

LISTING 10.2 Arranging the Buttons with setBounds()

```
// create the buttons
Button  buttonNorth = new Button("North");
Button  buttonSouth = new Button("South");
Button  buttonEast = new Button("East");
Button  buttonWest = new Button("West");
// position them
buttonNorth.setBounds(60, 5, 40, 20);
buttonSouth.setBounds(60, 75, 40, 20);
buttonEast.setBounds(110, 40, 40, 20);
buttonWest.setBounds(10, 40, 40, 20);
```

Before adding the buttons to the panel, we register an action listener with each button so that we can handle button presses:

```
// register with them to listen for button presses
buttonNorth.addActionListener(new NorthActionListener());
buttonSouth.addActionListener(new SouthActionListener());
buttonEast.addActionListener(new EastActionListener());
buttonWest.addActionListener(new WestActionListener());
```

As we saw in Chapter 6, the new event model in Java 1.1 uses a source/listener technique. The buttons are the event sources; they generate events of type ActionEvent when they're pressed. The Button class provides an addActionListener method so that interested parties (listeners) can register with the button to listen for these action events. An action event listener must implement the ActionListener interface. When an action event occurs, the source sends the event to all registered listeners by calling the actionPerformed() method declared in ActionListener for each listener.

Our ArrowCustomizer class is the true interested party (the listener) in this case, but you'll note that it doesn't implement the ActionListener interface. If it did implement the ActionListener interface, we could register the ArrowCustomizer as a listener for each button by calling addActionListener with this as the argument. This really wouldn't work very well, however. All four buttons would end up calling the same method, actionPerformed(), in the ArrowCustomizer class. We would then have to look at the ActionEvent we were passed, determine which button generated it, and take the appropriate action from there.

10

It would be much nicer if we could get each button to call a different method in ArrowCustomizer; inner-classes allow us, in effect, to do this.

TIP: *Inner-classes were covered in more detail in Chapter 6. An inner-class automatically has access to the methods and fields of the class in which it is declared. This makes inner-classes very useful as adaptors. Adaptors are small helper objects that sit between two other objects and wire them together. Technically, the four inner-classes presented here are all adaptors.*

Skipping forward in the ArrowCustomizer class for a moment, four inner-classes are defined: NorthActionListener, SouthActionListener, EastActionListener, and WestActionListener. These inner-classes appear in Listing 10.3. Each of these classes implements the ActionListener interface. The setObject() method registers a newly created NorthActionListener object to handle events generated by the north button. A SouthActionListener object handles events generated by the south button, and so on. Each of these inner-classes calls setDirection() with the appropriate argument ("North," "South," "East," and "West") in its actionPerfomed() method. Note that setDirection() is a protected method in ArrowCustomizer; the Java compiler performs a little magic behind the scenes to give the inner-classes access to this method. See Chapter 6 for more information on inner-classes.

After the action listeners are registered with each button, we add them to our container:

```
// add them
add(buttonNorth);
add(buttonSouth);
add(buttonEast);
add(buttonWest);
```

The setObject method then uses the target Arrow object to create a new Arrow object named view. This Arrow object is used to show the user the currently selected direction of the target arrow:

```
view = (Arrow)target.getClass().newInstance();
```

Lastly, the setObject() method sets the direction of the view arrow to be the same as the target arrow, positions it between the four buttons, and adds it to the component:

```
view.setDirection(target.getDirection());
view.setBounds(60, 30, 40, 40);
add(view);
```

10

LISTING 10.3 Inner-Classes for ArrowCustomizer

```
class NorthActionListener implements ActionListener {
    public void actionPerformed(ActionEvent e) {
      setDirection("North");
    }
  }

  class SouthActionListener implements ActionListener {
    public void actionPerformed(ActionEvent e) {
      setDirection("South");
    }
  }

  class EastActionListener implements ActionListener {
    public void actionPerformed(ActionEvent e) {
      setDirection("East");
    }
  }

  class WestActionListener implements ActionListener {
    public void actionPerformed(ActionEvent e) {
      setDirection("West");
    }
  }
```

The `preferredSize()` method comes after `setObject()`. This is a standard method overridden from `Component` which is called by the environment and allows us to specify the initial size of our component:

```
public Dimension preferredSize() {
    return new Dimension(16Ø, 1ØØ);
  }
```

10

NOTE: *The JDK 1.1 documentation for* `preferredSize()` *claims that it's deprecated by* `getPreferredSize()`. *This means that* `preferredSize()` *is the old name used prior to version 1.1, but* `getPreferredSize()` *should now be used instead. Several methods in the AWT were renamed like this with "get" and "set" to be consistent with JavaBeans. Unfortunately, in the final re-*

lease of the JDK 1.1, the actual code is written backwards; `preferredSize()` *is in effect deprecating* `getPreferredSize()` *rather than being deprecated by* `getPreferredSize()`. *The net result is that* `getPreferredSize()` *often does not work as advertised; if you use it, your component may not be sized properly. For the time being, use* `preferredSize()` *instead.*

Next, the `setDirection()` method we mentioned earlier is defined. This method sets the direction of the target and view Beans and then informs any listeners that a property change has occurred:

```
protected void setDirection(String newDir) {
    target.setDirection(newDir);
    view.setDirection(newDir);
    support.firePropertyChange(   , null, null);
}
```

Remember that a customizer must provide `addPropertyChangeListener()` and `removePropertyChangeListener()` methods. When a property is modified, the customizer must send a property change event to each registered listener. The JDK provides a class, `PropertyChangeSupport`, which handles all the dirty work of adding and removing property change listeners and sending a property change event to each registered listener. `ArrowCustomizer` contains a data field, `support`, which is an instance of `PropertyChangeSupport`. The `addPropertyChangeListener()` method in `ArrowCustomizer` calls `support.addPropertyChangeListener()` to add listeners; `removePropertyChangeListener()` calls `support.removePropertyChangeListener()` to remove listeners; and `setDirection()` calls `support.firePropertyChange()` to inform the registered listeners of a property change (see Listing 10.4).

This leaves only the inner-classes for handling action events from the buttons, the `addPropertyChangeListener()` and `removePropertyChangeListener()` methods, and the `support`, `target`, and `view` data fields, all of which we've already covered.

Changing BeanInfo

We touched on this topic briefly in Chapter 9 when discussing feature descriptors. A `BeanDescriptor` contains information about the class of the Bean and the class of the customizer for the Bean. The default `BeanDescriptor` for a Bean has no customizer. To provide one for our `Arrow` Bean, we must supply a `BeanInfo` object with a `getBeanDescriptor()` method.

In Chapter 7, we provided a `BeanInfo` class for our Arrow Bean, but it didn't supply the `getBeanDescriptor()` method. All we need to do is add this method

10

**LISTING 10.4 The addPropertyChangeListener(),
removePropertyChangeListener(), and setDirection() Methods**

```
public void addPropertyChangeListener(PropertyChangeListener l) {
  support.addPropertyChangeListener(l);
}

public void removePropertyChangeListener(PropertyChangeListener l)
{
  support.removePropertyChangeListener(l);
}
// …
protected void setDirection(String newDir) {
  target.setDirection(newDir);
  view.setDirection(newDir);
  support.firePropertyChange("", null, null);
}
```

---

to the original descriptor to install our customizer, as shown in Listing 10.5. This is
identical to the original `ArrowBeanInfo`, except that a `getBeanDescriptor()`
method is provided which simply returns a newly created `BeanDescriptor` object. The class of the `Arrow` Bean (`Arrow.class`) and the class of the customizer
(`ArrowCustomizer.class`) are passed to the constructor of the
`BeanDescriptor`.

Trying Out ArrowCustomizer

To try out the Arrow Bean customizer, compile `Arrow.java`,
`ArrowBeanInfo.java`, `ArrowCustomizer.java`, and `DirectionEditor.java`
using `javac`. Next create a JAR file named `Arrow.jar` which contains all of the
compiled .class files (notice that compiling the four source files will produce more
than four class files because of the inner-classes; make sure you include all of them
in the JAR file). You may install this new JAR file into the BeanBox by simply plac-
ing it in the jars directory of the BDK directory on your machine. See Chapter 4
for details on creating a JAR file.

10

TIP: *To compile most of the examples in this book, you will need to set the
CLASSPATH environment variable on your system to point to the directory
which contains the source code for the examples. If you're using Windows 95,*

LISTING 10.5 BeanInfo for Arrow with Customizer Support

```java
// BeanInfo for Arrow
// ArrowBeanInfo.java

package HTPJB.Chap10.Arrow;

import java.beans.*;

public class ArrowBeanInfo extends SimpleBeanInfo {
  public PropertyDescriptor[] getPropertyDescriptors() {
    try {
      PropertyDescriptor pd = new PropertyDescriptor("direction",
                                                     Arrow.class);
      pd.setPropertyEditorClass(DirectionEditor.class);
      PropertyDescriptor result[] = { pd };
      return result;
    } catch (Exception ex) {
      System.err.println("ArrowBeanInfo: unexpected exeption: " +
ex);
      return null;
    }
  }
  public BeanDescriptor getBeanDescriptor() {
    return new BeanDescriptor(Arrow.class, ArrowCustomizer.class);
  }
}                                                                    ■
```

---

*for example, and the source code for the examples is installed on your machine
at c:\Source, execute the following command from the command line:*

```
set CLASSPATH=c:\Source.
```

Figure 10.3 shows the BeanBox with an Arrow Bean and the customizer running. Note that the Edit menu has a "Customize…" item. The BeanBox adds this item for Beans which have customizers. Click on one of the direction buttons, and the arrow between the buttons should change to indicate the currently selected direction. Notice that the Arrow Bean in the BeanBox also updates.

10

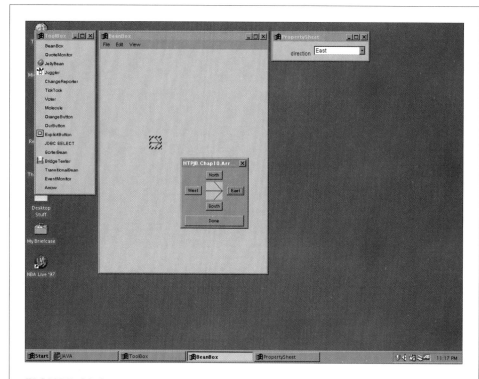

FIGURE 10.3

The Arrow Bean's customizer

Watch the direction property editor in the PropertySheet window as you manipulate the direction of the arrow from the customizer. It also updates in real time as you're changing the direction! We didn't specifically write any code to make the direction property editor do this, but we did provide code to generate property change events. The property sheet registers itself with our customizer as a property change listener. Whenever our customizer modifies the direction property, it sends a property change event to the property sheet, and the direction property editor updates. Pretty nice!

Summary

In this chapter, we learned how a Bean can obtain information about the environment it's being used in, such as whether there's a graphical user interface (GUI) available or whether the current user is an end-user or a program designer. We also examined customizers, which allow complex Beans to be manipulated and configured in a very high-level, user-friendly manner.

Part *3*

Building Your Own Beans

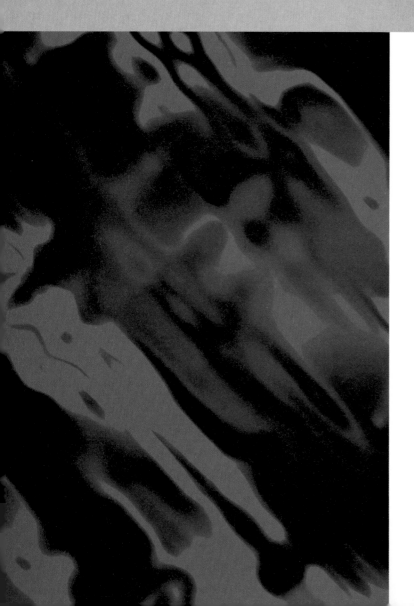

Chapter 11

An Image Button Bean

▶ **Designing the Image Button Bean**

▶ **Constructing the Image Button Bean**

▶ **Using the Image Button Bean**

11

Although you've learned a great deal about the JavaBeans technology throughout the book thus far, you've yet to learn the specifics of how to build a complete Bean from scratch. Since you now understand the fundamentals surrounding JavaBeans, it's time to press onward and begin learning how to build your own Beans. This chapter leads you through the design and implementation of a complete Bean, an Image Button Bean, which has a wide range of uses in application development.

Unlike previous chapters, this chapter is geared toward creating a fully functional JavaBean component. For this reason, the chapter takes a very hands-on approach to covering the knowledge and techniques necessary to build a Bean of your own. By the end of this chapter, you will not only understand the details surrounding the construction of your own Beans, you will also have a very versatile Bean that can be used in your own applications.

In this chapter, you will learn

▶ How to design an Image Button Bean

▶ How to construct an Image Button Bean

▶ How to use an Image Button Bean

Designing the Image Button Bean

The first step in building any Bean is to come up with a preliminary design, which is usually arrived at after some amount of brainstorming. This design should be worked out to a certain degree of detail before you embark on the actual coding of the Bean. The Bean we'll develop in this chapter is an Image Button Bean, which functions much like the standard Java AWT button but adds the additional functionality of displaying an image along with the text label. Since the goal of this chapter is to show you how a Bean is developed from scratch, I decided not to derive the Image Button Bean from the AWT `Button` class. This means that the Image Button Bean has to implement all of its own button functionality from scratch.

There are a few things about the Image Button Bean that set it apart from the standard AWT button. Like the AWT button, the Image Button Bean allows you to make any text of your choice the label for the button. However, the Image Button Bean also allows you to set the font for the label, using any of a variety of different typefaces in virtually any size. The Image Button Bean also supports changing the background and foreground colors. The background color corresponds to the face of the button, while the foreground color determines the color of the label text. The most important feature in the Image Button Bean, however, is the capability to display an image along with the button's label text. Since the Bean's size can vary based on the image, label text, and font, the Bean also supports an auto size feature that causes the Bean to automatically size itself to accommodate the image and label text.

The Image Button Bean also supports a feature that allows it to be used to represent an on/off state, much like a checkbox. In this mode, instead of automatically raising after you click it with the mouse, the button remains down. Another mouse click restores it to its normal position. This feature is sometimes useful in toolbars where some buttons reflect a two-state option. When used in this mode, the Image Button Bean functions as a two-state switch.

Now that you have an idea of what the Image Button Bean does, let's move on to designing some of its specifics. The design of a Bean can be broken down into three major parts: properties, methods, and events. The rest of this section focuses on the Image Button Bean and the design of its major functional parts.

Properties

The properties for the Image Button Bean must accurately and efficiently represent the functionality of the Bean. Fortunately, you don't have to specifically provide all the properties for the Image Button Bean yourself. The reason for this is that you are going to derive the Bean from an existing AWT class, Canvas, which will provide a great deal of the overhead, including some very useful properties. The Canvas class represents a rectangular area onto which you can draw or trap input events from the user. The Canvas class is derived from Component, which provides the base functionality typically required of graphical Beans, including background color, foreground color, name, and font properties.

Even though the Canvas and Component parent classes help by providing basic properties like the background and foreground colors, you still have to provide some properties of your own. Since you know the Image Button Bean will have a label and an image, you can start off the properties with a string label property and a string property for the image name. You may be wondering why I'm suggesting a string property for the image name, since Java provides an Image class for representing images. The reason is that images are always referenced by name, meaning that a name is used to load an image as a resource. Because of this, it is much easier to represent an image at the property level with a string name rather than with an Image object.

Beyond the string properties for the label and image, you also know the Bean needs to support a sticky mode, which can easily be represented by a boolean property. The functionality of the Sticky mode requires another boolean property to keep track of whether the Bean is up or down. The last property necessary to round out the Image Button Bean is a boolean property that controls the Auto Size mode for the Bean. These five properties, combined with the inherited properties provided by the parent Canvas and Component classes, are sufficient for modeling the functionality required of the Bean.

The following are the properties specifically required of the Image Button Bean:

▶ Label

▶ Image name

▶ Sticky mode (on/off)

▶ Button state (up/down)

▶ Auto size (on/off)

Methods

With the properties behind you, much of the work of designing the Image Button Bean is completed. The next step is determining the public methods required of the Bean. The most logical place to begin is with the accessor methods for the Bean. Since you already know the properties for the Bean, it's pretty easy to determine the accessor methods you need. The label, image name, Sticky mode, and auto size properties for the Bean are all readable and writeable, so you will need a pair of accessor methods for each of them. The property representing the Bean's up/down state is a little different, since the state is determined by the user clicking the button with the mouse. In other words, this property shouldn't be directly writeable like the other properties, and should instead always be set indirectly by the user visually interacting with the button. So for this property you only need a getter method.

If the auto size feature is enabled, the Bean is supposed to resize itself based on the image, label text, and font. This implies that the setter methods for each of these properties must somehow notify the Bean to resize itself. This is not a problem for the image name and label properties, since you will be writing them yourself, but what about the inherited font property? The solution is overriding the setter method for the font property. This setter method is defined in the Component class, along with the font property itself. By overriding it in the Image Button Bean, you can easily resize the Bean after setting the new font value.

> NOTE: *Overriding setter methods for inherited properties is a fairly common chore in JavaBeans programming. This is due to the fact that derived Beans often have new functionality that is directly impacted by a modified inherited property.*

Although accessor methods play an important role in any Bean, they typically don't tell the whole story in terms of a Bean's public methods. In other words, most Beans provide additional public methods beyond their accessor methods.

The Image Button Bean is a good example of this because it needs two public methods in addition to its accessor methods. The first of these, paint(), is over-ridden from the parent Canvas class to allow the Bean to paint itself. The paint() method is pretty much required of all graphical Beans since it provides a central location for the placement of a Bean's drawing code. The other public method required of the Bean isn't quite as obvious as paint(). It is the PreferredSize() method, which calculates and returns the preferred size of the Bean based on its current state. This method is only necessary because the Image Button Bean has a preferred size based on the image, label text, and font. The pre-ferred size is used by the auto size feature to resize the Bean.

The following are the public methods required of the Image Button Bean:

- ▶ Label property getter/setter methods
- ▶ Image name property getter/setter methods
- ▶ Sticky mode property getter/setter methods
- ▶ Auto Size mode property getter/setter methods
- ▶ Button state property getter method
- ▶ Overridden font property setter method
- ▶ Overridden paint() method
- ▶ Overridden PreferredSize() method

Events

The last design aspect of the Image Button Bean you need to address is events. Since the Bean is a button, it must be capable of firing action events whenever a user clicks it. This is what allows the Bean to be wired to other Beans or applica-tions in order to trigger them based on a button click. Since the event fired in this case is an action event, part of supporting it is providing event listener registration methods. A pair of these methods is all you need to support the addition and re-moval of action event listeners.

The details surrounding the actual firing of the action event are another issue altogether. The Bean is required to support some type of mechanism by which an action event is passed on to all the listeners registered. This mechanism must be handled via a single event-processing method that dispatches the event to each listener.

The final area of interest relating to events is how the Bean processes events for itself. It's one thing to be able to broadcast events to others, but the Image Button Bean must also manage events that occur within itself. For example, when the user clicks the mouse on the Bean, it needs to change its appearance to show the button pressing down. The events that must be responded to by the Bean consist of focus changes, mouse clicks, mouse drags, and key presses. The focus change events must be processed because the button draws a focus rectangle on its surface whenever it has focus. The mouse click and drag events must be processed in order for the Bean to change its state appropriately and act like a button. Finally, the key press events must be processed in order for the Bean to have a keyboard interfaceBean and simulate a mouse button click for keys like the Enter key. These events are processed in individual event processor methods that are overridden from the Bean's parent class.

The following are the event-related methods required of the Image Button Bean:

▶ Action event listener registration methods

▶ Action event processing method for firing events

▶ Focus event processing method

▶ Mouse click event processing method

▶ Mouse drag event processing method

▶ Key press event processing method

Constructing the Image Button Bean

With the preliminary design finished, you're now ready to move on to the code for the Image Button Bean. You will probably be pleasantly surprised by how little difference there is between the code for Beans and the code for normal Java classes. Beans are in fact normal Java classes with support for a few extra facilities such as introspection and serialization. In many cases these extra facilities are handled automatically, so the Bean code really does look just like a normal Java class.

Throughout this section you'll learn about different parts of the code for the Image Button Bean. As you read through the section, please feel free to check out the complete source code for the Bean, which is included on the CD-ROM accompanying this book. The main code for the Image Button Bean is in the `ImageButton` class, which appears on the CD-ROM in the file named ImageButton.java.

 ON THE CD: *The source code for the Image Button Bean is on the CD-ROM included with this book.*

Properties and Member Variables

The place to start in developing the Image Button Bean is laying out the properties. The following are the member variable properties for the Bean, based on the initial design:

```
private String   label;
private String   imageName;
private boolean  sticky;
private boolean  autoSize;
private boolean  down;
```

As you can see, these member variables directly correspond to the properties mentioned earlier in the initial design. Notice that they are all built-in Java types, which means that property editors are already provided by JavaBeans for each of them. This means you don't have to put forth any additional effort to provide visual editing support for the Image Button Bean's properties. Along with these properties, the Bean also requires a few other member variables for internal use:

```
private transient Image          image;
private transient int            imgWidth, imgHeight;
private transient ActionListener actionListener = null;
private boolean                  hasFocus;
```

The `image` member represents the actual image being displayed on the button. The image name property is used to load a physical image into the `image` member. The `imgWidth` and `imgHeight` members keep track of the width and height of the image. The `actionListener` member is an `ActionListener` interface that is used to keep track of action event listeners. This member is used by the action event processing method to fire events to each listener. The `hasFocus` member is used to keep track of the focus state of the Bean. The focus is important to keep up with because it impacts the visual appearance of the Bean.

Constructors

The Image Button Bean provides two constructors: a default constructor and a detailed constructor that takes all five properties as arguments. Listing 11.1 shows the code for both of these constructors.

The first constructor simply calls the second constructor with default property values. The second constructor is responsible for actually doing all the work. This constructor begins by calling the super-class constructor, and then moves on to setting all the properties. Notice that the two inherited properties, font and background color, are set by calling their setter methods instead of directly setting the member variables. This is a result of the fact that properties are always declared as private, meaning that you are required to use a setter method to access them. In

11

LISTING 11.1 The Constructors for the Image Button Bean

```java
public ImageButton() {
  this("OK", "OK.gif", true, false, false);
}

public ImageButton(String l, String in, boolean as, boolean s,
  boolean d) {
  // Allow the superclass constructor to do its thing
  super();

  // Set properties
  label = l;
  autoSize = as;
  sticky = s;
  down = d;
  setFont(new Font("Dialog", Font.PLAIN, 12));
  setBackground(Color.lightGray);
  setImageName(in);

  // Enable event processing
  enableEvents(AWTEvent.FOCUS_EVENT_MASK | AWTEvent.MOUSE_EVENT_MASK |
    AWTEvent.MOUSE_MOTION_EVENT_MASK | AWTEvent.KEY_EVENT_MASK);
}
```

this case, it works out well because the Image Button Bean provides its own setter method for the font property. The image name property also uses a setter method, since the setter method must load the physical image associated with the name.

With the properties set, the constructor moves on to enabling a group of events for the Bean to process by calling the enableEvents() method. Without calling this method, the Bean would be incapable of directly trapping any events. The purpose of selectively enabling certain events is to optimize the event-handling procedure by looking only for events that you are specifically interested in. In this case, the Image Button Bean is interested in focus, mouse, mouse move, and key events.

Accessor Methods

The next functional part of the Bean is the accessor methods, which provide access to Bean properties. Listing 11.2 shows the code for the label property's accessor methods.

11

The `getLabel()` getter method is pretty self-explanatory; it simply returns the value of the `label` member variable. The `setLabel()` setter method is slightly more involved in that it checks the `autoSize` member and calls the `sizeToFit()` method after setting the `label` member variable. The `sizeToFit()` method, which you will learn about in detail a little later in this chapter, is responsible for determining the ideal button size based on the image, label text, and font.

LISTING 11.2 The Label Property's Accessor Methods

```
public String getLabel() {
  return label;
}

public void setLabel(String l) {
  label = l;
  if (autoSize)
    sizeToFit();
}
```

The accessor methods for the image name property, `getImageName()` and `setImageName()`, are responsible for getting and setting the image name of the Bean (see Listing 11.3).

The `getImageName()` method is very minimal and simply returns the value of the `imageName` member variable. The `setImageName()` method is a little more involved in that it first sets the `imageName` member, then loads the image corresponding to this name. The `setImageName()` method uses the `loadImage()` method, which you will learn about a little later in this chapter, to handle the loading of the image. `setImageName()` finishes by checking the `autoSize` member variable and resizing the Bean if necessary.

The accessor methods for the sticky property, `isSticky()` and `setSticky()`, are very minimal; they simply get and set the value for the `sticky` member variable, with no additional functionality. The accessor methods for the auto size property, `isAutoSize()` and `setAutoSize()`, are very similar except that the `setAutoSize()` method resizes the Bean in addition to setting the `autoSize` member variable. Like the getter methods for these two properties, the getter method for the button

LISTING 11.3 The Accessor Methods for the Image Name Property

```
public String getImageName() {
  return imageName;
}

public void setImageName(String in) {
  imageName = in;

  // Load the image
  image = loadImage(imageName);
  if (autoSize)
    sizeToFit();
}
```

state property, isDown(), simply returns the value of the down member variable. Things get a little more interesting when you get to the overridden setter method for the font property, setFont():

```
public void setFont(Font f) {
  super.setFont(f);
  if (autoSize)
    sizeToFit();
}
```

The whole point of overriding this method is to make sure the Bean is resized if it is in Auto Size mode and a change occurs in the value of the font property. Notice that the super-class setFont() method is called to perform the actual setting of the property before the Bean is resized with a call to sizeToFit().

Public Methods

There are two important public methods in the Bean that you need to learn about now: paint() and PreferredSize(). The first one is the paint() method, which is used to paint the visual appearance of the Bean. This is the source code for the paint() method appears in Listing 11.4.

LISTING 11.4 The paint() Method

```
public synchronized void paint(Graphics g) {
  Dimension d = getSize();

  // Calculate the width & height of the image
  if (image != null) {
    image_height = image.getHeight(this);
    image_width = image.getWidth(this);
  }

  // Calculate the vertical spacing around image and foreground text
  g.setFont(getFont());
  FontMetrics fm = g.getFontMetrics();
  int         vSpacing = Math.max(SPACING, (d.height - image_height -
              fm.getMaxAscent() - fm.getMaxDescent()) / 3);

  // Paint the background with 3D effects
  g.setColor(getBackground());
```

CONTINUES

LISTING 11.4 The `paint()` Method (Continued)

```
    g.fillRect(1, 1, d.width - 2, d.height - 2);
    g.draw3DRect(0, 0, d.width - 1, d.height - 1, !down);
    g.setColor(Color.darkGray);
    if (down) {
      g.drawLine(1, d.height - 3, 1, 1);
      g.drawLine(1, 1, d.width - 3, 1);
    }
    else {
      g.drawLine(2, d.height - 2, d.width - 2, d.height - 2);
      g.drawLine(d.width - 2, d.height - 2, d.width - 2, 1);
    }

    // Paint the image
    if (image != null) {
      if (down)
        g.drawImage(image, ((d.width - image_width) / 2) + 2, vSpacing +
          1, this);
      else
        g.drawImage(image, (d.width - image_width) / 2, vSpacing, this);
    }

    // Paint the foreground text
    g.setColor(getForeground());
    if (down)
      g.drawString(label, ((d.width - fm.stringWidth(label)) / 2) + 2,
        d.height - vSpacing - fm.getMaxDescent() + 1);
    else
      g.drawString(label, ((d.width - fm.stringWidth(label)) / 2),
        d.height - vSpacing - fm.getMaxDescent());

    // Paint the focus rect
    if (hasFocus) {
      g.setColor(Color.gray);
      g.drawRect(SPACING - 1, SPACING - 1, d.width - (2 * (SPACING - 1)),
        d.height - (2 * (SPACING - 1)));
    }
  }
```

The paint() method starts off by getting the width and height of the Bean and calculating the vertical spacing between the image, label text, and borders. It then fills the background and paints a 3D effect around the edges. Notice that the 3D effect is painted differently depending on the value of the down member variable. The paint() method paints the image next by calling the drawImage() method, which is defined in the Graphics class. Like the 3D effects, the image is drawn based on the value of the down member variable. This code is what gives the effect of the image appearing to move down when the button is pushed. The paint() method then paints the foreground label text by selecting the appropriate font and calling the drawString() method. The down member variable is again referenced to determine where the label text is drawn. Finally, if the hasFocus member variable is set to true, a focus rectangle is drawn on the Bean to indicate that it has the input focus.

The PreferredSize() method is used to determine the ideal size of the Bean. The ideal size of the Bean is basically the size that provides the most appealing visual balance between the image, label text, and borders. The calculation of this size takes into account the image size, label text, and font. Listing 11.5 shows the code for the PreferredSize() method.

LISTING 11.5 The `getPreferredSize()` Method

```
public Dimension PreferredSize() {
  // Calculate the preferred size based on label text and image sizes
  FontMetrics fm = getFontMetrics(getFont());
  int height = 2 * SPACING,
      width = 0;
  if (image != null)
    height += SPACING + fm.getMaxAscent() + fm.getMaxDescent() +
      IMAGE_SIZE;
  else
    height += fm.getMaxAscent() + fm.getMaxDescent();
  width = Math.max(fm.stringWidth(label) + 2 * SPACING, (height * 3) /
    2);

  return new Dimension(width, height);
}
```

Event Registration Methods

The event registration methods in the Image Button Bean are used to allow the addition and removal of listeners for the Bean's action events. Here is the code for these methods:

```
public synchronized void addActionListener(ActionListener l) {
  actionListener = AWTEventMulticaster.add(actionListener, l);
}

public synchronized void removeActionListener(ActionListener l) {
  actionListener = AWTEventMulticaster.remove(actionListener, l);
}
```

These methods use the `AWTEventMulticaster` class to add and remove action listeners from the `actionListener` member variable, which is the multicast action listener used to keep up with who receives action events. Even though the `actionListener` member variable is defined in the Bean as an `ActionListener` interface, it is actually being used to represent a chain of multicast event listeners. This functionality is handled entirely by the `AWTEventMulticaster` class, which takes on the responsibility of managing the list of listeners.

Event Processing Methods

The Image Button Bean provides a variety of event-processing methods. This is primarily due to the fact that the Bean must listen for different types of input events to function properly. The first of these methods, `processActionEvent()`, isn't related to processing input events, however. The `processActionEvent()` method is instead used to dispatch action events to all of the registered action event listeners. Here is the code for this method:

```
protected void processActionEvent(ActionEvent e) {
  // Deliver the event to all registered action event listeners
  if (actionListener != null)
    actionListener.actionPerformed(e);
}
```

The `processActionEvent()` method simply calls the `actionPerformed()` method on the `actionListener` member variable, which results in the event being dispatched to all the registered listeners. The `actionPerformed()` method is the only method defined in the `ActionListener` interface, and is typically called any time an action occurs in an event source such as a Bean. In the case of the Image Button Bean, an action is defined as a button push, but an action can mean other things in other Beans.

There are four other event-processing methods used by the Image Button Bean, which all act differently than `processActionEvent()`. The code for the first of these methods, `processFocusEvent()`, is shown in Listing 11.6.

This method is called whenever the focus for the Bean changes. Its only function is to monitor changes in the Bean's focus and update the appearance of the Bean accordingly. The `processMouseEvent()` method is a little more interesting in that it responds to mouse button presses and releases. The code for this method appears in Listing 11.7.

The `processMouseEvent()` method is responsible for trapping mouse button presses and releases and making sure the Bean behaves properly. When the mouse button is pressed, the `down` member variable is toggled and the Bean is repainted. When the mouse button is released, the `down` and `sticky` member variables are checked to determine the state of the button. If the Bean isn't in Sticky mode and it is down, an action event is fired via the `fireActionEvent()` method, which you will learn about in a moment. The `down` member variable is then set to false and the Bean is repainted.

The `processMouseMotionEvent()` method (Listing 11.8) is used to respond to events related to the movement of the mouse.

The `processMouseMotionEvent()` method is responsible for detecting mouse drags and making sure the Bean behaves properly. The only purpose of

---

LISTING 11.6 The processFocusEvent() Method

```java
protected void processFocusEvent(FocusEvent e) {
  // Get the new focus state and repaint
  switch(e.getID()) {
    case FocusEvent.FOCUS_GAINED:
      hasFocus = true;
      repaint();
      break;

    case FocusEvent.FOCUS_LOST:
      hasFocus = false;
      repaint();
      break;
  }

  // Let the superclass continue delivery
  super.processFocusEvent(e);
}
```

LISTING 11.7 The processMouseEvent() Method

```java
protected void processMouseEvent(MouseEvent e) {
  // Track mouse presses/releases
  switch(e.getID()) {
    case MouseEvent.MOUSE_PRESSED:
      down = !down;
      repaint();
      break;

    case MouseEvent.MOUSE_RELEASED:
      if (down && !sticky) {
        fireActionEvent();
        down = false;
        repaint();
      }
      break;
  }
}
```

LISTING 11.8 The processMouseMotionEvent() Method

```java
protected void processMouseMotionEvent(MouseEvent e) {
  // Track mouse drags
  if (e.getID() == MouseEvent.MOUSE_DRAGGED && !sticky) {
    Point pt = e.getPoint();
    if ((pt.x < 0) || (pt.x > getSize().width) ||
      (pt.y < 0) || (pt.y > getSize().height)) {
      if (down) {
        down = false;
        repaint();
      }
    }
    else if (!down) {
      down = true;
      repaint();
    }
  }
}
```

responding to mouse drags is ensuring that the button raises up when the mouse is dragged off it, providing it's not in Sticky mode. In Sticky mode, drags have no meaning because the button changes state as soon as the mouse button is pressed. If the button isn't in Sticky mode, the coordinates of the mouse are checked to see if they fall within the button's bounding rectangle. If they don't, the Bean button is restored to its raised position by setting the down member to false. If the mouse is within the bounding rectangle for the button and the button is raised, the down member is set to true.

The last of the event-processing methods is processKeyEventMethod(), which is used to respond to key presses. The code for this method is shown in Listing 11.9.

The processKeyEventMethod() method is used to provide a keyboard interface for the Bean. If the Bean has input focus and the Return key or the spacebar is pressed, it is treated just like a mouse click on the Bean. The mouse click is simulated by setting the down member to true, firing an action event by calling fireActionEvent(), and then setting the down member to false.

LISTING 11.9 The processKeyEventMethod() Method

```java
protected void processKeyEvent(KeyEvent e) {
  // Simulate a mouse click for certain keys
  if (e.getKeyCode() == KeyEvent.VK_ENTER ||
    e.getKeyChar() == KeyEvent.VK_SPACE) {
    if (sticky) {
      down = !down;
      repaint();
    }
    else {
      down = true;
      repaint();
      fireActionEvent();
      down = false;
      repaint();
    }
  }
}
```

Support Methods

The Image Button Bean uses three private support methods that you haven't learned about yet: sizeToFit(), fireActionEvent(), and loadImage(). These methods provide functionality that is only needed by the Bean internally, which is why they are private. Nevertheless, they play a vital role in the inner workings of the Bean. The code for the sizeToFit() method appears in Listing 11.10.

The sizeToFit() method is responsible for sizing the Bean to fit the image and label text with enough space between the borders so the button looks visually appealing. The PreferredSize() method is used to get the ideal button size, which is then used to resize the Bean. Note that calling the setSize() method alone isn't sufficient to resize the Bean; you must also notify the Bean's parent to lay out the Bean again by calling the invalidate() and doLayout() methods on the parent.

The fireActionEvent() method is also important to the internal functioning of the Bean. Here is its code:

```
private void fireActionEvent() {
  processActionEvent(new ActionEvent(this,
    ActionEvent.ACTION_PERFORMED, null));
}
```

fireActionEvent() is a very simple method: it consists of a single call to the processActionEvent() method. The purpose of providing the fireActionEvent() method is to clean up the task of firing an action event by hiding the creation of the ActionEvent object passed into processActionEvent(). This isn't a big deal, but it does make the code calling fireActionEvent() in other methods a little cleaner.

The loadImage() method (Listing 11.11) is responsible for loading an image using a resource name for the image.

The loadImage() method takes an image name as its only argument and uses it to load an image as a resource. The URL (uniform resource locator) for the image is first determined by calling the getResource() method. The getContent() method is then called on this URL to get the actual image, which is returned from loadImage().

Speaking of the loadImage() method, the Image Button Bean comes with four different images that are used in a variety of situations. These images are named

---

LISTING 11.10   The sizeToFit() Method

```
private void sizeToFit() {
  // Resize to the preferred size
  Dimension d = PreferredSize();
  setSize(d.width, d.height);
  Component p = getParent();
  if (p != null) {
    p.invalidate();
    p.doLayout();
  }
}
```

LISTING 11.11   The `loadImage()` Method

```
private Image loadImage(String name) {
  try {
    URL url = getClass().getResource(name);
    return createImage((ImageProducer)url.getContent());
  }
  catch (Exception e) {
    System.err.println("Couldn't load the image " + name + ".");
    return null;
  }
}
```

`OK.gif`, `Cancel.gif`, `Plus.gif`, and `Minus.gif`, and are shown in Figure 11.1. You are free to create images of your own and use them with the Bean.

Additional Overhead

We've now covered all the source code for the Image Button Bean itself. Although the `ImageButton` class is all you really need to have a fully functioning Bean, there is one other class of importance: `ImageButtonBeanInfo`. This class is a Bean information class used to provide explicit information about the graphical icons for the Image Button Bean. The complete source code for the `ImageButtonBeanInfo` class appears in Listing 11.12.

The only method defined in the `ImageButtonBeanInfo` class is `getIcon()`, which is typically called by application builder tools to retrieve an icon representing the Bean. Notice that two different icons based on different resolutions are provided by the Bean information class. The first icon is 16 by 16 pixels in size, while the second is 32 by 32 pixels. This allows application builder tools some flexibility as to how they graphically represent Beans for selection. The BeanBox utility that comes with the BDK specifically uses the 16 by 16 size icons. Both of the Bean icons are provided as GIF 89A images, which is standard for Java. Figure 11.2 shows what the icons for the Image Button Bean look like.

One final part of the Image Button Bean is required before the Bean can be used in an application builder tool. I'm referring to the manifestation file required of the JAR file that the Bean is placed in. Beans must be distributed in a JAR file along with an appropriate manifestation file describing the contents of the JAR file. You'll learn more about JAR files and their role in JavaBeans in Chapter 4. The code for the Image Button Bean's manifestation file, ImageButton.mf, is as follows:

```
Manifest-Version: 1.0
```

FIGURE 11.1

The standard images provided with the Image Button Bean

LISTING 11.12   The ImageButtonBeanInfo Class

```java
// ImageButtonBeanInfo Class
// ImageButtonBeanInfo.java

package HTPJB.Chap11.ImageButton;

// Imports
import java.beans.*;

public class ImageButtonBeanInfo extends SimpleBeanInfo {
  // Get the appropriate icon
  public java.awt.Image getIcon(int iconKind) {
    if (iconKind == BeanInfo.ICON_COLOR_16x16) {
      java.awt.Image img = loadImage("ImageButtonIcon16.gif");
      return img;
    }
    if (iconKind == BeanInfo.ICON_COLOR_32x32) {
      java.awt.Image img = loadImage("ImageButtonIcon32.gif");
      return img;
    }
    return null;
  }
}
```

```
Name: HTPJB/Chap11/ImageButton/ImageButton.class
Java-Bean: True
```

FIGURE 11.2

The Bean information icons for the Image Button Bean

As you can see, the manifestation file is very simple; you just provide the name of your Bean class and specify that it is in fact a Bean. This is the only additional overhead you have to place in the JAR file in order for application builder tools to be able to extract information about your Bean. To build a JAR file containing the Image Button and its resources, execute the following command in the directory containing the HTPJB directory:

```
jar cfm ImageButton.jar HTPJB\Chap11\ImageButton\ImageButton.mf
HTPJB\Chap11\ImageButton\*.class HTPJB\Chap11\ImageButton\*.gif
```

TIP: *If you don't like the idea of typing in such a big command, feel free to create a batch file that does the work for you. Then, if you need to rebuild the JAR file, you can just run the batch file.*

This command uses the JAR archiving utility, which ships with the JDK, to create a JAR file containing the Image Button Bean and its resources. Don't forget that the complete source code and related resources for the Image Button Bean, including a JAR file for the Bean, are located on the CD-ROM included with this book.

Using the Image Button Bean

Congratulations, it's finally time to test your Bean! The first step in using a Bean in a visual environment such as the BeanBox is to add the Bean to the environment. To add the Image Button Bean to the BeanBox, you must copy the JAR file you created to the jars directory beneath your BDK installation, because this is where the BeanBox looks for Beans to add to its ToolBox. Upon being executed, the BeanBox automatically checks the jars directory to see if any new Beans have been added. So in order to add a Bean to the BeanBox you must copy its JAR file to the jars directory.

Once you've copied the JAR file for the Image Button Bean to the jars directory, try running the BeanBox by executing the `run.bat` batch file. The BeanBox should appear at this point with your Image Button Bean added to the ToolBox. Figure 11.3 shows what the ToolBox looks like with the Bean added.

Notice in the figure that the last Bean in the ToolBox is the Image Button Bean, complete with the 16-by-16 icon you specified in the Bean information class. Go ahead and add an Image Button Bean to the BeanBox by clicking on it in the ToolBox and then clicking the main container window. Figure 11.4 shows the newly added Image Button Bean. Now that the Bean has been added to the container window, you can really start seeing the power of JavaBeans. Check out Figure 11.5, which shows the PropertySheet window for the Image Button Bean.

The PropertySheet window shows all the properties for the Bean, including the inherited foreground color, background color, font, and name properties, along with your own sticky, label, image name, and auto size properties. All of these properties

FIGURE 11.3

The BeanBox ToolBox window with the Image Button Bean added

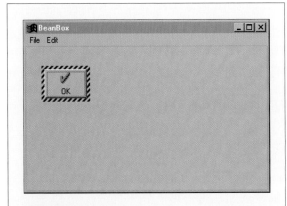

FIGURE 11.4

The BeanBox main container window with an Image Button Bean added are fully editable using the PropertySheet window. Before you start editing any properties, however, go ahead and add another Image Button Bean to the main container window below the first Bean. Then use the PropertySheet window to change the label for the first Bean to "Start" and the label for the second Bean to "Stop". When you've done that, change the image name for the second Bean to "Cancel.gif". Figure 11.6 shows what the PropertySheet window looks like after you've edited the second Image Button Bean. Figure 11.7 shows what the main container window looks like with these two modified Image Button Beans.

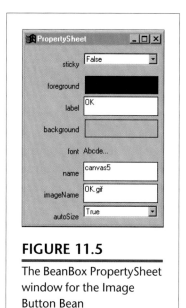

FIGURE 11.5

The BeanBox PropertySheet window for the Image Button Bean

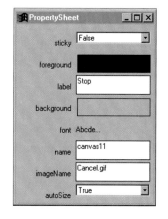

FIGURE 11.6

The BeanBox PropertySheet window for the second modified Image Button Bean

Now add a Juggler Bean to the main container window by selecting the Juggler Bean from the ToolBox and then clicking on the main container window. The Juggler Bean is a demo Bean provided with the BDK that is capable of displaying an animation. Figure 11.8 shows what the main container window looks like after you've added the Juggler Bean. The purpose of adding the Juggler Bean in this example is to enable you to control it with the Image Button Beans. This is done by connecting the action events for the buttons to public methods of the

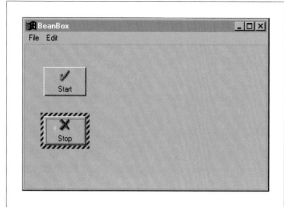

FIGURE 11.7

The BeanBox main container window with two modified Image Button Beans

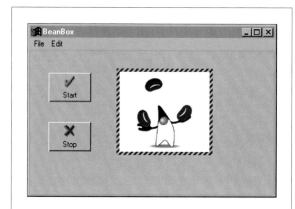

FIGURE 11.8

The BeanBox main container window with Image Button Beans and a Juggler Bean

Juggler Bean. To do this, select the first button and click the Edit menu in the BeanBox. You'll see an "Events" menu item that has a group of event types beneath it. Select the "action" menu item and then the "actionPerformed" command beneath it. Figure 11.9 shows what the BeanBox looks like while you're selecting this command.

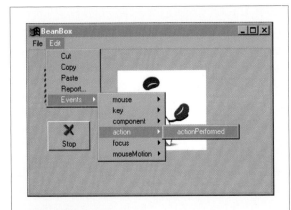

FIGURE 11.9

The actionPerformed command being selected in the BeanBox

After selecting the command, you'll see a line originating from the button that moves as you move the mouse around. Move the mouse over the Juggler Bean and click to connect the Image Button Bean's action event to the Juggler Bean. You'll be presented with a dialog box showing the available target methods defined in the Juggler Bean. Figure 11.10 shows this dialog box. Select the startJuggling() method from the list displayed in the dialog box and click OK. You will then see the dialog box shown in Figure 11.11, which lets you know that the connection between the event and the method is being generated and compiled.

What happened here is that the BeanBox generated code to handle the connection of the button's action event to the startJuggling() method in the Juggler Bean. This code actually comes in the form of a temporary adaptor class, which is compiled on the fly so it can be used to immediately connect the event and method.

Go ahead and connect the other button to the Juggler Bean using the same approach,

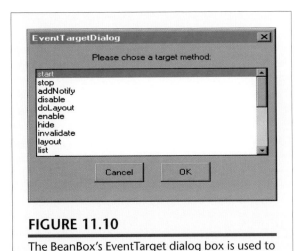

FIGURE 11.10

The BeanBox's EventTarget dialog box is used to connect events with public methods.

FIGURE 11.11

The BeanBox's EventTarget dialog box is also used to convey information about the generation and compilation of an event/method connection.

except this time select the `stopJuggling()` method as the target method. The end result of these connections is that the Juggler Bean's animation can be stopped and started by clicking the two Image Button Beans. Try clicking each button to see how it impacts the Juggler Bean. I think you'll agree that the results are pretty neat!

Summary

This chapter departed from discussion of theory to take a very hands-on approach to JavaBeans. More specifically, you spent the entire chapter developing a complete Bean from scratch. The Bean you developed is an Image Button Bean which exhibits the functionality required of a typical graphical Bean. Aside from exploring the actual code required to bring the Bean to life, you also learned the importance of the brainstorming and design phase of Bean development. It's always advantageous to spend some time on the design end of things before you jump into the details of turning out code.

This chapter hopefully opened your eyes to what it takes to build a real working Bean. If you're like me, you were probably surprised at how similar Bean development is to normal Java development. In reality, few Beans require a significant coding effort to implement Bean-specific functionality. Typically, a Bean information class is about the extent of what you will have to implement in terms of additional Bean overhead. This relative lack of overhead is due to the automatic nature of JavaBeans, which I hope you now have a deeper appreciation for.

Chapter 12

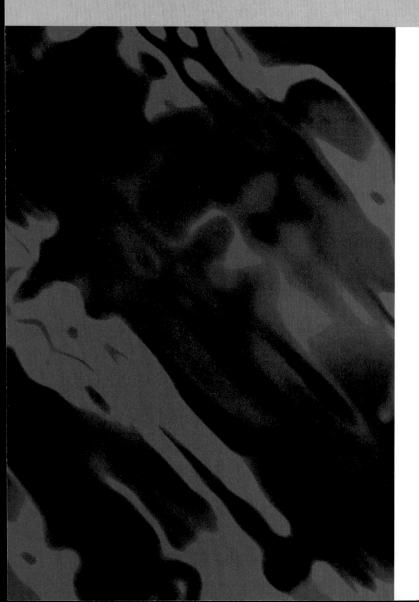

A Needle Gauge Bean

- ▶ Designing the Needle Gauge Bean
- ▶ Constructing the Needle Gauge Bean
- ▶ Using the Needle Gauge Bean

In this chapter, you'll learn how to design and build a Bean that provides graphical output that resembles a speedometer in a car or the VU meter found in many old stereos. You'll begin the chapter by designing the Bean at a purely conceptual level, and then move on to implementing the code required to support the functionality in the Bean. You'll finish up by testing out the Bean in the BeanBox test container that comes with the Beans Development Kit.

Although Beans will ultimately find usage in many different scenarios, graphical output Beans are one of the most immediately appealing types of Bean for developers. This is primarily due to the fact that graphical output Beans make it easy to present information to users with a lot of flair and relatively little work. With a powerful set of graphical output Beans, it is rarely necessary to code your own `paint()` method in an application; you just choose a Bean that provides the type of output you need and plug it in. This saves you from having to write application code to draw a graph or display an image, for example; you let Beans do all the work.

NOTE: *The notion of "plugging in" a piece of software is sometimes a source of confusion. Plugging in a piece of software refers to the inclusion of a software component in an application as a discrete, pre-built unit. This can be accomplished either through visual tools or by inserting a minimal amount of code by hand.*

The Needle Gauge Bean you'll design and develop in this chapter is a very good example of a graphical output Bean, in that it presents a bounded numeric value in a graphical form that is familiar to most users. If you've ever owned a stereo more than ten years old you no doubt remember the VU meters that were used to display audio signal levels. Even more familiar are automobile speedometers, which were all needle gauges until fairly recently. The immediate intuitiveness provided by needle gauges makes them very nice output displays.

In this chapter, you'll learn:

▶ How to design a Needle Gauge Bean

▶ How to construct a Needle Gauge Bean

▶ How to use a Needle Gauge Bean

Designing the Needle Gauge Bean

As you learned in the previous chapter, the design process is a critical part of creating Beans. Without a sound design, a great deal of your coding efforts would ultimately

12

go to waste. A good preliminary design helps you gain a better perspective on the big picture of your Bean. In other words, taking the time to design a Bean well at a concept level helps prevent major rewrites during the coding of the Bean.

The Bean you develop in this chapter is a Needle Gauge Bean, which functions similarly to the speedometer on most automobiles. Like many graphical Beans, the Needle Gauge Bean will inherit from the standard AWT `Canvas` class, which provides much of the core functionality for graphical output. If you recall from the previous chapter, the `Canvas` class derives from `Component`, which provides a variety of properties such as background color, foreground color, name, and font. The Needle Gauge Bean needs all of these properties as well as a few of its own. To understand how these properties are used, however, you need to fully understand how the Bean itself works.

Like a speedometer in an automobile, the Needle Gauge Bean consists of an arc with a needle that can turn on a central axis along the arc. The arc is marked with divisions that display numeric values. For example, if you wanted to mimic an automobile speedometer with the Needle Gauge Bean, the gauge would be labeled with numbers corresponding to the range of speeds possible. So, for my Honda Civic, the gauge would start with 0 miles per hour and have numbered divisions all the way up to 120 miles per hour. Feel free to adjust this number upward if you drive a sports car! The divisions on the gauge would occur on 20 mile per hour intervals, which is enough to indicate the current speed. As the speed changes, the needle swings back and forth to reflect it in the gauge. That sums up the basic functionality of the Needle Gauge Bean.

The Needle Gauge Bean supports the display of text as a label to signify what it represents, and also allows you to set the font for the label, which can be one of a variety of different typefaces in virtually any size. This font is also used when drawing the numeric values associated with each division on the gauge. The Bean also supports changing the background and foreground colors. The background color corresponds to the area surrounding the gauge, while the foreground color determines the color of the label text and division numbers. The background color of the gauge itself is always white, and the needle is always red.

Since the Needle Gauge Bean potentially could be updated very rapidly, it is important that its display be very smooth when updating. For instance, imagine if the gauge were updated numerous times a second in response to a live data feed. In this case, the Bean would be redrawing itself constantly, which could easily result in flicker. It's important that the Bean not flicker, so it must use an offscreen buffer when drawing itself. If you aren't familiar with offscreen buffers, don't panic; you'll learn about them a little later in the chapter when you dig into the code for the Bean. For now, just understand that an offscreen buffer allows you to update a Bean rapidly with no resulting flicker.

Now that you have an idea of how the Needle Gauge Bean works, let's move on to designing its specifics. As you learned in the previous chapter, the design of a Bean can be broken down into three major parts: properties, methods, and events. The rest of this section is devoted to the Needle Gauge Bean and the design of its major functional parts.

Properties

The properties for the Needle Gauge Bean are perhaps the most important part of the Bean, since they largely determine how it is interacted with externally. Since the Bean inherits a few properties from its parent class, you don't have to specifically provide all the properties yourself. The Bean is derived from an existing AWT class, Canvas, which indirectly provides a great deal of overhead, including some very useful properties. The Canvas class represents a rectangular area onto which you can draw or trap input events from the user. The Canvas class is derived from Component, which provides the base functionality typically required of graphical Beans, including background color, foreground color, name, and font properties.

Even though the Canvas and Component parent classes do their share in providing basic properties like the background and foreground colors, you still have to provide some properties of your own. Since you know the Needle Gauge Bean needs a label, you can start off the properties with a string label property. You also know that the value of the gauge always falls within a given range of numbers. This results in two more properties: low and high values for the gauge's range. Associated with the range are divisions, which determine the resolution of the gauge. Using the earlier speedometer example, the low value is 0, the high value is 120, and the number of divisions is 6 (20 miles per hour between divisions). Although these properties are required of the Bean, they wouldn't be very meaningful without a property representing the value of the gauge.

The last property required of the Bean is more of a frill: the raised property. The raised property is a Boolean property that determines the look of the 3D effect used for the border of the Bean. This property allows you to tweak the appearance of the Bean a little, which is unrelated to the Bean's core functionality but nevertheless provides an additional feature without much work. If the raised property is set to true, the 3D border makes the Bean appear to be raised from the screen, while a value of false makes the Bean appear to be inset. This property, combined with the other properties you just learned about and the inherited properties provided by the parent Canvas and Component classes, is sufficient for modeling the functionality required of the Bean.

The following are the properties required of the Needle Gauge Bean:

▶ Label

▶ Low value in range

▶ High value in range

▶ Number of divisions

▶ Value

▶ Raised (true/false)

Methods

Now that you have an idea of the properties required of the Bean, you're ready to move on to determining the public methods for the Bean. The public methods for a Bean together comprise the interface used to access the Bean externally, so it's important to give them careful consideration. The most logical place to begin assessing these methods is with the accessor methods for the Bean. Since you already know the properties for the Bean, it's pretty easy to determine the accessor methods you need. All of the properties are readable and writeable, so you will need a pair of accessor methods for each of them.

> **NOTE:** *Accessor methods are important because they provide the only direct means of getting and setting Bean properties. Accessor methods are always public methods, but they play such a unique role in JavaBeans that it is worth acknowledging them separately from the other public methods in a Bean.*

Although accessor methods play an important role in any Bean, they usually aren't the only public methods required of the Bean. Providing an interface to a Bean's properties isn't quite enough to meet the requirements of most Beans. In other words, most Beans provide additional public methods beyond their accessor methods. The Needle Gauge Bean is a good example of this because it needs six public methods in addition to its accessor methods. The first two of these, `update()` and `paint()`, are overridden from the parent `Canvas` class to allow the Bean to paint itself. The `paint()` method is required of all graphical Beans since it is responsible for drawing the graphical representation of a Bean. The `update()` method is required to streamline the painting process and help eliminate flicker.

The other public methods required of the Needle Gauge Bean aren't inherited like `update()` and `paint()`. I'm referring to the `incValue()` and `decValue()` methods, which provide a means of incrementing and decrementing the value represented by the gauge. Of course, you can always set the value property directly, but these methods provide an alternate means of changing the value. There are actually two sets of these methods: One set takes an argument of type double representing the amount by which to increment or decrement the value, while the other set takes no argument and increments or decrements the value by a default amount determined by the range and number of divisions for the gauge.

TIP: *Providing two sets of methods for altering the value of the Needle Gauge Bean gives users more flexibility in working with the Bean.*

These are the public methods required of the Needle Gauge Bean:

▶ Label property getter/setter methods

▶ Low value property getter/setter methods

▶ High value property getter/setter methods

▶ Number of divisions property getter/setter methods

▶ Value property getter/setter methods

▶ Raised property getter/setter methods

▶ Overridden `update()` method

▶ Overridden `paint()` method

▶ Increment value method (by a specified amount)

▶ Decrement value method (by a specified amount)

▶ Increment value method (by a default amount)

▶ Decrement value method (by a default amount)

Events

The Needle Gauge Bean is purely a graphical output Bean, meaning that it responds to no input events from the user and fires no events of its own. For this reason, the Bean requires no event-related methods. Don't be too let down, because there's still plenty of work to be done even without the task of processing and managing events.

NOTE: *Just in case you're a little confused about how the Bean can function without using events, understand that the Bean is manipulated by a user directly changing the value property, which in turn causes the needle to change position.*

Constructing the Needle Gauge Bean

With the basic design finished, you're now ready to dive into the code for the Needle Gauge Bean. Throughout this section you'll learn about different parts of the code for the Bean. To help make the code more digestible, most of it is presented in the form of individual member declarations or method listings. As you read through the section, please feel free to check out the complete source code for the Bean, which is included on the CD-ROM that came with this book. The main code for the Needle Gauge Bean is in the `NeedleGauge` class, which appears on the CD-ROM in the file NeedleGauge.java.

ON THE CD: *The source code for the Needle Gauge Bean is on the CD-ROM included with this book.*

Properties and Member Variables

The first area to attack when developing the Needle Gauge Bean is the properties. Listing 12.1 shows the member variable properties for the Bean.

As you can see, these member variables directly relate to the properties mentioned earlier in the initial Bean design. It is important to note that they are all built-in Java types, which means that property editors are already provided for them by JavaBeans. Along with these properties, the Bean also requires a few other member variables for internal use:

LISTING 12.1 The Member Variable Properties for the Needle Gauge Bean

```
private boolean      raised;
private String       label;
private double       loVal;
private double       hiVal;
private int          divisions;
private double       value;      ■
```

```
private transient Dimension offSize;
private transient Image     offImage;
private transient Graphics  offGrfx;
```

These members are all used in providing the offscreen buffer functionality necessary to keep the Bean from flickering during rapid updates. The `offSize` member is the size of the offscreen buffer used to draw the Bean, the `offImage` member is the image for the buffer, and the `offGrfx` member is the graphics context for the buffer. We'll see how these members are used in implementing the offscreen buffer a little later in the chapter.

Constructors

The Needle Gauge Bean provides two constructors: a default constructor and a detailed constructor that takes all six properties as arguments. The code for both of these constructors appears in Listing 12.2.

The first constructor simply calls the second constructor with default property values. The second constructor actually does the work of initializing the Bean and getting all the properties set correctly. Notice that the inherited background color property is set by calling its setter method instead of directly setting the member variable. You are required to use a setter method to access inherited properties, since they are declared as private in the parent class. Once the properties are set, the constructor sets the Bean to a default size, which is admittedly somewhat arbitrary.

Accessor Methods

The Needle Gauge Bean's accessor methods provide a means of accessing and modifying the Bean's properties. Listing 12.3 shows you how to get and set the Bean's raised property.

LISTING 12.2 The Constructors for the Needle Gauge Bean

```java
public NeedleGauge() {
  this(false, "Needle Gauge", 0.0, 10.0, 5, 0.0);
}

public NeedleGauge(boolean r, String l, double lv, double hv, int d,
  double v) {
  // Allow the superclass constructor to do its thing
  super();

  // Set properties
  raised = r;
  label = l;
  loVal = lv;
  hiVal = hv;
  divisions = d;
  value = v;
  setBackground(Color.lightGray);

  // Set a default size
  setSize(120, 80);
}
```

As you can see, there is nothing magical about these methods; they simply get and set the value of the raised property. It is important to notice that the `setRaised()` method calls `repaint()` after setting the property. This is done to force the Bean to repaint itself whenever the property changes. Otherwise, the Bean wouldn't immediately reflect the changing property value in its appearance.

The label property's accessor methods are similar to those for the raised property in that they are very minimal. Listing 12.4 shows the code for these methods. These methods are practically identical to the accessor methods for the raised property, except that they operate on the label property. There isn't much more that can be said about these methods, so let's move on to the accessor methods for the low and high value properties.

These methods (Listing 12.5) are responsible for getting and setting the low and high value properties for the gauge's numeric range. Both of the getter methods are very simple: They just return the value of the member variable associated with each property. The setter methods are slightly more involved because they have

LISTING 12.3 The Accessor Methods for the Raised Property

```
public boolean isRaised() {
  return raised;
}

public void setRaised(boolean r) {
  raised = r;
  repaint();
}                                    ■
```

LISTING 12.4 The Label Property's Accessor Methods

```
public String getLabel() {
  return label;
}

public void setLabel(String l) {
  label = l;
  repaint();
}                                    ■
```

to ensure that the low value is always less than the high value. They also force a repaint so that the Bean's appearance reflects the new range.

The accessor methods for the divisions property are very straightforward, as Listing 12.6 shows. These methods are pretty self-explanatory at this point, so let's move on to the last property in the Needle Gauge Bean. This is the value property, which represents the value the gauge is set to. The code for the accessor methods for this property appears in Listing 12.7.

The getter method for the value property is extremely simple, as you've probably come to expect. The setter method is more interesting because it must set the property while constraining it within the acceptable range of values for the gauge. This is handled with the `min()` and `max()` methods provided by the `Math` class. After setting the property, the setter method forces a repaint so the Bean's appearance is

LISTING 12.5 The Accessor Methods for the Low and High Value Properties

```
public double getLoVal() {
  return loVal;
}

public void setLoVal(double lv) {
  loVal = lv;
  if (value < loVal)
    value = loVal;
  repaint();
}

public double getHiVal() {
  return hiVal;
}

public void setHiVal(double hv) {
  hiVal = hv;
  if (value > hiVal)
    value = hiVal;
  repaint();
}
```

LISTING 12.6 The Accessor Methods for the Divisions Property

```
public int getDivisions() {
  return divisions;
}

public void setDivisions(int d) {
  divisions = d;
  repaint();
}
```

LISTING 12.7 The Accessor Methods for the Value Property

```
public double getValue() {
  return value;
}

public void setValue(double v) {
  value = Math.max(loVal, Math.min(hiVal, v));
  repaint();
}
```

---

updated. That wraps up the accessor methods for the Bean; let's move on to the other public methods!

Public Methods

As you learned earlier in the chapter while designing the Needle Gauge Bean, there are six public methods in the Bean beyond the accessor methods. The first one is the update() method, which is called whenever the Bean needs to be repainted, such as when the repaint() method is called. The default update method in the Component class erases the background and then calls the paint() method. Since you are going to be using an offscreen buffer to eliminate flicker, you don't want the background erased. Therefore, the update() method is overridden solely to avoid erasing the background. This is the code for the update() method:

```
public void update(Graphics g) {
  paint(g);
}
```

The update() method consists of a single call to the paint() method. By only calling the paint() method and not erasing the background, update() eliminates the flicker typically associated with the erase/repaint approach. Of course, this change pushes the responsibility of erasing and repainting the Bean on to the paint() method.

The paint() method completely takes care of drawing the Bean's appearance, which includes managing an offscreen buffer. Before getting into the code for the paint() method, let's consider what an offscreen buffer is and how it works in terms of the Needle Gauge Bean. An offscreen buffer is essentially a drawing surface, or image, in memory. You can graphically manipulate an offscreen buffer just as you would the graphics context for a Bean, but it impacts the buffer in memory rather than the Bean's appearance on the screen. By performing all of a Bean's graphical operations on an offscreen buffer, you can reduce the drawing of the

Bean on the screen to one draw. In other words, the only time you draw to the screen is when you draw the completed offscreen buffer. The point of using this approach is to avoid the flicker problem that arises when you perform lots of drawing operations to the screen rapidly. The offscreen buffer approach requires just as many drawing operations, but most of them occur purely in memory. Now that you understand a little better how this process works, here's a list of the steps in using an offscreen buffer to draw a Bean:

1   Create/erase the offscreen buffer

2   Draw at will to the offscreen buffer

3   Draw the offscreen buffer to the screen

The `paint()` method in the Needle Gauge Bean uses this offscreen buffer approach to eliminate flicker. Listing 12.8 shows the source code for the `paint()` method.

LISTING 12.8 The paint() Method

```
public synchronized void paint(Graphics g) {
  Dimension d = getSize();

  // Create the offscreen graphics context
  if (offGrfx == null || (offSize.width != d.width) ||
    (offSize.height != d.height)) {
    offSize = d;
    offImage = createImage(d.width, d.height);
    offGrfx = offImage.getGraphics();
  }

  // Paint the background with 3D effects
  offGrfx.setColor(getBackground());
  offGrfx.fillRect(1, 1, d.width - 2, d.height - 2);
  offGrfx.draw3DRect(0, 0, d.width - 1, d.height - 1, raised);
  offGrfx.setColor(getForeground());

  // Paint the clock
  drawNeedleGauge(offGrfx);

  // Paint the image onto the screen
  g.drawImage(offImage, 0, 0, null);
}
```

12

The `paint()` method starts off by getting the size of the Bean, which is used throughout the method for drawing the needle gauge. The `paint()` method then checks to see if the offscreen buffer needs to be created, and creates it if necessary. In addition to creating the buffer image itself, the `paint()` method also sets the size of the buffer and creates the graphics context for the buffer. These are both necessary for the proper functioning of the offscreen buffer.

With the offscreen buffer in place, the background and 3D effects are drawn. Notice that the 3D effect is painted differently based on the value of the `raised` member variable. Even more important to note is the fact that all of this drawing takes place on the `offGrfx` graphics context, which belongs to the offscreen buffer. This means that all of the drawing is taking place on the offscreen buffer in memory rather than the screen.

After the background and 3D effects have been drawn, the needle gauge itself is drawn with a call to the `drawNeedleGauge()` method. Again, notice that the `offGrfx` graphics context is passed to the `drawNeedleGauge()` method, which results in the drawing taking place on the offscreen buffer. You'll learn about the `drawNeedleGauge()` method in just a moment. At this point, the offscreen buffer is finished and ready to be drawn to the screen. This is accomplished with a call to the `drawImage()` method.

The `update()` and `paint()` methods are the only overridden public methods in the Needle Gauge Bean. The Bean also implements four other public methods that are used to modify the value of the gauge. These methods are `incValue()` and `decValue()`, each of which comes in two varieties: One takes an argument of type double as the amount by which to increment or decrement the value, while the other takes no arguments and increments or decrements the value by a default amount determined by the range and number of divisions. The code for these methods appears in Listing 12.9.

The first pair of methods take an argument of type double that is used to increment or decrement the value of the gauge. These methods are careful to constrain the new value within the acceptable range before setting it. Once the newly incremented/decremented value has been set, a repaint is forced on the Bean so that it reflects the new value.

The second pair of methods take no arguments and use a default amount to increment or decrement the value of the gauge. This default amount is calculated based on the range and number of divisions for the Bean, and is actually passed to one of the other increment/decrement methods to change the value. This is convenient because it keeps you from having to rewrite the code that constrains the value within the gauge's range.

Support Methods

You're just about finished with the code for the Needle Gauge Bean itself. There is only one method you haven't covered: the `drawNeedleGauge()` method. This method is solely responsible for drawing the needle gauge on a provided graphics context. Listing 12.10 shows the code for the `drawNeedleGauge()` method.

> **NOTE:** *The* `SPACING` *value used in the* `drawNeedleGauge()` *method is an integer constant defined in the* `NeedleGauge` *class that determines the spacing between different parts of the gauge.*

Wow, what a method! Before you get scared and close the book, let me calm your fears a little by saying that this code is not as complex as it first looks. The method begins by getting the size of the Bean and calculating the radius for the gauge based on this size. The radius of the gauge is ultimately responsible for the size of the gauge. The calculation of the radius is important because the method tries to fit the gauge into the Bean's rectangular area in the best way possible while keeping the perspective of the gauge intact. Once the radius is determined, the center point of the gauge is calculated. This is the point where the needle itself originates, as you will soon see.

With these preliminary calculations out of the way, the `drawNeedleGauge()` method moves on to drawing the basic gauge. The gauge at this point consists of a white-filled semicircle (arc) with black borders and a small black semicircle near its

LISTING 12.9 The incValue() and decValue() Methods

```
public void incValue(double i) {
  value = Math.max(loVal, Math.min(hiVal, value + i));
  repaint();
}

public void decValue(double d) {
  value = Math.max(loVal, Math.min(hiVal, value - d));
  repaint();
}

public void incValue() {
  incValue((hiVal - loVal) / divisions);
}

public void decValue() {
  decValue((hiVal - loVal) / divisions);
}
```

LISTING 12.10   The drawNeedleGauge() Method in the NeedleGauge Class

```java
private void drawNeedleGauge(Graphics g) {
  Dimension d = getSize();
  g.setFont(getFont());
  FontMetrics fm = g.getFontMetrics();
  int   radius = Math.min(d.height - (SPACING * 3) -
    (fm.getMaxAscent() + fm.getMaxDescent()), (d.width / 2) -
    (SPACING * 2));
  Point center = new Point(d.width / 2, d.height - (SPACING * 2) -
    (fm.getMaxAscent() + fm.getMaxDescent()));

  // Draw the gauge
  g.setColor(Color.white);
  g.fillArc(center.x - radius + 1, center.y - radius + 1,
    (radius * 2) - 2, (radius * 2) - 2, 0, 180);
  g.setColor(Color.black);
  g.drawArc(center.x - radius, center.y - radius, radius * 2,
    radius * 2, 0, 180);
  g.drawArc(center.x - (radius / 8), center.y - (radius / 8),
    radius / 4, radius / 4, 0, 180);
  g.drawLine(center.x - radius, center.y, center.x + radius,
center.y);

  // Draw the divisions
  for (int i = 0; i <= divisions; i++) {
    // Draw a mark
    double markAngle = ((double)i / divisions * 0.9 * Math.PI) -
      (0.9 * Math.PI / 2);
    g.setColor(Color.black);
    g.drawLine(center.x + (int)(Math.round(0.95 * radius *
      Math.sin(markAngle))), center.y - (int)(Math.round(0.95 *
      radius * Math.cos(markAngle))), center.x +
      (int)(Math.round(radius * Math.sin(markAngle))), center.y -
      (int)(Math.round(radius * Math.cos(markAngle))));

    // Draw a number, as long as it will fit
    if (fm.getAscent() - fm.getDescent() < (radius / divisions)) {
      String markText = String.valueOf(loVal + (((double)i /
```

CONTINUES

**LISTING 12.10 The drawNeedleGauge() Method in the NeedleGauge Class
(Continued)**

```
                divisions) * (hiVal - loVal)));
        int decPos = markText.indexOf(   , 1);
        String trimmedText = markText.substring(0, decPos) +    +
                markText.substring(decPos + 1, decPos + 2);
            g.setColor(getForeground());
            g.drawString(trimmedText, center.x + (int)(Math.round(0.7 *
                radius * Math.sin(markAngle))) - (fm.stringWidth(trimmedText)
    /
                2), center.y - (int)(Math.round(0.7 * radius *
                Math.cos(markAngle))) + ((fm.getAscent() - fm.getDescent()) /
                2));
            }
        }


        // Draw the needle and center
        double angle = (((value - loVal) / (hiVal - loVal)) * 0.9 *
            Math.PI) - (0.9 * Math.PI / 2);
        g.setColor(Color.red);
        g.drawLine(center.x, center.y, center.x + (int)(Math.round(0.65 *
            radius * Math.sin(angle))), center.y - (int)(Math.round(0.65 *
            radius * Math.cos(angle))));
        g.setColor(Color.darkGray);
        g.fillOval(center.x - 2, center.y - 2, 4, 4);


        // Draw the label text
        g.setColor(getForeground());
        g.drawString(label, (d.width - fm.stringWidth(label)) / 2,
            d.height - SPACING - fm.getMaxDescent());
    }
```

---

center. The semicircles and borders are drawn using the drawArc() method, which is made available by the Graphics class. The drawArc() method provides an easy way to draw semicircles.

With the basic gauge drawn, the drawNeedleGauge() method then draws the divisions on the gauge. This is perhaps the messiest code in the method, simply because it relies heavily on trigonometric functions to figure out where to draw

12

the division marks and numbers. One of the more interesting aspects of this code is that it only draws the division numbers if they will fit. The division numbers are drawn in the Bean's font, which means they could feasibly be set too large to be displayed on the gauge. The code that draws the division numbers attempts to determine if they will fit before drawing any of them.

Once the division marks and numbers are drawn, the `drawNeedleGauge()` method draws the needle and center of the gauge. This is accomplished by calculating the angle of the needle based on the value of the gauge, and then drawing a red line at this angle and a gray circle at the center of the gauge. The last chore of the `drawNeedleGauge()` method is to draw the label text below the gauge in the Bean's font. This is accomplished with a call to the `drawString()` method.

Additional Overhead

You've now developed all the source code for the Needle Gauge Bean. Although the `NeedleGauge` class is all that is required to have a fully functioning Bean, there is one other class you need to make the Bean complete: `NeedleGaugeBeanInfo`. This class is a Bean information class used to provide explicit information about the graphical icons for the Needle Gauge Bean. The complete source code for the `NeedleGaugeBeanInfo` class appears in Listing 12.11.

The only method defined in the `NeedleGaugeBeanInfo` class is `getIcon()`, which is usually called by application builder tools to retrieve an iconic representation of the Bean. Notice that two icons are actually provided by the Bean information class based on different resolutions. The first icon is 16-by-16 pixels in size, while the second is 32-by-32 pixels. The BeanBox utility that comes with the BDK specifically uses the 16-by-16 size icons, but other application builder tools are free to use either (or both) of them. Both of the Bean icons are provided as GIF 89A images, which is standard for Java. Figure 12.1 shows what the icons for the Needle Gauge Bean look like.

There is one additional thing the Needle Gauge Bean needs before it can be used in an application builder tool: a manifest file. As you may recall from the previous chapter, a manifest file is required in the JAR file that the Bean is placed in for distribution. The code for the Needle Gauge Bean's manifest file, NeedleGauge.mf, is as follows:

```
Manifest-Version: 1.0

Name: HTPJB/Chap12/NeedleGauge/NeedleGauge.class
Java-Bean: True
```

The manifest file for the Needle Gauge Bean is very simple: You just provide the name of the Bean class and specify that it is in fact a Bean. This is the only additional overhead you have to place in the JAR file in order for application builder

LISTING 12.11   The Complete Source Code for the NeedleGaugeBeanInfo Class

```
// NeedleGaugeBeanInfo Class
// NeedleGaugeBeanInfo.java

package HTPJB.Chap12.NeedleGauge;

// Imports
import java.beans.*;

public class NeedleGaugeBeanInfo extends SimpleBeanInfo {
  // Get the appropriate icon
  public java.awt.Image getIcon(int iconKind) {
    if (iconKind == BeanInfo.ICON_COLOR_16x16) {
      java.awt.Image img = loadImage("NeedleGaugeIcon16.gif");
      return img;
    }
    if (iconKind == BeanInfo.ICON_COLOR_32x32) {
      java.awt.Image img = loadImage("NeedleGaugeIcon32.gif");
      return img;
    }
    return null;
  }
}
```

tools to be able to extract information about the Bean. For information on how to build a JAR file for the Bean, refer to Chapter 4, "Packaging Beans with JAR Files." Keep in mind that the complete source code and related resources for the Needle Gauge Bean, including a JAR file for the Bean, are located on the CD-ROM included with this book.

FIGURE 12.1

The Bean information icons for the Needle Gauge Bean

Using the Needle Gauge Bean

After all that hard work you just did developing the Needle Gauge Bean, you're no doubt ready to see it in action. As in the previous chapter, you're going to try out the Bean in the BeanBox test container that ships with the BDK. The first step in using a Bean in a visual environment such as the BeanBox is to add the Bean to the environment. You add the

12

Needle Gauge Bean to the BeanBox by copying the JAR file for the Bean to the *jars* directory beneath your BDK installation. The BeanBox looks in this directory for new Beans to add to its ToolBox. When executed, the BeanBox automatically checks the *jars* directory to see if any new Beans need to be added.

Once you've copied the JAR file for the Needle Gauge Bean to the *jars* directory, try running the BeanBox by executing the `run.bat` batch file provided with the BeanBox. The BeanBox should appear at this point with your Needle Gauge Bean added to the ToolBox. Figure 12.2 shows what the ToolBox looks like with the Bean added.

Notice in the figure that the last Bean in the ToolBox is the Needle Gauge Bean, which is represented by the 16-by-16 icon you specified in the Bean information class. You should also see the Image Button Bean you added in the previous chapter. Try adding a Needle Gauge Bean to the BeanBox by clicking on it in the ToolBox and then clicking on the main container window. Figure 12.3 shows main container window with the newly added Needle Gauge Bean.

FIGURE 12.2

The BeanBox ToolBox window with the Needle Gauge Bean added

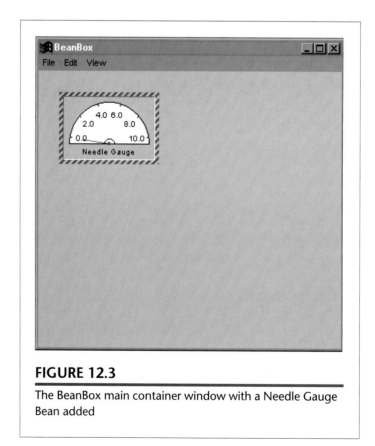

FIGURE 12.3

The BeanBox main container window with a Needle Gauge Bean added

With the Bean added to the container window, you can take a look at the properties for it. Check out Figure 12.4, which shows the PropertySheet window for the Needle Gauge Bean.

The PropertySheet window shows all the properties for the Bean, including the inherited foreground color, background color, font, and name properties along with your own raised, label, high value, low value, divisions, and value properties. All of these properties can be edited using the PropertySheet window. Go ahead and try editing the Bean by changing the foreground color to blue, the label text to "Richter Scale", the divisions to 10, and the font to 24-point Times Roman. You also need to make the Bean larger for the label and division numbers to fit with the larger font. Figure 12.5 shows what the PropertySheet window looks like after you've edited the Needle Gauge Bean. Figure 12.6 shows what the main container window looks like with the modified Needle Gauge Bean.

Now add two Image Button Beans to the main container window just below the needle gauge by selecting them from the ToolBox and then clicking on the

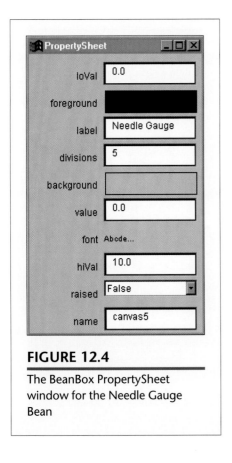

FIGURE 12.4

The BeanBox PropertySheet window for the Needle Gauge Bean

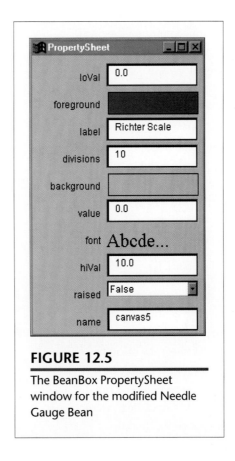

FIGURE 12.5

The BeanBox PropertySheet window for the modified Needle Gauge Bean

main container window. Modify one of them so that its label property is set to "Bigger" and its image property is set to "Plus.gif." Then modify the other Image Button Bean so that its label is set to "Smaller" and its image property is set to "Minus.gif." Figure 12.7 shows what the main container window looks like after you've added the two Image Button Beans.

The purpose of adding the Image Button Beans is to allow you to control the Needle Gauge Bean with them. This is done by connecting the action events for the buttons to public methods of the Needle Gauge Bean. To do this, select the first button and click the Edit menu in the BeanBox. You'll see an Events menu item that has a group of event types beneath it. Select the Action event menu item and then the actionPerformed command beneath it. You'll see a line originating from the button that moves as you move the mouse around. Move the mouse over the Needle Gauge Bean and click to connect the Image Button Bean's action event to the Needle Gauge Bean. You'll be presented with a dialog box showing the available target methods defined in the Needle Gauge Bean. Figure 12.8 shows this dialog box.

Figure 12.8 shows the incValue() method highlighted; select this method and click OK. This wires the first button to the incValue() method of the Needle Gauge Bean. Now repeat this process for the other button, but connect it to the decValue() method of the Needle Gauge Bean. Now try clicking each button and watching how it impacts the needle gauge. Pay close attention to the fact that there is no flicker no matter how fast you click. The flicker issue would be even more important if the Needle Gauge Bean were being controlled by an application that updated it rapidly, which it likely will be in many cases.

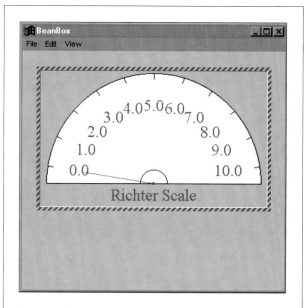

FIGURE 12.6

The BeanBox main container window with the modified Needle Gauge Bean

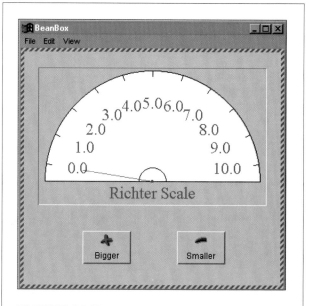

FIGURE 12.7

The BeanBox main container window with the Needle Gauge Bean and two Image Button Beans

Summary

This chapter took you through the development of a Bean that acts as a graphical needle gauge. This is a very practical output Bean that could be used in a variety of different applications. For example, the Needle Gauge Bean could be used to represent available system resources such as memory and hard disk space.

You spent the first part of the chapter working out the design of the Bean in conceptual terms. You then jumped into the actual code required to make the Bean a reality. After developing the code for the Bean, you got a chance to put it through its paces in the BeanBox. You even learned how to integrate the Needle Gauge Bean with the Image Button Bean you developed in the previous chapter.

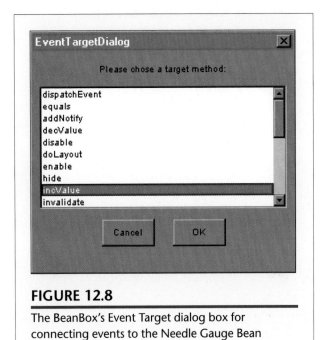

FIGURE 12.8

The BeanBox's Event Target dialog box for connecting events to the Needle Gauge Bean

12

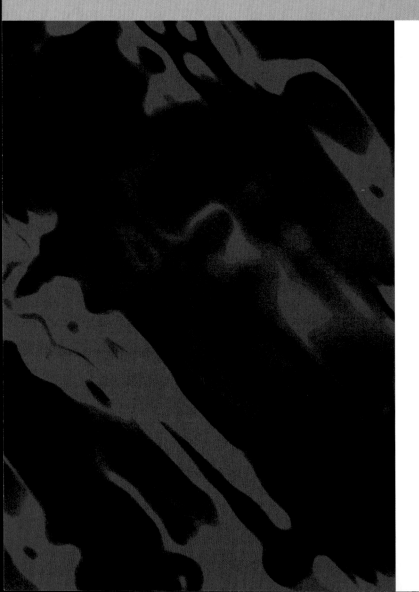

Chapter *13*

A Clock Bean

- ▶ Designing the Clock Bean

- ▶ Constructing the Clock Bean

- ▶ Using the Clock Bean

In this chapter, you'll learn how to design and build a Bean that acts as a graphical clock. You'll start by working through a preliminary design of the Bean. You'll then move on to developing the actual code for the Bean, which directly supports the functionality covered in the Bean's design. You'll wrap up by testing the Bean in the BeanBox test container that comes with the BDK.

As you learned in the previous chapter, graphical output Beans have a wide range of uses in application development. The Bean you'll develop in this chapter is a graphical output Bean, but not one you would use to output information in a traditional sense. The Bean is a clock that displays the current time in either analog or digital form. Although the information displayed by the clock is determined entirely by the clock and not by information from the user, it still makes for an interesting Bean because it automatically updates itself at regular intervals.

In this chapter, you'll learn:

- ▶ How to design a Clock Bean

- ▶ How to construct a Clock Bean

- ▶ How to use a Clock Bean

Designing the Clock Bean

Let's begin the overall development of the Clock Bean by working on its conceptual design. This is hopefully becoming a familiar process for you since you performed it in the previous two chapters. I also hope you've managed to see the benefits of spending some initial time designing a Bean before jumping into the coding.

The Clock Bean you'll develop in this chapter works very much like clocks you probably have around your house or office. The primary difference is that the Bean clock can display the time in either analog or digital form, which is a pretty neat feature. Like most graphical Beans, the Clock Bean will inherit from the standard AWT `Canvas` class, which derives from `Component`. The clock needs all of the inherited properties provided by `Canvas` as well as a couple of its own. Before getting into the properties, however, let's take a look at how the Bean works.

The Clock Bean needs to function exactly like an analog or digital clock in the real world. Knowing this, it makes sense that the clock should update itself every second. When the clock is in analog mode, the hour, minute, and second hands need to sweep an appropriate amount as seconds tick away. When it's in digital mode, the numbers being displayed must be updated with each passing second. Since Beans are self-contained entities, it's apparent that the clock needs some way of triggering itself to update once every second. This is handled by having the Bean implement the `Runnable` interface, which gives it a `run()` method executing within a thread. It is then possible for the `run()` method to trigger an update every second.

In analog mode, the clock is presented as a circle with hour marks and numbers, much like the needle gauge divisions you saw in the previous chapter. The clock supports a font for displaying the hour numbers, which can be one of a variety of different typefaces and sizes. The background color for the Bean is used in the area surrounding the clock, while the foreground color determines the color of the hour number text. The background color of the clock itself is always white, while the hour and minute arms are black and the second arm is red.

Even though the clock is only updating itself once per second, you want to make sure there is no chance it will produce flicker when repainting itself. Since you learned how to implement an offscreen buffer that fixes this problem in the previous chapter, it only makes sense to add the same support to the Clock Bean. Just in case your short-term memory is a little rusty, an offscreen buffer was used in the Needle Gauge Bean in the previous chapter to eliminate flicker when rapidly updating the Bean.

Now that you understand the basic functionality of the Clock Bean, you're ready to move on to some more specific design issues. As you learned in the previous two chapters, the design of a Bean can be broken down into three major parts: properties, methods, and events. The rest of this section is devoted to the design of the Clock Bean's major functional parts.

Properties

The properties for the Clock Bean are much simpler than the properties for the two other Beans (Image Button and Needle Gauge) you've developed in the book thus far. Since the Clock Bean inherits a most of its properties from the parent `Canvas` class, you need to specifically provide only a couple of properties. If you recall from the previous two chapters, the `Canvas` class is derived from `Component`, which provides background color, foreground color, name, and font properties.

The two additional properties required of the Clock Bean are very straightforward. You've already seen the first one, the raised property, in the Needle Gauge Bean from the previous chapter. If you recall, the raised property was used to control the look of a 3D effect around the Bean's border. The other property required of the Clock Bean is a mode property that keeps track of whether the Bean is in analog or digital mode. Since the mode is always one of two states (analog or digital), it can be stored in a Boolean member variable. You'll get to that a little later in this chapter when you see the code for the Clock Bean.

To summarize, these are the two properties required of the Clock Bean:

▶ Raised (true/false)

▶ Mode (analog/digital)

Methods

With the properties squared away, you're ready to design the public methods for the Bean; the accessor methods are the best place to start because they are directly related to the properties you just defined. Since you just worked through the required properties for the Bean, determining the accessor methods is a very straightforward process. All of the properties for the Clock Bean are readable and writeable, so you will need a pair of accessor methods for each of them. That was pretty easy!

Accessor methods are important because they directly relate to a Bean's properties, but they are rarely sufficient to provide a rich interface for a fully functioning Bean. Because the Clock Bean is a fully functioning Bean, it stands to reason that it needs more than accessor methods to operate. In fact, the Clock Bean needs three public methods in addition to its accessor methods. The first of these, run(), is a method you've no doubt seen before if you have any experience with multithreaded Java programming. The run() method acts as a thread's central path of execution, meaning that it is the ideal place to set up a periodic trigger for clock updates. The other two public methods required of the Bean, update() and paint(), should be familiar to you from developing the Needle Gauge Bean in the previous chapter. The paint() method is responsible for drawing the graphical representation of the Bean, while the update() method is used to help implement an offscreen buffer.

To summarize, the public methods required of the Clock Bean are

- ▶ Raised property getter/setter methods

- ▶ Mode property getter/setter methods

- ▶ Overridden run() method

- ▶ Overridden update() method

- ▶ Overridden paint() method

Events

Event methods are only required if a Bean needs to respond to input events or to fire events of its own. Since the Clock Bean is purely a graphical output Bean (like the Needle Gauge Bean in the previous chapter), the Clock Bean requires no event-related methods.

Constructing the Clock Bean

Now that the basic design is finished, you know what's next! That's right, it's time to roll up your sleeves and get busy coding the Clock Bean. Fortunately, the detailed coding of the Bean flows logically from the design you just performed. The properties and methods you laid out in the Bean's design translate directly to functional pieces of source code, as you will soon see. Also, since the Clock Bean operates without any interaction from the user, it is simpler than the previous Bean examples.

> **NOTE:** *Technically, users can interact with the Clock Bean in a development environment by altering its properties. However, the Clock Bean operates in a runtime setting without any user interaction.*

This section focuses on developing the code for the Clock Bean. To make the code easier to understand and follow, most of it is presented in the form of individual member declarations or method listings. As you read through the section, you may want to check out the complete source code for the Bean, which is included on the CD-ROM accompanying this book. The main code for the Clock Bean is in the Clock class, which appears on the CD-ROM in the file Clock.java.

 ON THE CD: *The complete code for the Clock Bean is included on the CD-ROM.*

Properties and Member Variables

The starting point for Bean coding is defining the properties. This is due to the fact that properties determine the overall functional makeup of a Bean. With the properties defined, much of the rest of a Bean's coding becomes trivial. The member variable properties for the Clock Bean are

```
private boolean raised;
private boolean digital;
```

These two member variables directly correspond to the properties discussed earlier in the design of the Bean. The only thing that's a little tricky here is the digital member variable, which represents the mode of the clock. Why didn't I just call it mode? Well, since we're using a Boolean value to represent the property, its name should clearly reflect what it represents. If the member variable were named mode, true and false values would have no obvious meaning. With the variable named `digital`, it becomes more apparent that a true setting means the clock is in digital mode, while a false setting means it is in analog mode. Pretty simple!

TIP: *You might be wondering why I used a Boolean member variable for the clock's mode to begin with. Since the mode can only be in one of two states (digital or analog), it makes things simpler to use a data type that supports the same number of states.*

Since both of the properties are built-in Java types, their property editors are already provided by JavaBeans, which saves you from having to create your own. In addition to these public properties, the Bean requires a few other private member variables for internal use:

```
private transient Dimension offSize;
private transient Image     offImage;
private transient Graphics  offGrfx;
private transient Thread    clockThread;
```

The first three members should look somewhat familiar, since they are all used in providing the offscreen buffer functionality for the Bean, which you learned about in the previous chapter while developing the Needle Gauge Bean. To recap, the `offSize` member is the size of the offscreen buffer used to draw the Bean, `offImage` is the image for the buffer, and `offGrfx` is the graphics context for the buffer. The last member, `clockThread`, is the thread used to control the updating of the clock. The `clockThread` member is very critical to the functioning of the clock because it provides the mechanism by which the clock can be automatically updated each second. Notice that all of these member variables are defined as being transient, meaning that they aren't to be stored away as part of the Clock Bean's internal state. This is logical, since all of them are re-created and initialized based on the specific instance of the Bean when it is created.

Constructors

The Clock Bean provides two constructors: a default constructor and a detailed constructor that takes both properties as arguments. Listing 13.1 shows the code for both of these constructors.

The first constructor takes no arguments and simply calls the second constructor with default property values. The second constructor does the work of initializing the Bean and getting all the properties set correctly, including creating and starting the update thread. The `Thread` object is created using the `new` operator, and then the `start()` method is called on it to get the ball rolling. The `start()`

LISTING 13.1 The Constructors for the Clock Bean

```
public Clock() {
  this(false, false);
}

public Clock(boolean r, boolean d) {
  // Allow the superclass constructor to do its thing
  super();

  // Set properties
  raised = r;
  digital = d;
  setBackground(Color.lightGray);

  // Set a default size
  setSize(100, 100);

  // Create the clock thread
  clockThread = new Thread(this, "Clock");
  clockThread.start();
}
```

method starts the thread and directly results in the execution of the overridden
run() method defined in the Bean. You'll learn about the run() method and how
it controls the clock's display in a moment.

Accessor Methods

Accessor methods form the next piece of the Clock Bean development puzzle. The
first property defined in the Bean is the raised property; the code for its accessor
methods appears in Listing 13.2. The mode property's accessor methods (Listing
13.3) are also very minimal.

NOTE: *Incidentally, there is no special reason why the Bean properties and
their associated accessor methods appear in the order they do here. I discuss
properties and accessor methods in the order that they occurred to me while designing and developing the Bean.*

LISTING 13.2 The Accessor Methods for the Raised Property

```
public boolean isRaised() {
  return raised;
}

public void setRaised(boolean r) {
  raised = r;
  repaint();
}
```

NOTE: *This code is exactly the same as the accessor method code for the raised property in the Needle Gauge Bean from the previous chapter. Why did I bother showing it to you again? Well, because it's easy to get lost when you see code listing after code listing. So, at the risk of being repetitive, I wanted to make sure you know what's going on inside of the Clock Bean.*

LISTING 13.3 The Accessor Methods for the Mode Property

```
public boolean isDigital() {
  return digital;
}

public void setDigital(boolean d) {
  digital = d;
  repaint();
}
```

As you can see, these methods are practically identical in function to the accessor methods for the raised property, except they operate on the digital member variable. That's it for the Clock Bean's accessor methods. So far you've put together code for the Bean's properties, constructors, and accessor methods. Next on the agenda are the Bean's public methods.

Public Methods

The Clock Bean uses three public methods in addition to the accessor methods. The first one is the run() method, which is responsible for triggering updates once every second. The run() method is called automatically by the Java runtime system once the thread has been created and started. The code for the run() method in the Clock Bean is shown in Listing 13.4.

LISTING 13.4 The run() Method

```
public void run() {
  while (clockThread != null) {
    repaint();
    try {
      // Sleep for a second
      clockThread.sleep(1000);
    } catch (InterruptedException e) {
      System.out.println(e);
    }
  }
}
```

You may be thinking that this seems like a small amount of code to be performing such an important function as triggering the Bean at regular intervals. However, the structure of Java's multithreading support makes it very easy to implement this type of functionality. The run() method consists of a while loop that is always executing as long as the clockThread member variable isn't null. Each time through the loop the Bean is repainted, which means the clock's appearance is updated to reflect the current time. The one-second interval is established by the call to the sleep() method, which causes the thread to cease execution for a specified period of time (in milliseconds). In other words, the thread pauses for a second and then starts the loop over, which results in another repaint. Pretty slick!

NOTE: *Since the* sleep() *method is called from within a thread that runs asynchronously, it doesn't halt the execution of code outside the thread in any way. In other words, the one-second pause only impacts the code within the thread.*

One of the other public methods used by the Clock Bean is the `update()` method, which you learned about while developing the Needle Gauge Bean in the previous chapter. Just in case you don't remember how simple the code is for this method, here it is again:

```
public void update(Graphics g) {
  paint(g);
}
```

Remember, too, why the `update()` method is needed. In a typical Bean, the `update()` method erases the background of the Bean and then calls the `paint()` method. Since you are implementing an offscreen buffer in the Clock Bean, you want to override the `update()` method so it doesn't erase the background before calling `paint()`. The `update()` method is overridden solely to avoid erasing the background.

The `paint()` method is completely responsible for drawing the Bean, which includes the creation and manipulation of the offscreen buffer. Just in case you don't remember the steps required to use an offscreen buffer in a Bean, here they are again:

1 Create/erase the offscreen buffer

2 Draw at will to the offscreen buffer

3 Draw the offscreen buffer to the screen

The `paint()` method in the Clock Bean uses this offscreen buffer approach to eliminate flicker. The source code for the `paint()` method appears in Listing 13.5. The majority of this code is the overhead required to manage the offscreen buffer. The only things significant to the Clock Bean are the calls to the `drawDigitalClock()` and `drawAnalogClock()` methods, which are conditional parts of an `if` statement controlled by the `digital` member variable. These methods are private methods responsible for drawing the clock on a provided graphics context. In this case, the `offGrfx` graphics context is passed to the methods, which results in the drawing taking place on the offscreen buffer. You'll learn about the `drawDigitalClock()` and `drawAnalogClock()` methods in just a moment. After the clock's been drawn to the offscreen buffer, the buffer is finished and ready to be drawn to the screen, which is accomplished with a call to the `drawImage()` method.

Support Methods

The final code we need to cover for the Clock Bean is the code for the `drawDigitalClock()` and `drawAnalogClock()` methods. These methods are responsible for drawing the clock on a provided graphics context. The `drawDigitalClock()` method draws a digital representation of the clock, while

LISTING 13.5. The paint() Method

```java
public synchronized void paint(Graphics g) {
  Dimension d = getSize();

  // Create the offscreen graphics context
  if (offGrfx == null || (offSize.width != d.width) ||
    (offSize.height != d.height)) {
    offSize = d;
    offImage = createImage(d.width, d.height);
    offGrfx = offImage.getGraphics();
  }

  // Paint the background with 3D effects
  offGrfx.setColor(getBackground());
  offGrfx.fillRect(1, 1, d.width - 2, d.height - 2);
  offGrfx.draw3DRect(0, 0, d.width - 1, d.height - 1, raised);
  offGrfx.setColor(getForeground());

  // Paint the clock
  if (digital)
    drawDigitalClock(offGrfx);
  else
    drawAnalogClock(offGrfx);

  // Paint the image onto the screen
  g.drawImage(offImage, 0, 0, null);
}
```

the drawAnalogClock() method draws a circular analog clock. Listing 13.6 shows the source code for the drawDigitalClock() method.

NOTE: *The* SPACING *value used in the* drawDigitalClock() *method is an integer constant defined in the* Clock *class that determines the positioning of the time text.*

The drawDigitalClock() method draws the clock with the hours, minutes, and seconds separated by colons, much like you see on digital alarm clocks. It starts off by creating a Calendar object that is used to determine the current time.

LISTING 13.6 The drawDigitalClock() Method

```
private void drawDigitalClock(Graphics g) {
  Dimension d = getSize();

  // Get the time as a string
  Calendar      now = Calendar.getInstance();
  int           h = now.get(Calendar.HOUR) % 12;
  StringBuffer  time = new StringBuffer("");
  if (h == 0)
    time.append("12:");
  else
    time.append(String.valueOf(h) + ":");
  String  s = String.valueOf(now.get(Calendar.MINUTE));
  if (s.length() < 2)
    time.append("0" + s + ":");
  else
    time.append(s + ":");
  s = String.valueOf(now.get(Calendar.SECOND));
  if (s.length() < 2)
    time.append("0" + s);
  else
    time.append(s);

  // Draw the time
  g.setColor(getForeground());
  g.setFont(getFont());
  FontMetrics fm = g.getFontMetrics();
  g.drawString(time.toString(), (d.width - (SPACING * 2) -
    fm.stringWidth(time.toString())) / 2, (d.height - (SPACING * 2) +
    fm.getAscent() - fm.getDescent()) / 2);
}
```

13

The current hour is first determined by calling the get() method on the Calendar object and passing the Calendar.HOUR mask. A string buffer is then created and the hour is appended to it. The current minute and second are then determined and appended to the string buffer in a similar fashion. This results in a string version of the time in a format ready to be displayed.

The time string is then drawn to the graphics context with a call to the drawString() method. The drawDigitalClock() method is careful to first select the font, however. The font metrics are also retrieved and used to center the string in the graphics context. That's all it takes to draw the time in digital form!

Drawing an analog clock is a little more work, as you might have guessed. The rather substantial code for the drawAnalogClock() method is shown in Listing 13.7. This method begins by calculating the radius and center of the clock based on the size of the Bean. The calculation of the radius is significant because the drawAnalogClock() method tries to size the clock appropriately within the Bean's rectangular area. Once the radius has been determined, the basic shape of the clock is drawn with a black border and white background.

LISTING 13.7 The drawAnalogClock() Method

```
private void drawAnalogClock(Graphics g) {
  int    radius = (Math.min(getSize().height, getSize().width) -
                  (SPACING * 2)) / 2;
  Point center = new Point(getSize().width / 2, getSize().height /
2);

  // Draw the clock shape
  g.setColor(Color.black);
  g.drawOval(center.x - radius, center.y - radius, radius * 2,
    radius * 2);
  g.setColor(Color.white);
  g.fillOval(center.x - radius + 1, center.y - radius + 1,
    (radius * 2) - 2, (radius * 2) - 2);

  // Draw the hour marks and numbers
  g.setFont(getFont());
  FontMetrics fm = g.getFontMetrics();
  for (int h = 1; h < 13; h++) {
    // Draw an hour mark
    double hourAngle = h * Math.PI / 6.0;
    g.setColor(Color.black);
    g.drawLine(center.x + (int)(Math.round(0.9 * radius *
      Math.sin(hourAngle))), center.y - (int)(Math.round(0.9 * radius
    *
      Math.cos(hourAngle))), center.x + (int)(Math.round(radius *
      Math.sin(hourAngle))), center.y - (int)(Math.round(radius *
      Math.cos(hourAngle))));
```

CONTINUES

LISTING 13.7 The drawAnalogClock() Method (Continued)

```java
      // Draw an hour number, as long as it will fit
      if (fm.getAscent() - fm.getDescent() < (radius / 4)) {
        String num = String.valueOf(h);
        g.setColor(getForeground());
        g.drawString(num, center.x + (int)(Math.round(0.7 * radius *
          Math.sin(hourAngle))) - (fm.stringWidth(num) / 2), center.y -
          (int)(Math.round(0.7 * radius * Math.cos(hourAngle))) +
          ((fm.getAscent() - fm.getDescent()) / 2));
      }
    }


    // Draw the hour hand
    Calendar now = Calendar.getInstance();
    g.setColor(Color.black);
    g.drawLine(center.x, center.y, center.x + (int)(Math.round(radius *
      0.4 * Math.sin((now.get(Calendar.HOUR) % 12) * Math.PI / 6.0 +
      (Math.PI * now.get(Calendar.MINUTE) / 360.0)))), center.y -
      (int)(Math.round(radius * 0.4 * Math.cos((now.get(Calendar.HOUR)
%
      12) * Math.PI / 6.0 + (Math.PI * now.get(Calendar.MINUTE) /
      360.0)))));

    // Draw the minute hand
    g.drawLine(center.x, center.y, center.x + (int)(Math.round(0.8 *
      radius * Math.sin(now.get(Calendar.MINUTE) * Math.PI / 30.0))),
      center.y - (int)(Math.round(0.8 * radius *
      Math.cos(now.get(Calendar.MINUTE) * Math.PI / 30.0))));

    // Draw the second hand and center
    g.setColor(Color.red);
    g.drawLine(center.x, center.y, center.x + (int)(Math.round(0.6 *
      radius * Math.sin(now.get(Calendar.SECOND) * Math.PI / 30.0))),
      center.y - (int)(Math.round(0.6 * radius *
      Math.cos(now.get(Calendar.SECOND) * Math.PI / 30.0))));
    g.setColor(Color.black);
    g.fillOval(center.x - 2, center.y - 2, 4, 4);
  }
```

13

13

The next step is drawing the hour marks and numbers, which is the ugliest code in the method. This code is practically identical to the code used in the Needle Gauge Bean in the previous chapter, so I won't go through a detailed explanation. Like the code in the Needle Gauge Bean, this code only draws the hour numbers if they will fit. After drawing the hour marks and numbers, the `drawAnalogClock()` method draws the hour, minute, and second hands. It does this by using a `Calendar` object and calling its `get()` method, just as was done in the `drawDigitalClock()` method. The calculations for drawing the hands are very similar to those used for drawing the needle in the needle gauge.

> **NOTE:** *The* `Calendar` *class is provided in the* `java.util` *package and is useful for determining information about a date and time.*

Additional Overhead

You've now finished developing the source code for the Clock Bean, but there are a few finishing touches remaining. You still need to define a `ClockBeanInfo` class so the Bean has graphical icons associated with it for use in application builder tools. The complete source code for the `ClockBeanInfo` class appears in Listing 13.8.

The `ClockBeanInfo` class is very similar to the Bean information classes associated with the two other Beans you've developed in the book thus far. It defines a single method, `getIcon()`, which provides an iconic representation of the Bean. Two icons are provided by the Bean information class to support two different resolutions. Figure 13.1 shows what the icons for the Clock Bean look like.

The Clock Bean still needs a manifest file so that it can be built into a distributable JAR file. The code for the Clock Bean's manifest file, Clock.mf, is as follows:

```
Manifest-Version: 1.0

Name: HTPJB/Chap13/Clock/Clock.class
Java-Bean: True
```

FIGURE 13.1

The Bean information icons for the Clock Bean

The manifest file for the Clock Bean is very similar to manifest files you've seen for other Beans in the book. Remember that this manifest file must be used when you're building a JAR file containing the Bean. For information on how to build a JAR file for the Bean, refer to Chapter 4, "Packaging Beans with JAR Files." Keep in mind that the complete source code and related resources for the Clock Bean, including a JAR file for the Bean, are located on the CD-ROM included with this book.

13

LISTING 13.8 The ClockBeanInfo Class

```
// ClockBeanInfo Class
// ClockBeanInfo.java

package HTPJB.Chap13.Clock;

// Imports
import java.beans.*;

public class ClockBeanInfo extends SimpleBeanInfo {
  // Get the appropriate icon
  public java.awt.Image getIcon(int iconKind) {
    if (iconKind == BeanInfo.ICON_COLOR_16x16) {
      java.awt.Image img = loadImage("ClockIcon16.gif");
      return img;
    }
    if (iconKind == BeanInfo.ICON_COLOR_32x32) {
      java.awt.Image img = loadImage("ClockIcon32.gif");
      return img;
    }
    return null;
  }
}
```

Using the Clock Bean

It's finally time for the most exciting part of building your own Bean: testing it!
You're going to test out the Clock Bean using the BeanBox test container, which
you are hopefully getting more comfortable with by now. If you recall, the first
step in using a Bean in a visual environment such as the BeanBox is to add the
Bean to the environment. You add the Clock Bean to the BeanBox by copying the
JAR file for the Bean to the jars directory beneath your BDK installation. When the
BeanBox is executed, it automatically looks in the jars directory to see if any new
Beans need to be added.

NOTE: *The BeanBox doesn't actually check for "new" Beans when it looks in
the jars directory; it actually loads all the Beans in the jars directory.*

Once you've copied the JAR file for the Clock Bean to the jars directory, run the BeanBox by executing the `run.bat` batch file provided with the BeanBox. The BeanBox should appear at this point with your Clock Bean added to the ToolBox. Figure 13.2 shows what the ToolBox looks like with the Clock Bean added.

The figure shows that the last Bean in the ToolBox is now the Clock Bean, which is represented by the 16-by-16 icon you specified in the Bean information class. You should also see the Image Button and Needle Gauge Beans you added in the previous two chapters. Try adding a Clock Bean to the BeanBox by clicking on it in the ToolBox and then clicking in the main container window. Figure 13.3 shows the main container window with the newly added Clock Bean.

With the Bean added to the container window, you can check out its properties. Figure 13.4 shows the PropertySheet window for the Clock Bean. The PropertySheet window shows all the properties for the Bean, including the inherited foreground color, background color, font, and name properties, along with your own raised and mode (digital) properties. All of these properties can be edited using the PropertySheet window. Go ahead and try editing the Bean by changing

FIGURE 13.2

The BeanBox ToolBox window with the Clock Bean added

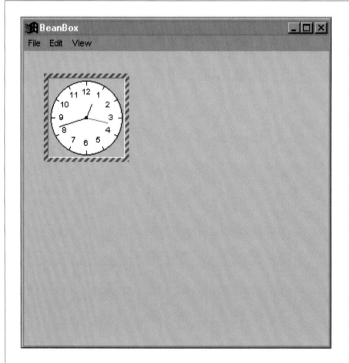

FIGURE 13.3

The BeanBox main container window with a Clock Bean added

the foreground color to blue, the raised property to true, and the font to 36-point Times New Roman. Figure 13.5 shows what the PropertySheet window looks like after you've edited the Clock Bean. Figure 13.6 shows what the main container window looks like after you've modified the properties for the Bean.

Now try setting the digital (mode) property to true; the whole look of the clock should change. Figure 13.7 shows what the clock looks like after you've changed it to digital mode.

Summary

In this chapter, you designed and developed a Bean that acts as a graphical clock. The Clock Bean has the capability to display the current time in either digital or analog form. One interesting thing about the Clock Bean is that it automatically updates itself every second, which gives it a degree of autonomy that you haven't seen in other Beans.

13

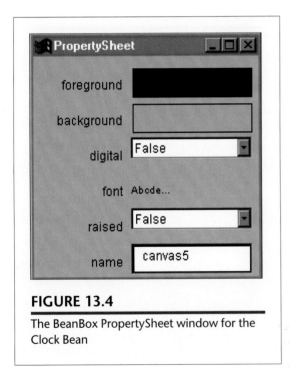

FIGURE 13.4

The BeanBox PropertySheet window for the Clock Bean

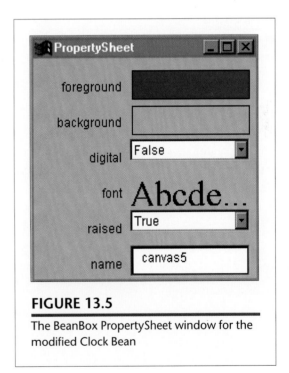

FIGURE 13.5

The BeanBox PropertySheet window for the modified Clock Bean

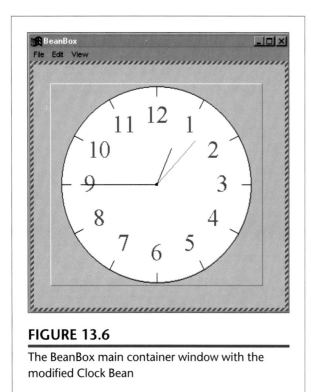

FIGURE 13.6

The BeanBox main container window with the modified Clock Bean

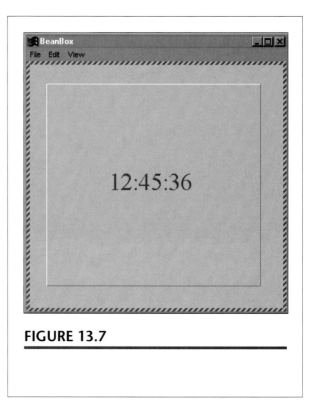

FIGURE 13.7

You began the chapter by designing the Clock Bean from a purely conceptual perspective. This allowed you to get a solid idea of what the Bean was to accomplish before digging into the details of the source code. From there, you went on to creating the actual code for the Bean. With the code in place, you tested out the Bean in the BeanBox.

Chapter *14*

An Image Enhancer Bean

▶ **Image Filtering Basics**

▶ **Designing the Image Enhancer Bean**

▶ **Constructing the Image Enhancer Bean**

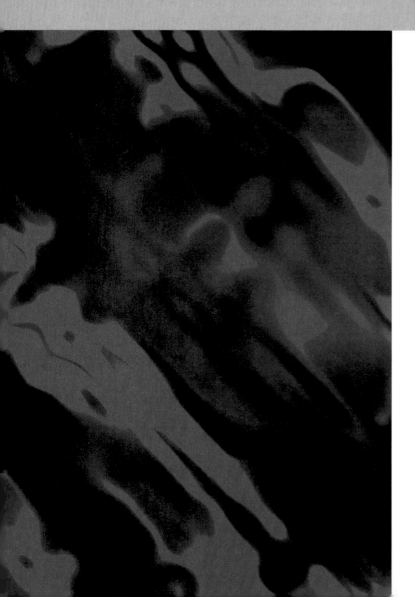

In this chapter, you'll learn how to design and build a Bean that can manipulate images in real time. You'll begin the chapter by working through a preliminary design of the Bean, and then you'll progress to developing the actual code for the Bean. As you work through the code, you'll see the value of having the code closely follow the conceptual design of the Bean. You'll finish up the chapter by testing the Bean in the faithful BeanBox test container.

The Image Enhancer Bean you develop in this chapter is interesting in that it allows you to process an image in real time based on a variety of different attributes such as brightness and alpha level. These attributes are altered via simple Bean properties, which in turn cause the image to be filtered. The filtering itself is handled through Java's standard image processing support, which helps make things easier to implement. I think you'll find this Bean an interesting departure from the Beans you've developed thus far, so let's get started!

In this chapter, you'll learn

- ▶ The basics of Java image filtering

- ▶ How to design an Image Enhancer Bean

- ▶ How to construct an Image Enhancer Bean

- ▶ How to use an Image Enhancer Bean

14

Image Filtering Basics

Before jumping into the design of the Image Enhancer Bean, you need to understand a little about image filtering and how it fits into Java. *Image filtering*, which is also sometimes referred to as *image processing*, is the process of altering the individual pixels of an image according to a particular algorithm. Java provides a simple yet powerful framework for filtering images. In Java, image processing objects are called *image filters*, and they serve as a way to isolate and generalize the filtering of an image without worrying about the details associated with the source or destination of the image data.

A Java image filter can be thought of as a pipe into which all the data for an image must enter and exit on its way from a source to a destination. While the individual pixels of an image are passing through an image filter, they can be altered by the filter in any way. By design, image filters are structured to be self-contained components. The image filter model supported by Java is based on three logical components: an image producer, an image filter, and an image consumer. The image producer makes the raw pixel data for an image available, the image filter in turn filters this data, and the resulting filtered image data is passed on to the image consumer (which is usually where it has been requested).

Java's support for image filters is scattered across several classes and interfaces in the `java.awt.image` package. You don't necessarily have to understand all these classes to be able to work with image filters, but it's important that you understand at least a few of them in order to build the Image Enhancer Bean. These are a few of the relevant classes and interfaces in the `java.awt.image` package that provide support for image filtering:

▶ ImageProducer

▶ FilteredImageSource

▶ ImageFilter

▶ RGBImageFilter

The `ImageProducer` interface describes the methods necessary to extract image pixel data from `Image` objects. The `FilteredImageSource` class implements the `ImageProducer` interface and produces filtered image data. The filtered image data it produces is based on the image and the specific filter object passed in `FilteredImageSource`'s constructor. `FilteredImageSource` provides a very simple way to apply image filters to `Image` objects.

The Java image filter model operates under the concept of an image source sending image data through an image filter on its way to an image consumer. The `ImageFilter` class provides the basic functionality of an image filter that operates on the image data being delivered from an image producer to an image consumer. `ImageFilter` objects are specifically designed to be used in conjunction with `FilteredImageSource` objects.

The `ImageFilter` class is implemented as a null filter, meaning that it passes image data through unmodified. This may seem strange, but the function of the `ImageFilter` class is only to provide the overhead for processing the data in an image. The actual modification of pixel data is left up to derived filter classes. This turns out to be a very nice design, because it enables you to create new image filters by simply deriving from `ImageFilter` and overriding only a few methods.

The `ImageFilter` class operates on an image using the color model defined by the image producer. The `RGBImageFilter` class, on the other hand, derives from `ImageFilter` and implements an image filter specific to the default RGB (Red/Green/Blue) color model. A color model is a Java object that provides methods for translating from pixel values to the corresponding red, green, and blue color components of an image. Color models are used extensively in the internal implementations of the various Java image filtering classes. The `RGBImageFilter` class provides the overhead necessary to process image data in a single method that converts pixels one at a time in the default RGB color model. Like `ImageFilter`, `RGBImageFilter` is meant to be used in conjunction with the `FilteredImageSource` image producer.

> **NOTE:** *The RGB color model is the most popular color model used in computer graphics systems. In the RGB color model, colors are represented by red, green, and blue color components. The combination of these components results in an RGB color. Different colors are obtained by varying the amount of each component.*

The seemingly strange thing about `RGBImageFilter` is that it is an abstract class, so you can't instantiate objects from it. In other words, you can't directly use the `RGBImageFilter` class to filter an image. This isn't a problem because the RGBImageFilter class is designed as a base class for fully functioning filter classes. RGBImageFilter is abstract because of a single abstract method, `filterRGB()`. The `filterRGB()` method is used to convert a single input pixel to a single output pixel in the default RGB color model. `filterRGB()` is the workhorse method that handles filtering the image data; each pixel in the image is sent through this method for processing. To create your own RGB image filters, all you must do is derive from `RGBImageFilter` and implement the `filterRGB()` method. This is the technique you'll use later in this chapter when you implement image filters for the Image Enhancer Bean.

> **NOTE:** *The `RGBImageFilter` class allows you to effectively create image filters by writing a single method, `filterRGB()`.*

Designing the Image Enhancer Bean

As in the other Beans in the book, the development of the Image Enhancer Bean begins with its conceptual design. Spending initial design time on a Bean before jumping into the coding is very beneficial.

The Image Enhancer Bean functions as an image processor, meaning that it alters pixels in an image based on a particular set of rules. These rules are spelled out by the image filters used in the Image Enhancer Bean, which are built on the standard Java image filtering framework. Like the Beans in earlier chapters, the Image Enhancer Bean will inherit from the standard AWT `Canvas` class, which derives from `Component`. Unlike the other Beans, the Image Enhancer Bean requires only one of the inherited properties provided by `Canvas`: the name property. You'll learn how to exclude the unneeded inherited properties later in the chapter. The Image Enhancer Bean also needs a few properties of its own. Before getting into these properties in detail, though, let's go ahead and take a look at how the Bean works.

The Image Enhancer Bean provides the capability to process a given image through several different filters. The filters are selected and applied by modifying the Bean's properties. The resulting filtered image is drawn in the Bean's display area, and is updated any time a property that impacts the filtering is changed. Since the filters are controlled entirely through the Bean's properties, the Bean is entirely responsible for managing the filters and applying them as necessary. From this description it is clear that the Image Enhancer Bean functions as both a real-time image processor and an image viewer.

The Image Enhancer Bean supports three different filters: a color filter, an alpha filter, and a brightness filter. The color filter provides a means of filtering out individual colors (red, green, blue) of an image. The alpha filter provides a means of adjusting the transparency, or alpha level, of an image. And the brightness filter gives you a way to adjust the brightness level of an image. The neat thing about the Image Enhancer Bean is that it allows you to apply all three of these filters to an image at once.

With the basic functional design of the Bean now complete, let's move on to some more specific design issues. The Image Enhancer Bean can be broken down into three major parts: properties, methods, and events. The rest of this section covers the design of the Image Enhancer Bean's major functional parts.

Properties

The properties for the Image Enhancer Bean directly control the filtering of the image, which makes them a very critical part of the Bean's design. Properties are always a critical part of a Bean's design, but play an even larger role in this case because they directly control the type of image manipulation performed by the Bean. For this reason, the properties required of the Image Enhancer Bean are directly related to the filtering capabilities supported by the Bean.

The Bean still needs to inherit a property from its parent `Component` class. The inherited property is the name property, which allows you to assign the Bean a unique name. The first new property required by the Bean is the image name property, which keeps track of the name of the image being filtered/viewed. It's important to understand the difference between the inherited name property and the new image name property. The inherited name property represents the name of the Bean itself, while the image name property represents the name of the image being filtered by the Bean. Unlike the name property, the image name property is actually the name of an image file.

The next three properties are all related to the color filter: the red, green, and blue properties. These three properties are Boolean values that determine whether each color is included in the image or filtered out. The alpha property is next, and is responsible for how the alpha filter is applied to the image. The last property required of the Image Enhancer Bean is the brightness property, which determines how the brightness filter is applied to the image. That wraps up the properties needed by the Bean.

To recap a little, these are the properties required of the Image Enhancer Bean:

▶ Image name

▶ Red (filtered/unfiltered)

▶ Green (filtered/unfiltered)

▶ Blue (filtered/unfiltered)

▶ Alpha

▶ Brightness

Methods

Now that the properties are laid out, it's time to design the public methods required of the Bean. With the properties fresh on your mind, let's start with their accessor methods. Fortunately, as you've learned in previous chapters, determining the accessor methods is a very simple process. All of the properties for the Image Enhancer Bean are readable and writeable, so you will need a pair of accessor methods for each of them. That's really all you need to know at this stage of the game; you'll get into the gory details of each method a little later in the chapter.

Since the Image Enhancer Bean does more than just manage its own properties, it makes sense that it should need more than accessor methods to function properly. The Image Enhancer Bean in fact requires two other public methods, `paint()` and `PreferredSize()`, which are both overridden from a parent class. The `paint()` method, which you are probably intimately familiar with by now, is responsible for drawing the graphical representation of the Bean. The `PreferredSize()` method is responsible for determining the preferred size of the Bean based on its current state. The preferred size of the Bean is simply the size of the image being filtered and displayed by the Bean.

> **NOTE:** *Since accessor methods are really just property interfaces, practically all Beans require other methods to perform any real function.*

These are the public methods required of the Image Enhancer Bean:

▶ Image name property getter/setter methods

▶ Red property getter/setter methods

▶ Green property getter/setter methods

- ▶ Blue property getter/setter methods

- ▶ Alpha property getter/setter methods

- ▶ Brightness property getter/setter methods

- ▶ Overridden `paint()` method

- ▶ Overridden `PreferredSize()` method

Events

The Image Enhancer Bean is purely a graphical output Bean. This means that it responds to no input events from the user and fires no events of its own. Therefore no event-related methods are required.

Constructing the Image Enhancer Bean

With the basic design under your belt, you know what's next! That's right, it's time to get dirty with the details of coding the Image Enhancer Bean. Although the code for the Bean itself is very straightforward, you'll have to do a decent amount of work building the three image filters used by the Bean. Don't worry right now, though, because they are last on your list of concerns. For now, let's focus on developing the code for the Image Enhancer Bean itself.

To make the code for the Bean easier to understand and follow, most of it is presented in the form of individual member declarations or method listings. As you read through this section, you may want to check out the complete source code for the Bean, which is included on the CD-ROM that accompanies this book. The main code for the Image Enhancer Bean is in the `ImageEnhancer` class, which appears on the CD-ROM in the file ImageEnhancer.java.

 ON THE CD: *The source code for the Image Enhancer Bean is on the CD-ROM included with this book.*

Properties and Member Variables

The best place to start with the Bean's code is defining the properties. The following are the member variable properties for the Bean:

```
private String   imageName;
private boolean  red, green, blue;
private int      alpha;
private int      brightness;
```

The first member variable, imageName, keeps track of the name of the image being filtered and displayed. The remaining member variables are associated with the three image filters used by the Bean. The red, green, and blue members are Boolean values that determine whether the colors are included in or filtered out of the image. The alpha member is an integer value that determines the degree to which the alpha level is filtered in the image. The alpha level of an image specifies how transparent or opaque the image appears. The alpha member variable can have a value ranging from 0 to 9, where 0 means the image is completely transparent (invisible) and 9 means the image is completely opaque (visible). The default value for the alpha member is 9. The last property member variable is brightness, which determines how bright the image is via the brightness image filter. The brightness member is an integer in the range of -100 to 100, where -100 means the brightness of the image is decreased by 100% and 100 means the brightness is increased by 100%. The default value for the brightness member is 0.

Since these properties have built-in Java types, their property editors are already provided by JavaBeans. In addition to these public properties, the Image Enhancer Bean requires a couple of private member variables for internal use:

```
private transient Image srcImage, dstImage;
```

These two member variables are used to manage the image being filtered. The srcImage member is used to store the original image, or source image, in its unfiltered state. When it comes time to filter the image, the source image is copied to the dstImage member, which is passed on to the filters. This filtered image is in turn drawn to the screen. It is necessary to keep these images separate because the filters always need to be applied to an original, unfiltered image in order to avoid compounding previous filter effects. Both of these member variables are defined as transient, which means they aren't stored away as part of the Bean's internal state when the Bean is serialized.

Constructors

Everything begins with the Bean's constructors, which is where the property member variables are initialized. The Image Enhancer Bean provides two constructors: a default constructor and a detailed constructor that takes all of the properties as arguments. Listing 14.1 shows the code for both of these constructors.

NOTE: *The* ALPHA_MAX *value used in the* ImageEnhancer *constructor is an integer constant defined in the* ImageEnhancer *class that determines the maximum value of the alpha property.*

LISTING 14.1 The Constructors for the Image Enhancer Bean

```
public ImageEnhancer() {
  this("Pear.gif", true, true, true, ALPHA_MAX, 0);
}

public ImageEnhancer(String in, boolean r, boolean g, boolean b, int a,
  int br) {
  // Allow the superclass constructor to do its thing
  super();

  // Set properties
  red = r;
  green = g;
  blue = b;
  alpha = a;
  brightness = br;
  setImageName(in);

  // Get things rolling
  filterImage();
}
```

The first constructor takes no arguments and merely calls the second constructor with default property values. You might notice that the first default property value is "Pear.gif", which is the default image name used by the Bean. This GIF image is included with the Bean as a default just in case you don't have any images of your own to try out. You'll get to test the Bean with this image later in the chapter. Figure 14.1 shows what the Pear.gif image looks like.

The second constructor handles the details of initializing the Bean and setting all the properties to the values passed as arguments. Once the properties are set, the constructor calls the filterImage() method to filter the image based on the initial property values. You'll learn about the filterImage() method a little later in the chapter; for now, just understand that it filters the image based on the Bean's present state.

FIGURE 14.1

The default pear image for the Image Enhancer Bean

Accessor Methods

A pair of accessor methods is required for each property in the Bean. These methods serve as the external interface for each property, which means that the accessor methods are responsible for controlling the different filters. The first property defined in the Bean is the image name property, whose accessor method pair is shown in Listing 14.2.

The `getImageName()` method is pretty minimal and simply returns the value of the `imageName` member variable. The `setImageName()` method is a little more involved in that it first sets the `imageName` member and then loads the image corresponding to this name. The `setImageName()` method uses the `loadImage()` method, which you'll learn about a little later in this chapter, to handle the loading of the image. Since images don't conform to any particular size, it is important to resize the Bean whenever the image is changed. This is handled in `setImageName()` with a simple call to the `sizeToFit()` method, which you used while developing the Image Button Bean in Chapter 11.

> **LISTING 14.2 The Accessor Methods for the Image Name Property**
>
> ```
> public String getImageName() {
>   return imageName;
> }
>
>
> public void setImageName(String in) {
>   imageName = in;
>
>   // Load the image
>   srcImage = loadImage(imageName);
>   if (srcImage != null)
>     dstImage = srcImage;
>   sizeToFit();
> }
> ```

The accessor methods for the red, green, and blue color properties are all very similar, as Listing 14.3 shows. The getter methods for the color properties are all very straightforward: They simply return the appropriate color property setting. The setter methods have to do a little more since they impact how the image is filtered. Each setter method first checks to make sure the value of the property has really changed, which ensures that the image isn't filtered unnecessarily. The new property value is then set, after which the setter methods call the `filterImage()` method to filter the image based on the new property value.

The accessor methods for the alpha property are similar to those for the color properties, as Listing 14.4 shows. The getter method for the alpha property doesn't hold any surprises, but the setter method is a little different than its color property counterparts. The difference is how the alpha property is constrained to the 0 to 9 range of values. This is accomplished by using the `min()` and `max()` methods provided by the `Math` class. Incidentally, the upper range value of 9 is provided by the `ALPHA_MAX` constant, which is defined as follows:

```
private static final int  ALPHA_MAX = 9;
```

LISTING 14.3 The Accessor Methods for the Red, Green, and Blue Color Properties

```
public boolean isRed() {
  return red;
}

public void setRed(boolean r) {
  if (r != red) {
    red = r;
    filterImage();
  }
}

public boolean isGreen() {
  return green;
}

public void setGreen(boolean g) {
  if (g != green) {
    green = g;
    filterImage();
  }
}

public boolean isBlue() {
  return blue;
}

public void setBlue(boolean b) {
  if (b != blue) {
    blue = b;
    filterImage();
  }
}
```

The last accessor methods defined in the Image Enhancer Bean belong to the brightness property. The source code for these methods appears in Listing 14.5. These accessor methods are a lot like the ones for the alpha property in that they constrain the brightness to a particular range. In this case, the range is -100 to 100.

LISTING 14.4 The Accessor Methods for the Alpha Property

```
public int getAlpha() {
  return alpha;
}

public void setAlpha(int a) {
  if (a != alpha) {
    alpha = Math.max(0, Math.min(a, ALPHA_MAX));
    filterImage();
  }
}                                                        ■
```

Again, the `min()` and `max()` methods are used to enforce the range of acceptable brightness values. Like the color and alpha setter methods, the `setBrightness()` method calls `filterImage()` to filter the image after setting the property. That wraps up the accessor methods for the Bean.

LISTING 14.5 The Accessor Methods for the Brightness Property

```
public int getBrightness() {
  return brightness;
}

public void setBrightness(int br) {
  if (br != brightness) {
    brightness = Math.max(-100, Math.min(br, 100));
    filterImage();
  }
}                                                        ■
```

Public Methods

In addition to accessor methods, the Image Enhancer Bean requires two other public methods: `paint()` and `PreferredSize()`. The first method, `paint()`, is used to paint the visual appearance of the Bean, which in this case is simply the filtered image. This is the source code for the `paint()` method:

```
public synchronized void paint(Graphics g) {
```

14

```
    if (dstImage != null)
      g.drawImage(dstImage, 0, 0, this);
  }
```

As you can see, the `paint()` method is pretty simple. It basically just makes sure the destination image is valid, then draws it to the screen. The `paint()` method really has nothing to do with the actual filtering of the image; it simply draws the resulting image if it is available.

The `PreferredSize()` method should sound at least vaguely familiar to you since you used it in the Image Button Bean in Chapter 11. Actually, the `PreferredSize()` method for the Image Enhancer Bean is very different from the one used in the Image Button Bean, although its purpose is basically the same. In general, the `PreferredSize()` method is used to determine the ideal size for a Bean. For the Image Enhancer Bean, this size is simply the size of the image being filtered and displayed. Listing 14.6 shows the code for the `PreferredSize()` method.

LISTING 14.6 The PreferredSize() Method

```
public Dimension PreferredSize() {
  if (srcImage != null) {
    // Set the preferred size to image size
    int width = srcImage.getWidth(this),
        height = srcImage.getHeight(this);
    if (width > 0 && height > 0)
      return new Dimension(width, height);
  }

  // Otherwise set the preferred size to default image size
  return new Dimension(200, 150);
}
```

The `PreferredSize()` method first checks to make sure the source image is valid. If not, it returns the size of the default image, Pear.gif. Otherwise, the size of the Bean is determined based on the width and height of the current source image.

Support Methods

The Image Enhancer Bean uses three private support methods to take care of internal business: `sizeToFit()`, `loadImage()`, and `filterImage()`. These methods provide functionality that is only needed by the Bean internally, which explains why they are private. The code for the sizeToFit() method appears in Listing 14.7.

LISTING 14.7 The sizeToFit() Method

```
private void sizeToFit() {
  // Resize to the preferred size
  Dimension d = PreferredSize();
  setSize(d.width, d.height);
  Component p = getParent();
  if (p != null) {
    p.invalidate();
    p.doLayout();
  }
}
```

The sizeToFit() method is responsible for sizing the Bean to fit the image. This method is identical to the one used in the Image Button Bean in Chapter 11. The sizeToFit() method actually pushes the details of determining the size of the Bean onto the PreferredSize() method. It's important that sizeToFit() notify the Bean's parent to lay out the Bean again by calling the invalidate() and layout() methods after resizing the Bean.

The loadImage() method is responsible for loading an image given a resource name for the image. Listing 14.8 shows the code for this method. Like

---

LISTING 14.8 The loadImage() Method

```
private Image loadImage(String name) {
  try {
    URL url = getClass().getResource(name);
    return createImage((ImageProducer)url.getContent());
  }
  catch (Exception e) {
    System.err.println("Couldn't load the image " + name + ".");
    return null;
  }
}
```

sizeToFit(), the loadImage() method is exactly the same as the one used in the Image Button Bean in Chapter 11. The loadImage() method takes an image name as its only argument and uses it to load the image as a resource.

The final method required by the Image Enhancer Bean is without a doubt the most interesting method in the Bean. I'm referring to the filterImage() method, which is responsible for doing the work of filtering the source image to arrive at a destination image. The source code for the filterImage() method appears in Listing 14.9.

LISTING 14.9 The filterImage() Method

```
private void filterImage() {
  if (srcImage != null) {
    dstImage = srcImage;

    // Apply the color filter
    dstImage =
      createImage(new FilteredImageSource(dstImage.getSource(),
      new ColorFilter(!red, !green, !blue)));

    // Apply the alpha filter
    dstImage =
      createImage(new FilteredImageSource(dstImage.getSource(),
      new AlphaFilter((alpha * 255) / ALPHA_MAX)));

    // Apply the brightness filter
    dstImage =
      createImage(new FilteredImageSource(dstImage.getSource(),
      new BrightnessFilter(brightness)));

    // Redraw the image
    repaint();
  }
}
```

The filterImage() method first checks to make sure the source image is valid. If so, it copies the original source image to the destination image. This ensures that none of the filtering impacts the original image. The filterImage() method then applies each of the three filters to the destination image using a

`FilteredImageSource` object. The `FilteredImageSource` object requires a filter, which is applied to the given image. In this case, instances of the three different filter classes (`ColorFilter`, `AlphaFilter`, `BrightnessFilter`) are used in conjunction with the `FilteredImageSource` object. You'll build these filter classes a little later in the chapter. Once all the filtering is finished, the `repaint()` method is called to force the Bean to draw the newly filtered image.

Additional Overhead

You've now finished developing the source code for the Image Enhancer Bean itself, but there is still a decent amount of work to be done. First off, you need to define an `ImageEnhancerBeanInfo` class so the Bean has graphical icons associated with it for use in application builder tools. Additionally, the `ImageEnhancerBeanInfo` class is used to hide unwanted inherited properties in

---

LISTING 14.10   The Complete Source Code for the ImageEnhancerBeanInfo Class

```java
// ImageEnhancerBeanInfo Class
// ImageEnhancerBeanInfo.java

package HTPJB.Chap14.ImageEnhancer;

// Imports
import java.beans.*;

public class ImageEnhancerBeanInfo extends SimpleBeanInfo {
  // Get the appropriate icon
  public java.awt.Image getIcon(int iconKind) {
    if (iconKind == BeanInfo.ICON_COLOR_16x16) {
      java.awt.Image img = loadImage("ImageEnhancerIcon16.gif");
      return img;
    }
    if (iconKind == BeanInfo.ICON_COLOR_32x32) {
      java.awt.Image img = loadImage("ImageEnhancerIcon32.gif");
      return img;
    }
    return null;
  }
```

CONTINUES

14

14

LISTING 14.10   The Complete Source Code for the ImageEnhancerBeanInfo Class (Continued)

```java
// Explicit declare the properties
public PropertyDescriptor[] getPropertyDescriptors() {
  try {
    PropertyDescriptor
      // Inherited properties
      foreground = new
        PropertyDescriptor("foreground", ImageEnhancer.class),
      background = new PropertyDescriptor("background",
        ImageEnhancer.class),
      font = new PropertyDescriptor("font", ImageEnhancer.class),
      name = new PropertyDescriptor("name", ImageEnhancer.class),
      // New properties
      imageName = new PropertyDescriptor("imageName",
        ImageEnhancer.class),
      red = new PropertyDescriptor("red", ImageEnhancer.class),
      green = new PropertyDescriptor("green", ImageEnhancer.class),
      blue = new PropertyDescriptor("blue", ImageEnhancer.class),
      alpha = new PropertyDescriptor("alpha", ImageEnhancer.class),
      brightness = new PropertyDescriptor("brightness",
        ImageEnhancer.class);

    // Hide the foreground, background, and font properties
    foreground.setHidden(true);
    background.setHidden(true);
    font.setHidden(true);

    PropertyDescriptor[] pd = { foreground, background, font, name,
      imageName, red, green, blue, alpha, brightness};
    return pd;
  }
  catch (IntrospectionException e) {
    throw new Error(e.toString());
  }
}
}
```

the Bean. Listing 14.10 contains the complete source code for the ImageEnhancerBeanInfo class.

The ImageEnhancerBeanInfo class is similar in some ways to the Bean information classes associated with other Beans you've developed in the book. The first method it defines is getIcon(), which provides an iconic representation of the bean. Two icons are provided by the Bean information class that provide support for different resolutions. Figure 14.2 shows what the icons for the Image Enhancer Bean look like.

Just in case you're having trouble figuring out what the icons are, I'll clue you in by noting that they are scaled-down versions of the default Pear.gif image. This makes for kind of a neat touch since the Bean will always appear displaying the Pear.gif image upon creation.

The ImageEnhancerBeanInfo class also has a getPropertyDescriptors() method, which explicitly specifies the properties exposed by the Bean. The purpose of implementing this method is to exclude all but one of the inherited properties from the Bean. This is necessary because the inherited foreground, background, and font properties have no usage in the Image Enhancer Bean. Notice that the remaining inherited property, name, is not hidden, so it remains exposed.

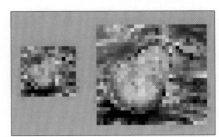

FIGURE 14.2

The Bean information icons for the Image Enhancer Bean

In addition to the ImageEnhancerBeanInfo class, the Image Enhancer Bean also needs a manifest file so that it can be built into a distributable JAR file. A manifest file is required so that the Bean class is identified in the JAR file. The code for the Image Enhancer Bean's manifest file, ImageEnhancer.mf, is as follows:

```
Manifest-Version: 1.0

Name: HTPJB/Chap14/ImageEnhancer/ImageEnhancer.class
Java-Bean: True
```

The manifest file for the Image Enhancer Bean is very similar to manifest files you've seen for other Beans in the book. This manifest file must be used when you're building a JAR file containing the Bean. For information on how to build a JAR file for the Bean, please refer to Chapter 4, "Packaging Beans with JAR Files."

ON THE CD: *The complete source code and related resources for the Image Enhancer Bean, including a JAR file for the Bean, are located on the CD-ROM included with this book.*

At this point, the Image Enhancer Bean is still missing one major component: the image filter classes. All of the image filters used by the Bean are derived from `RGBImageFilter`, which enables you to filter images through a single method, `filterRGB()`. You'll see that building a custom image filter is as easy as deriving your class from `RGBImageFilter` and implementing the `filterRGB` method. Let's give it a try!

The Color Image Filter

Possibly the simplest image filter imaginable is one that filters out the individual color components (red, green, and blue) of an image. The `ColorFilter` class does exactly that, as Listing 14.11 shows. The `ColorFilter` class is derived from `RGBImageFilter` and contains three Boolean member variables that determine which colors are to be filtered out of the image. These member variables are set by the parameters passed into the constructor. The member variable inherited from `RGBImageFilter`, `canFilterIndexColorModel`, is set to `true` to indicate that the color map entries can be filtered using `filterRGB()` if the incoming image is using an index color model.

LISTING 14.11   The ColorFilter Class

```java
class ColorFilter extends RGBImageFilter {
  boolean red, green, blue;

  public ColorFilter(boolean r, boolean g, boolean b) {
    red = r;
    green = g;
    blue = b;
    canFilterIndexColorModel = true;
  }

  public int filterRGB(int x, int y, int rgb) {
    // Filter the colors
    int r = red ? 0 : ((rgb >> 16) & 0xff);
    int g = green ? 0 : ((rgb >> 8) & 0xff);
    int b = blue ? 0 : ((rgb >> 0) & 0xff);

    // Return the result
    return (rgb & 0xff000000) | (r << 16) | (g << 8) | (b << 0);
  }
}
```

> **NOTE:** *An index color model relies on indexes into a fixed palette of colors to represent image colors. Index color models are more efficient than their counterparts, direct color models, but they rely on a fixed number of available colors.*

The `ColorFilter` class implements only one method, `filterRGB()`, which is an abstract method defined in `RGBImageFilter` that must be overridden in derived classes. The `FilterRGB()` method takes three parameters: the X and Y positions of the pixel within the image and the 32-bit integer color value. The only parameter you are concerned with is the color value, `rgb`.

The default RGB color model places the red, green, and blue color components in the lower 24 bits of the 32-bit color value. This makes it relatively easy to extract each color by shifting out of the `rgb` parameter. These individual components are stored in the local variables `r`, `g`, and `b`. Notice, however, that each color component is shifted only if it is not being filtered. For filtered colors, the color component is set to zero. The new color components are then shifted back into a 32-bit color value and returned from `filterRGB`. Notice that the alpha component of the color value is not altered, since the filter is only interested in the red, green, and blue components. The `0xff000000` mask takes care of this, because the alpha component resides in the upper byte of the color value.

That finishes up the color image filter. I think you'll agree that it wasn't too terribly complicated. It's a good thing because you have two more filters to go!

The Alpha Image Filter

The alpha component of a pixel specifies the transparency or opaqueness of the pixel. By altering the alpha values for an entire image, you can make it appear to fade in and out. This works because the alpha values range from totally transparent (invisible) to totally opaque (visible).

The `AlphaFilter` class filters the alpha components of an image according to the alpha level you supply in its constructor. Listing 14.12 displays the source code for the `AlphaFilter` class. The `AlphaFilter` class contains a single member variable, `alphaLevel`, that keeps up with the alpha level to be applied to the image. This member variable is initialized in the constructor, as is the `canFilterIndexModel` member variable.

Like the `ColorFilter` class, `AlphaFilter` implements only one method: the `filterRGB()` method. The `filterRGB()` method first extracts the alpha component of the pixel by shifting it into a local variable, `alpha`. This value is then scaled according to the `alphaLevel` member variable initialized in the constructor. The purpose of the scaling is to alter the alpha value based on its current value. If you were to just set the alpha component to the alpha level, you wouldn't be taking into account the original alpha component value.

LISTING 14.12   The AlphaFilter Class

```
class AlphaFilter extends RGBImageFilter {
  int alphaLevel;

  public AlphaFilter(int alpha) {
    alphaLevel = alpha;
    canFilterIndexColorModel = true;
  }

  public int filterRGB(int x, int y, int rgb) {
    // Adjust and return the alpha value
    return ((rgb & 0x00ffffff) | (alphaLevel << 24));
  }
}
```

The new alpha component is shifted back into the pixel color value and the result returned from filterRGB(). Notice that the red, green, and blue components are preserved by using the 0x00ffffff mask.

A Brightness Image Filter

The first two image filters you just developed were fairly simple. This last one is a little more complex, but it acts as a more interesting filter. The BrightnessFilter class implements an image filter that brightens or darkens an image based on a brightness percentage you provide in the constructor. Listing 14.13 shows the source code for the BrightnessFilter class.

The BrightnessFilter class contains one member variable, brightness, that keeps track of the percentage by which the brightness of the image is to be altered. This member variable is set via the constructor, along with the canFilterIndexModel member variable. The brightness member variable can contain values in the range -100 to 100. A value of -100 means the image is darkened by 100 percent, and a value of 100 means the image is brightened by 100 percent. A value of 0 doesn't alter the brightness of the image at all.

It should come as no surprise by now that filterRGB() is the only other method implemented by BrightnessFilter. In filterRGB(), the individual color components are first extracted into the local variables r, g, and b. The brightness effects are then calculated based on the brightness member variable. The new color components are then checked against the 0 and 255 boundaries and modified if necessary.

LISTING 14.13   The BrightnessFilter Class

```
class BrightnessFilter extends RGBImageFilter {
  int brightness;

  public BrightnessFilter(int b) {
    brightness = b;
    canFilterIndexColorModel = true;
  }

  public int filterRGB(int x, int y, int rgb) {
    // Get the individual colors
    int r = (rgb >> 16) & 0xff;
    int g = (rgb >> 8) & 0xff;
    int b = (rgb >> 0) & 0xff;

    // Calculate the brightness
    r += (brightness * r) / 100;
    g += (brightness * g) / 100;
    b += (brightness * b) / 100;

    // Check the boundaries
    r = Math.min(Math.max(0, r), 255);
    g = Math.min(Math.max(0, g), 255);
    b = Math.min(Math.max(0, b), 255);

    // Return the result
    return (rgb & 0xff000000) | (r << 16) | (g << 8) | (b << 0);
  }
}
```

Finally, the new color components are shifted back into the pixel color value and returned from filterRGB. Hey, it's not all that complicated after all! That wraps up the image filters required for the Image Enhancer Bean. After all this hard work, you're probably ready to see it in action. Read on!

14

Using the Image Enhancer Bean

The Image Enhancer Bean is no doubt the most involved Bean you've developed yet, which means the anticipation to see it work is probably a little higher. Well, it's finally time to reap the benefits of your efforts by giving the Bean a test drive. You're going to use the BeanBox test container to test the Image Enhancer Bean, much as you have tested Beans in previous chapters. If you recall, the first step in using a Bean in a visual environment such as the BeanBox is to add the Bean to the environment. You add the Image Enhancer Bean to the BeanBox by copying the JAR file for the Bean to the jars directory beneath your BDK installation. When executed, the BeanBox automatically looks in the jars directory to see if any new Beans need to be added.

Once you've copied the JAR file for the Image Enhancer Bean to the jars directory, run the BeanBox by executing the run.bat batch file provided with the BeanBox. The BeanBox should appear at this point with your Image Enhancer Bean added to the ToolBox. Figure 14.3 shows what the ToolBox looks like with the Bean added.

The figure shows that the last Bean in the ToolBox is the Image Enhancer Bean, which is represented by the 16-by-16 icon you specified in the Bean information class. You should also see the Image Button, Needle Gauge, and Clock Beans you added in previous chapters. Go ahead and try adding an Image Enhancer Bean to the BeanBox by clicking on it in the ToolBox and then clicking in the main container window. Figure 14.4 shows the main container window with the newly added Image Enhancer Bean.

Now that the Bean is in the container window, you can check out the properties for it. Figure 14.5 shows the PropertySheet window for the Image Enhancer Bean. The PropertySheet window shows all the properties for the Bean, including the inherited name property and the image name, red, green, blue, alpha, and brightness properties you defined. All of these properties can be edited using the PropertySheet window. Try out the color filter by setting the red property to false. This filters out the color red from the image, as Figure 14.6 shows.

Now try also filtering out blue by setting the blue property to false. Figure 14.7 shows what the image looks like with the colors red and blue filtered out.

Now take the alpha filter for a spin by setting the alpha property to 3. Keep in mind that the color filter is already in action, so the alpha filter is acting in addition to it. Figure 14.8 shows what the image looks like with the alpha value set to 3.

FIGURE 14.3

The BeanBox ToolBox window with the Image Enhancer Bean added

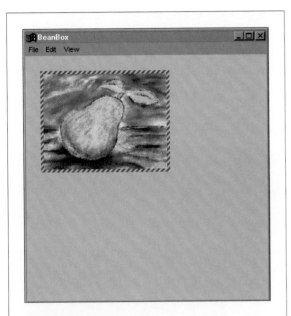

FIGURE 14.4

The BeanBox main container window with an Image Enhancer Bean added

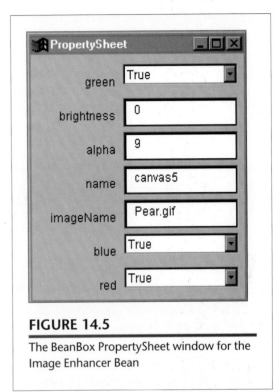

FIGURE 14.5

The BeanBox PropertySheet window for the Image Enhancer Bean

FIGURE 14.6

The Image Enhancer Bean with the color red filtered out

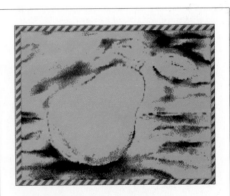

FIGURE 14.7

The Image Enhancer Bean with the colors red and blue filtered out

14

Notice how the image looks more transparent with the alpha filter at work on it. Let's move on to the brightness filter. To test the brightness filter, reset the Bean's properties to their default values and then set the brightness property to 50. Figure 14.9 shows what the image looks like with the brightness value set to 50.

To see how different brightness values impact the filtering of the image, try setting the brightness value to -40. Figure 14.10 shows what the image looks like with the brightness value set to -40.

That concludes the testing of the Image Enhancer Bean. By all means feel free to try out different combinations of property settings to see how the filters interact. I think you'll agree that this is a pretty neat Bean to tinker with.

Summary

This chapter introduced you to perhaps the most interesting Bean you've seen yet, an Image Enhancer Bean. In designing and developing the Image Enhancer Bean, you learned a great deal about the image filtering support provided by the Java AWT. This image filtering support makes the otherwise complex task of processing individual image pixels very straightforward and easy to carry out. The Image Enhancer Bean hopefully illustrates how you can easily leverage existing Java classes to create powerful Beans.

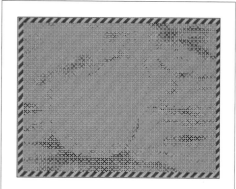

FIGURE 14.8

The Image Enhancer Bean with the colors red and blue filtered out and the alpha value set to 3

FIGURE 14.9

The Image Enhancer Bean with the brightness value set to 50

FIGURE 14.10

The Image Enhancer Bean with the brightness value set to -40

The chapter began with a quick primer on image filters, then moved on to the design of the Image Enhancer Bean. With a solid design in mind (and on paper), you shifted gears and developed the code for the Bean. Although a decent amount of coding work was required, I think you'll agree that the end result is pretty impressive. You got to enjoy the end result for yourself toward the end of the chapter by using the Bean in the BeanBox.

14

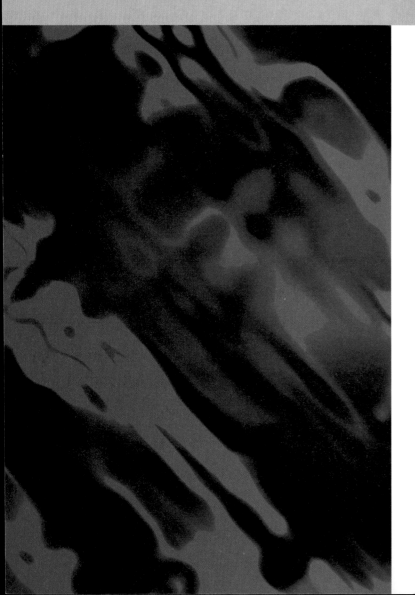

Chapter 15

A Timer Bean

▶ **Designing the Timer Bean**

▶ **Constructing the Timer Bean**

▶ **Using the Timer Bean**

In this chapter, you'll learn how to design and build an invisible Timer Bean that fires events at regularly timed intervals. You'll start off the chapter by performing a preliminary design of the Bean and then progress to developing the actual code for the Bean. You'll finish up the chapter by testing the Bean in the BeanBox test container, which you're probably starting to get a little sick of.

The Timer Bean you'll develop in this chapter is different from all the other Beans you've seen in the book because it has no graphical representation. The purpose of the Bean is to fire periodic events, so there really is no need for it to have an appearance. This type of Bean is known as an *invisible Bean* and often finds interesting uses alongside more traditional graphical (visible) Beans. The good news is that invisible Beans typically require much less overhead, since there is no drawing going on.

In this chapter, you'll learn

▶ How to design a Timer Bean

▶ How to construct a Timer Bean

▶ How to use a Timer Bean

Designing the Timer Bean

As you may have guessed, the development of the Timer Bean begins with its conceptual design. The Timer Bean is meant to function as a periodic trigger, generating events at regular intervals that can be processed by other interested Beans or applications. A good application of the Timer Bean is in providing the timing for a series of animated images. For example, you could wire the Timer Bean to an image Bean that changes the displayed image each time it receives an event from the Timer. Invisible Beans are very useful in roles like this where they control other Beans behind the scenes. Hey, that rhymes!

Since the Timer is basically just an event generator, it doesn't require any of the graphical overhead you've implemented in the other Beans throughout the book. For example, the Timer Bean will derive directly from the `Object` class instead of the `Canvas` or `Component` class, which means that it has no `update()` or `paint()` method. You may be wondering what happens to the Bean in a development setting, since it has no graphical appearance. There are no set rules regarding how visual development tools are to represent invisible Beans, but the BDK BeanBox provides a good example of how tools might solve the problem. The BeanBox displays a rectangle containing the name of an invisible Bean, which is sufficient for selecting the Bean and accessing its properties. Keep in mind that this only applies at design time; at runtime, invisible Beans are completely hidden from view.

15

Getting back to the design of the Timer Bean, the sole function of the Bean is to generate periodic events that can be used by other Beans or applications. Although this is the typical usage scenario for the Bean, there may be times when an application or Bean requires only one timed event. For example, an Alarm Bean might use the Timer Bean to trigger a single event after a given period of time has elapsed. To support this usage, it is necessary to add a one-shot mode to the Bean. When the Bean is in one-shot mode, it waits a specified period of time and fires a single event.

That pretty well sums up the basic design of the Timer Bean. You're probably thinking the Bean sounds pretty simple, and in a lot of ways you're right. It only seems fair that you end this five-chapter Bean-development tour de force with an easier Bean.

Properties

The properties for the Timer Bean are closely tied to the Bean's functionality as spelled out in the Bean's initial design. Since the Bean derives directly from the Object class, it doesn't inherit any properties. Contrast this with graphical Beans, which inherit a variety of properties from their parent Component class. In the absence of inherited properties, the Timer Bean still requires a few properties of its own: name, period, and one-shot.

The first property, name, is kind of strange in that it doesn't directly relate to the Bean's specific functionality. I'm referring to the name property, which represents the name of the Bean. Graphical Beans automatically inherit the name property from the Component class, but invisible Beans are responsible for providing it themselves. Why is it so important? Well, the name property serves as a unique identifier for instances of the Bean, meaning that if you are using two Timer Beans, they can easily be distinguished and referenced through their name properties. For example, one Timer Bean could be named minuteTimer, while another could be named dayCounter. You would reference the different Beans in code using these names.

The next property for the Timer Bean, and undoubtedly the most important, is the period property. The period property represents the period of time that elapses between timer events, in milliseconds. If you have an application that needs to be notified every second, you'll use the Timer Bean with the period property set to 1000 (milliseconds). In one-shot mode, the period property specifies the amount of time that elapses before a single event is triggered.

TIP: *The Timer Bean could be used as the timing mechanism in an application displaying an animation. In this type of application, the period property would determine the rate of animation, which is also referred to as the frame rate. The frame rate specifies how many frames of animation are displayed in succession per second. A minimal frame rate for smooth animation is 12 frames per second, which results in a timing period of 83 milliseconds (½ of a second).*

Speaking of one-shot mode, this brings us to the last property required of the Timer Bean: the one-shot property. The one-shot property is a Boolean property that determines whether the Bean is in one-shot mode or not.

To summarize, the following properties are required for the Timer Bean:

▶ Name

▶ Period

▶ One-shot (on/off)

Methods

With the properties laid out, you're ready to determine the public methods required of the Bean. The accessor methods are a good place to start, especially since they are so easy to define. All three properties for the Timer Bean are readable and writeable, so you will need a pair of accessor methods for each of them. That's all you need to know about the accessor methods at this point; you'll get into the details of them a little later in the chapter.

Other than event processing methods, which you'll learn about in just a moment, there is only one other public method required in the Timer Bean: the `run()` method. You relied on the `run()` method in building the Clock Bean back in Chapter 13. You are actually using the `run()` method for a similar purpose in the Timer Bean. The `run()` method acts as a thread's central path of execution, meaning that it is the ideal place for a periodic trigger as required by the Timer Bean. You'll learn the details of how this works a little later in the chapter when you get into the code for the Bean.

To summarize, the public methods required of the Timer Bean are

▶ Name property getter/setter methods

▶ Period property getter/setter methods

▶ One-shot property getter/setter methods

▶ Overridden `run()` method

Events

The last design aspect of the Timer Bean you need to address is events. Since the Bean acts as a periodic event generator, it must be capable of firing action events. This is what allows the Bean to be wired to other Beans or applications in order to trigger events after a given period of time has elapsed. Since the event fired in this case is an action event, part of supporting it is providing event listener registration methods. A pair of these methods is all that is required to support the addition and removal of action event listeners.

As you learned back in Chapter 11 while developing the Image Button Bean, Beans that generate events are required to support some type of mechanism by which events are passed to all the registered event listeners. This mechanism is handled in the Timer Bean by a single event processing method that dispatches the event to each listener.

To summarize, the following are the event-related methods required of the Timer Bean:

▶ Action event listener registration methods

▶ Action event processing method for firing events

Constructing the Timer Bean

Now that the basic design is finished, you're no doubt ready to move on to the fun stuff. So let's go ahead and jump into the details of coding the Timer Bean!

To make the code for the Bean easier to understand and follow, most of it is presented in the form of individual member declarations or method listings. As you read through this section, you may want to check out the complete source code for the Bean, which is included on the CD-ROM that accompanies this book. The main code for the Timer Bean is in the Timer class, which appears on the CD-ROM in the file Timer.java.

ON THE CD: *The complete code for the Timer Bean is included on the CD-ROM.*

Properties and Member Variables

As with the design for the Bean, the best place to start with the Bean's code is defining the properties. The following are the member variable properties for the Bean:

```
private String  name;
private int     period;  // in milliseconds
private boolean oneShot;
```

The first member variable, `name`, represents the unique string name of the Bean. Although a default name is generated whenever a Bean is created, it is expected that users will provide a meaningful name of their own. The next member, `period`, represents the amount of time (in milliseconds) that elapses between timer events. The last member, `oneShot`, determines whether the Bean is in one-shot mode or not. One-shot mode means that the Bean fires only one event after the time period specified by `period` elapses.

Since these properties are built-in Java types, their property editors are already provided by JavaBeans. In addition to these public properties, the Timer Bean requires a few private member variables for internal use:

```
private transient static int     numTimers = 0;
private transient Thread          timerThread;
private transient ActionListener actionListener = null;
```

The first member, `numTimers`, is a static member that keeps up with how many timers have been created in a given session. The only reason for keeping up with this number is to generate unique Timer Bean names for each Bean created. You'll see the specifics of how this is done a little later in the chapter. The `timerThread` member represents the thread used to control the timing of the events generated by the Bean. This member is very critical to the proper functioning of the Bean because it is completely responsible for providing the timing mechanism. The last member, `actionListener`, is an `ActionListener` interface that is used to keep track of action event listeners. This member is used by the action event processing method to fire events to each listener whenever the specified period of time has elapsed.

These three member variables are all defined as being transient, meaning that they aren't to be stored away as part of the Timer Bean's internal state.

NOTE: *Any member variables that hold temporary values should be defined as transient so they aren't stored away as part of a Bean's persistent state. Typically, transient member variables are easily initialized to suitable values when a Bean is created, regardless of whether other non-transient member variables are being persistently restored.*

Constructors

The property member variables are initialized in the Bean's constructors. The Timer Bean provides two constructors: a default constructor and a detailed constructor that takes all of the properties as arguments. Listing 15.1 shows the code for both of these constructors.

15

LISTING 15.1 The Constructors for the Timer Bean

```
// Constructors
public Timer() {
  this(new String("timer" + numTimers++), 1000, false);
}

public Timer(String n, int p, boolean os) {
  // Allow the superclass constructor to do its thing
  super();

  // Set properties
  name = n;
  period = p;
  oneShot = os;

  // Create the clock thread
  timerThread = new Thread(this, "Timer");
  timerThread.start();
}
```

The first constructor takes no arguments and simply calls the second constructor with default property values. One of these default property values is the name of the Bean, which is created by appending the current Timer Bean count (numTimers) to the string "timer". This results in Bean names of timer0, timer1, and so on, which are guaranteed to be unique.

The second constructor does the work of initializing the Bean and setting all the properties to the appropriate values, as well as handling the creation and starting of the timing thread. The Thread object is created using the new operator, and then the start() method is called on it to get things going. The start() method starts the thread and directly results in the execution of the overridden run() method defined in the Bean. You'll learn about the run() method and how it controls the Bean's timing in just a moment.

Accessor Methods

If you recall from the Timer Bean's design, a pair of accessor methods is required for each property in the Bean. The first property defined in the Bean is the name property, whose accessor method pair you can see in Listing 15.2. These accessor methods simply get and set the underlying member variable (name) representing the property.

LISTING 15.2 The Accessor Methods for the Name Property

```
public String getName() {
  return name;
}

public void setName(String n) {
  name = n;
}
```

Let's move on to the next property; the code for the period property's accessor methods appears in Listing 15.3. The getter method for the period property is pretty tame, but the setter method is a little more interesting. After setting the period member variable to the new property value, the setPeriod() method interrupts the thread with a call to the thread's interrupt() method if there is already a thread in progress. This is necessary so that the timing for the next event is changed to the new period. Otherwise, the thread would reflect its current state with time elapsed and probably not wait long enough for the next event.

LISTING 15.3 The Accessor Methods for the Period Property

```
public int getPeriod() {
  return period;
}

public void setPeriod(int p) {
  period = p;
  if (timerThread != null)
    timerThread.interrupt();
}
```

The last accessor method set for the Bean belongs to the one-shot property. The code for these accessor methods is shown in Listing 15.4. Like the accessor methods for the name property, these are about as simple as accessor methods get. I'll spare you the boredom of a detailed explanation!

15

LISTING 15.4 The Accessor Methods for the One-Shot Property

```
public boolean isOneShot() {
  return oneShot;
}


public void setOneShot(boolean os) {
  oneShot = os;
}
```

Public Methods

In addition to accessor methods, the Timer Bean requires only one other public method: run(). The run() method is responsible for triggering events once every period, or once at the end of one period if the Bean is in one-shot mode. The run() method is called automatically by the Java runtime system once the timer thread has been created and started. Listing 15.5 shows the code for the run() method.

LISTING 15.5 The run() Method

```
public void run() {
  while (timerThread != null) {
    // Sleep for the period
    try {
      timerThread.sleep(period);
    } catch (InterruptedException e) {
      // Restart the loop
      continue;
    }

    // Fire an action event
    fireActionEvent();

    if (oneShot)
      break;
  }
}
```

This run() method is similar in a lot of ways to the run() method in the Clock Bean you developed earlier in the book. The run() method consists of a while loop that is always executing as long as the timerThread member variable isn't null. Each time through the loop the fireActionEvent() method, which you'll learn about in a moment, is called to fire an event. The periodic interval is established by the call to the sleep() method, which causes the thread to cease execution for a specified period of time. In other words, the thread pauses for an amount of time determined by period, then it fires an event and starts all over. Notice that at the end of the loop the oneShot member is checked to see if the loop should continue. If the Bean is in one-shot mode, the loop breaks out so that no more events are fired.

The call to the sleep() method is encased within a try-catch clause that checks for InterruptedExceptions. An InterruptedException is thrown if the thread is interrupted by another thread while sleeping. If this occurs, the Timer Bean's thread simply continues sleeping.

Event Registration Methods

The event registration methods in the Timer Bean are used to allow the addition and removal of listeners for the Bean's action events. The code for these methods appears in Listing 15.6. They use the AWTEventMulticaster class to add and remove action listeners from the actionListener member variable, just as they did in the Image Button Bean in Chapter 11. If you recall from developing the Image Button Bean, the actionListener member variable is used to represent a chain of multicast event listeners. This functionality is handled entirely by the AWTEventMulticaster class, which takes on the task of managing the list of listeners.

LISTING 15.6 The Event Registration Methods for the Timer Bean

```
public synchronized void addActionListener(ActionListener l) {
  actionListener = AWTEventMulticaster.add(actionListener, l);
}

public synchronized void removeActionListener(ActionListener l) {
  actionListener = AWTEventMulticaster.remove(actionListener, l);
}
```

15

Event Processing Methods

The Timer Bean uses a single event processing method to facilitate the firing of action events: processActionEvent(). The processActionEvent() method is used to dispatch action events to all of the registered action event listeners. The following is the code for this method:

```
protected void processActionEvent(ActionEvent e) {
  // Deliver the event to all registered action event listeners
  if (actionListener != null)
    actionListener.actionPerformed(e);
}
```

The processActionEvent() method simply calls the actionPerformed() method on the actionListener member variable, which results in the event being dispatched to all the registered listeners. The actionPerformed() method is the only method defined in the ActionListener interface, and is typically called any time an action occurs in an event source such as a Bean. The Timer Bean defines an action as the elapsing of a period of time, but an action clearly can mean other things in other Beans, as it did in the Image Button Bean in Chapter 11.

Support Methods

The Timer Bean requires a single private support method, fireActionEvent(), which helps make firing action events a little easier. This is the source code for the fireActionEvent() method:

```
private void fireActionEvent() {
  processActionEvent(new ActionEvent(this,
    ActionEvent.ACTION_PERFORMED, null));
}
```

This method is very simple: it consists only of a call to the processActionEvent() method. The purpose of providing the fireActionEvent() method is to clean up the task of firing an action event by hiding the creation of the ActionEvent object passed into processActionEvent(). This isn't a necessity, but it does make the code in run() that calls fireActionEvent() a little cleaner.

Additional Overhead

You now have the source code for the Timer Bean itself completed, but I'm sure you realize that there is still some unfinished business. First off, you need to define a TimerBeanInfo class so the Bean has graphical icons associated with it for use in application builder tools. Listing 15.7 shows the complete source code for the TimerBeanInfo class.

LISTING 15.7 The TimerBeanInfo Class

```java
// TimerBeanInfo Class
// TimerBeanInfo.java

package HTPJB.Chap15.Timer;

// Imports
import java.beans.*;

public class TimerBeanInfo extends SimpleBeanInfo {
  // Get the appropriate icon
  public java.awt.Image getIcon(int iconKind) {
    if (iconKind == BeanInfo.ICON_COLOR_16x16) {
      java.awt.Image img = loadImage("TimerIcon16.gif");
      return img;
    }
    if (iconKind == BeanInfo.ICON_COLOR_32x32) {
      java.awt.Image img = loadImage("TimerIcon32.gif");
      return img;
    }
    return null;
  }
}
```

The TimerBeanInfo class is very similar to the Bean information classes associated with other Beans you've developed in the book. The only method it defines is getIcon(), which provides an iconic representation of the Bean. Two icons are provided by the Bean information class that provide support for different resolutions. Figure 15.1 shows what the icons for the Timer Bean look like.

In addition to the TimerBeanInfo class, the Timer Bean also needs a manifest file so that it can be built into a distributable JAR file. The code for the Timer Bean's manifest file, Timer.mf, is as follows:

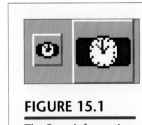

FIGURE 15.1

The Bean information icons for the Timer Bean

```
Manifest-Version: 1.0

Name: HTPJB/Chap15/Timer/Timer.class
Java-Bean: True
```

The manifest file for the Timer Bean is very similar to manifest files you've seen for other Beans in the book. This manifest file is required when you're building a JAR file containing the Bean. For information on how to build a JAR file for the Bean, please refer to Chapter 4, "Packaging Beans with JAR Files." Don't forget that the complete source code and related resources for the Timer Bean, including a JAR file for the Bean, are located on the CD-ROM accompanying this book. That finishes up the Timer Bean!

Using the Timer Bean

Now that you've put in the time to develop the Timer Bean, I'm sure you're ready to see it in action. You're going to use the BeanBox test container to test the Timer Bean, much as you have tested Beans in previous chapters. If you recall, the first step in using a Bean in the BeanBox is to add the Bean to the BeanBox environment by copying the JAR file for the Bean to the jars directory beneath your BDK installation. When executed, the BeanBox automatically looks in the jars directory to see if any new Beans need to be added.

Once you've copied the JAR file for the Timer Bean to the jars directory, run the BeanBox by executing the `run.bat` batch file provided with the BeanBox. The BeanBox should then appear with your Timer Bean added to the ToolBox. Figure 15.2 shows what the ToolBox looks like with the Bean added.

The figure shows that the last Bean in the ToolBox is the Timer Bean, which is represented by the 16-by-16 icon you specified in the Bean information class. You should also see the other Beans you added in previous chapters. Go ahead and try adding a Timer Bean to the BeanBox by clicking on it in the ToolBox and then clicking in the main container window. Figure 15.3 shows the main container window with the newly added Timer Bean.

Remember that you didn't add any capabilities to the Timer Bean for it to draw itself, so the BeanBox is displaying its own representation of the invisible Bean. With the Bean in the container window, you can now check out its properties. Figure 15.4 shows the PropertySheet window for the Timer Bean. The PropertySheet window shows all the properties for the Bean, which consist of the name, period, and one-shot properties you defined. All of these properties can be edited using the PropertySheet window. Notice that the name property is initially set to `timer0`. Try adding another Timer Bean to make sure that it takes on a unique name of its own.

FIGURE 15.2

The BeanBox ToolBox window with the Timer Bean added

Let's test out the timing functionality of the Timer Bean by wiring a couple of them to the Needle Gauge Bean from Chapter 12. Since you have already added two Timer Beans to the BeanBox, all you need to do is add a Needle Gauge Bean. Figure 15.5 shows the two Timer Beans with the Needle Gauge Bean.

Set the high value for the needle gauge to 100, then set the number of divisions to 25. Now click on the first Timer Bean to select it and then select the actionPerformed event from the Events menu under the main Edit menu. Figure 15.6 shows what the selection of this event looks like in the main container window.

Now click on the Needle Gauge Bean to select it as the event's recipient. You will be presented with an Event Target dialog box listing the methods that can be called on the Bean. Select the incValue() method and click the OK button. Figure 15.7 shows the Event Target dialog box for the Needle Gauge Bean.

You will be presented with a window stating that the event connection is being carried out. Once this window goes away, the first timer will be successfully wired to the needle gauge and you will see the gauge start incrementing once every second. This is due to the fact that the Timer Bean's default period is 1000 milliseconds, which is one second. Now wire the second timer to the needle gauge, but this time connect the event to the decValue() method. Once you've completed this, you'll see the two timers dueling over the needle gauge as they try to increment and decrement the value once every second.

Here is where the real fun begins: Try changing the periods for each of the timers to see how they impact the needle gauge. For example, try setting one of them slightly lower than the other and notice that the needle gauge will start moving in one direction.

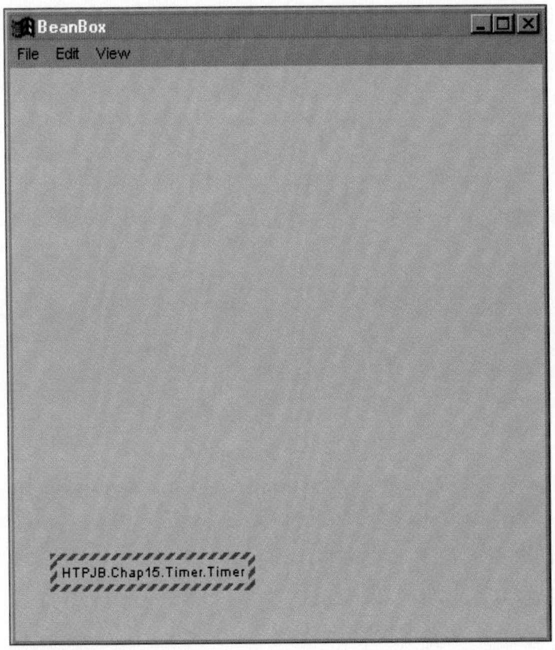

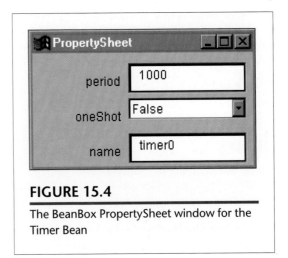

FIGURE 15.3

The BeanBox main container window with a Timer Bean added

15

FIGURE 15.4

The BeanBox PropertySheet window for the Timer Bean

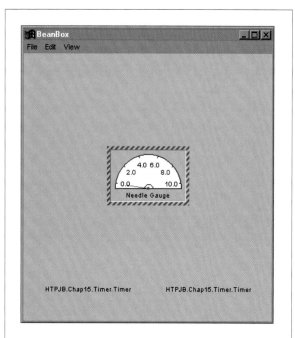

FIGURE 15.5

The BeanBox main container window with two Timer Beans and a Needle Gauge Bean added

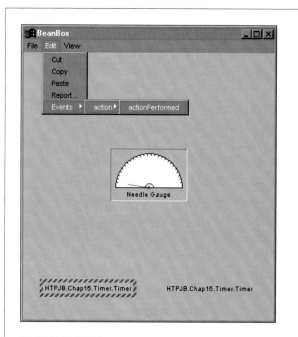

FIGURE 15.6

The BeanBox main container window while you select an `actionPerformed` event for a Timer Bean

This is due to the fact that one timer is firing events faster than the other, which results in the needle gauge's value changing more often in one direction. Be sure and spend some time trying out the Timer Bean because you may find it useful in some of your own projects.

Summary

This chapter focused on the design and development of yet another Bean, but this Bean was a little different than others you'd seen previously because it had no visible representation. The Bean you built in this chapter is an invisible Bean that fires events at regular intervals. Although invisible Beans aren't as popular or widely applicable as graphical Beans, the Timer

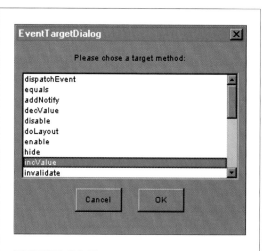

FIGURE 15.7

The Event Target dialog box for the Needle Gauge Bean.

Bean in particular has a wide range of uses in applications that require periodic timing.

You started off the chapter by deciding exactly how the Bean is supposed to work from a user's perspective. With a preliminary design in hand, you were then able to move on to creating the actual code for the Bean. You saw what a small amount of code, relatively speaking, it took to bring the Timer Bean to life. You finished up the chapter by trying out the Bean in the BeanBox.

15

Part *4*

Putting Beans to Work

Chapter 16: Distributed Computing with Beans, RMI, and CORBA

Chapter 17: Bridging JavaBeans to ActiveX

Chapter 18: Into the Future with JavaBeans

Chapter *16*

Distributed Computing with Beans, RMI, and CORBA

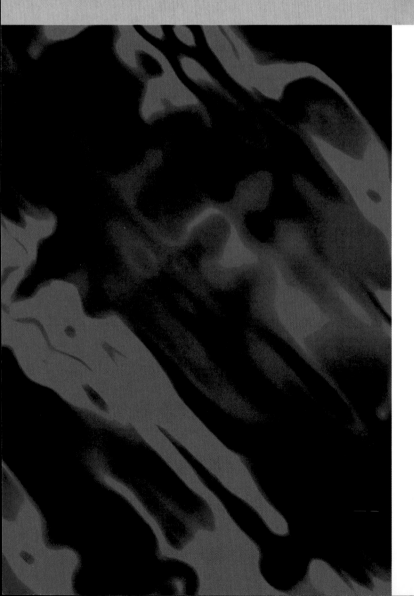

▶ **Beans in a Networked Environment—An Overview**

▶ **Getting Started**

▶ **Introduction to Remote Method Invocation**

▶ **Introduction to the Java IDL**

This chapter will introduce you to distributed-object computing using techniques such as Java remote method invocation and Java CORBA, thus providing a good foundation for developing distributed Java software. By following the code examples, you will build two distributed applications harnessing the full power of these technologies.

The JavaBeans architecture is well suited to the world of distributed computing and the era of the World Wide Web. The designers of Java have ensured that developers and Webmasters have at their disposal all the tools necessary to create fully distributed applications and applets which operate seamlessly across the network in a heterogeneous operating system environment. To this end, Javasoft has provided two primary network access mechanisms which are available to JavaBeans developers on all Java Virtual Machines:

▶ Java RMI (remote method invocation)

▶ Java IDL (interface definition language)

This chapter will explain the implementation of Java RMI and Java IDL in two separate applications, using a simple applet in each case. Both topics are fairly large and it would require more than a single chapter to cover all the important aspects of these two packages. You are encouraged to explore the potential of these tools by reading the documentation accompanying their release and other related sites on the Internet.

16

Beans in a Networked Environment—An Overview

Java *RMI*, or *remote method invocation*, allows the programmer to create distributed applications in which methods can be invoked either on the local machine or on remote hosts. In fact, RMI is analogous to remote procedure calls (RPCs) which are widely used in distributed computing today. Communication is restricted to taking place between two Java Virtual Machines only. Basically, the Java client program invokes the method on the remote server object either by looking up the name of the remote object in a bootstrap naming service or by receiving a reference to the remote object via an argument or return value.

The Common Object Request Broker Architecture (CORBA) is a standard architecture designed by the Object Management Group which allows developers to design interoperable software objects for heterogeneous computing networks. Irrespective of the language used to write the program, CORBA allows the exchange of object and method calls across the network by defining a common interface definition language (IDL). In turn, the Java IDL package provides a mapping whereby specifications written in IDL are mapped to interfaces using the Java-language equivalent. Developers will then typically use the Java stubs and skeletons generated by the IDL compiler to code both client and server sides. However, it is possible to mix components so that a Java client could interact with a server object written in C++ (or another language, for that matter).

Getting Started

Before we get started with explaining the details of RMI, we will develop a simple Bean component called MyBean which will be referred to throughout the chapter. By now the reader should be quite comfortable with developing Bean components and ready to use them in a network-based environment. Basically the Bean consists of Java AWT components, namely a Panel containing a Button, two TextFields, and two Labels. The Button is registered as a listener for the `java.awt.event.ActionListener` interface.

```
ConvButton.addActionListener(this);
```

Once the `ACTION_EVENT` is fired, MyBean, which implements the `ActionListener` interface, can invoke the `actionPerformed` method and send the event `MyBeanEvent` to all registered listeners. The `actionPerformed` method is shown in Listing 16.1.

LISTING 16.1 The actionPerformed Method

```
Public void actionPerformed (ActionEvent e)
{
  Vector v;
  // include user data with the event
  MyBeanEvent evt = new MyBeanEvent(this, getInputString());

  synchronized(this)
  {
    v = (Vector)listeners.clone();
  }
  for (int j = 0; j < v.size(); j++)
  {
    MyBeanListener mybl = (MyBeanListener)v.elementAt(j);
    mybl.convert(evt);
  }
}
```

The MyBeanEvent object has user-defined information encapsulated in the event state object which is typically used to pass data around in your programs. Here we use getInputString to attach user data to the event:

```
MyBeanEvent evt = new MyBeanEvent(this, getInputString());
```

In order for your programs to obtain this data, an accessor method such as getString must be defined in the MyBeanEvent object.

```
public String getString()
{
  return out_string;
}
```

Finally, it should be noted that MyBean also implements the java.io.Serializable interface. This is necessary if you want your Bean components to have persistence in their data when using network communication mechanisms like RMI. Listings 16.2 through 16.4 display the complete code for the MyBean component.

LISTING 16.2 MyBeanListener.java

```
import java.util.*;
public interface MyBeanListener extends java.util.EventListener
{
  public void convert(MyBeanEvent e);
}
```

Introduction to Remote Method Invocation

This section will introduce you to the basic concepts of Java RMI using the MyBean component developed in the "Getting Started" section. By following all the steps you will create an applet which invokes a method on a remote server to convert a string consisting of lowercase characters to uppercase and display the converted characters in the bottom Textfield component of MyBean.

LISTING 16.3 MyBeanEvent.java

```java
import java.util.*;
public class MyBeanEvent extends java.util.EventObject
{
  public MyBeanEvent(java.awt.Component source, String input)
  {
    super(source);
    out_string = input;
  }

  // provide accessor method
  public String getString()
  {
    return out_string;
  }

  private String out_string;
}
```

Write the Server Program

When the server program is complete, we will have two files: MyRmi.java, which is the remote interface, and MyRmiImpl.java, which is the actual implementation of the remote server object. We'll begin by writing the remote interface.

The Remote Interface

The remote interface is the same as the usual Java interface definition except that it must comply with the following:

▶ The remote interface must extend the `java.rmi.Remote` interface to identify itself as a remote object.

▶ The remote interface must be declared as public; otherwise it will not be accessible to any client.

▶ Every method specified in this interface must declare `java.rmi.RemoteException` in its `throws` clause. This exception allows for possible network-related communication problems.

Make sure that you specify all methods intended for remote invocation in this remote interface, as these methods will not be available otherwise. Listing 16.5 shows the remote interface definition.

LISTING 16.4 MyBean.java

```java
import java.awt.event.*;
import java.awt.*;
import java.io.*;
import java.util.Vector;

public class MyBean extends Panel implements ActionListener, Serializable
{
  public MyBean()
  {
    setLayout(null);
    convButton = new Button(ðBeanUpñ);
    add(convButton);
    convButton.addActionListener(this);
    convButton.setBounds(15, 10, 70, 25);

    inField = new TextField("mybean", 25);
    add(inField);
    inField.setBounds(200, 5, 150, 30);

    outField = new TextField("", 25);
    add(outField);
    outField.setBounds(200, 40, 150, 30);

    Label lower = new Label("Lower : ");
    add(lower);
    lower.setBounds(130, 5, 60, 25);
    Label upper = new Label("Upper : ");
    add(upper);
    upper.setBounds(130, 40, 60, 25);
  }

  public synchronized void addMyBeanListener(MyBeanListener l)
  {
    listeners.addElement(l);
  }

  public synchronized void removeMyBeanListener(MyBeanListener l)
  {
    listeners.removeElement(l);
```

CONTINUES

16

LISTING 16.4 MyBean.java (Continued)

```java
  }

  public void actionPerformed(ActionEvent e)
  {
    Vector v;
    //include user data with the event
    MyBeanEvent evt = new MyBeanEvent(this, getInputString());

    synchronized(this)
    {
      v = (Vector)listeners.clone();
    }
    for (int j = 0; j < v.size(); j++)
    {
      MyBeanListener mybl = (MyBeanListener)v.elementAt(j);
      mybl.convert(evt);
    }
  }

  public void setText(String str)
  {
     outField.setText(str);
  }

  private String getInputString()
  {
    String inputstring = inField.getText();
    if (inputstring.length() > 80)
      inputstring = inputstring.substring(0, 80);
    return inputstring;
  }

  private Vector listeners = new Vector();
  private Button convButton;
  private TextField inField;
  private TextField outField;
}
```

LISTING 16.5 MyRmi.java

```java
public interface MyRmi extends java.rmi.Remote
{
    String rmiconvert(String message) throws java.rmi.RemoteException;
}
```

Implement the Remote Interface

Next we write the `MyRmiImpl` class to implement the remote interface `MyRmi`.
Notice that our class also extends `java.rmi.server.UnicastRemoteObject`,
which allows us to create a non-replicated remote object communicating via TCP
streams. This class essentially provides support for a single point-to-point active
object reference, that is, a single remote server object. Here is the code segment il-
lustrating the above:

```java
import java.rmi.*;
import java.rmi.server.*;

public class MyRmiImpl extends UnicastRemoteObject
                       implements MyRmi
{
    . . . .
```

TIP: *Your remote objects should extend* `RemoteObject`, *typically via*
`UnicastRemoteObject`. *If you extend a remote object using a non-remote
class, the remote object must then be explicitly exported using the method*
`UnicastRemoteObject.exportObject(obj)`.

Export the Remote Object

The remote object will be automatically exported when the constructor
`MyRmiImpl` is invoked, as it will call the constructor of its superclass
`UnicastRemoteObject` and it is in this constructor that the `exportObject`
method is called (see UnicastRemoteObject.java in the JDK 1.1 source code). Now
the remote object can listen on an anonymous port for any incoming calls. Here is
the constructor code:

```java
public MyRmiImpl (String obj_name) throws RemoteException
{
```

16

```
        server = obj_name; // store server name
    }
```

NOTE: *The constructor throws the* `java.rmi.RemoteException` *to cater again for any possible network problems.*

Define the Remote Methods

Now we'll deal with the code that actually does the job for the client. These methods were previously listed in the remote interface `MyRmi`. Again, the method needs to throw the `RemoteException` to handle any possible network breakdowns. Here is the code for implementing the remote method:

```
public String rmiconvert(String message) throws RemoteException
{
    return (message.toUpperCase());
}
```

Make sure that any objects passed as arguments to or return values from remote methods implement the `java.io.Serializable` interface to preserve the persistence of the data. Recall the use of object serialization in Chapter 8 and how objects are written to and read from streams.

Security Manager

Java ensures that the security of your network is never breached by disallowing the loading of any RMI classes if there is no security manager running. The following code creates and installs the `RMISecurityManager`.

```
System.setSecurityManager(new RMISecurityManager());
```

Bind Remote Object to RMI Registry

RMI provides a bootstrap naming service which allows you to bind a URL of the form *//host/object_name* to the remote object. For example, the following code binds the URL of the remote object named `MyRmiServer` running on MyHost to a reference for the remote object.

```
java.rmi.Naming.rebind("//MyHost/MyRmiServer", remote_obj);
```

It is also possible, as we have done below in Listing 16.6, to omit "MyHost" from the string argument. RMI will then use the current host as the default. Obviously, you're free to substitute your favorite host machine name here. By calling `Naming.rebind`, RMI rebinds the name to a new object, effectively replacing any existing bindings using an identical name which could have potentially caused name resolution problems. Once the remote object is registered on the server, clients can consult the RMI registry, perform a name lookup to obtain the remote object reference, and then remotely invoke methods on the object. The following code statement illustrates the above points, while Listing 16.6 shows the entire code listing for the remote server object.

```
// first create an instance of the remote object
   MyRmiImpl remote_obj = new MyRmiImpl("MyRmiServer");
   Naming.rebind("MyRmiServer", remote_obj);
```

TIP: *By default, RMI creates a registry on port 1099. If you wish to use a different port, the following code segment shows you how to use another port instead of the default.*

```
   Naming.rebind("//MyHost:6789/MyRmiServer", remote_obj);
```

LISTING 16.6 MyRmiImpl.java

```java
import java.rmi.*;
import java.rmi.server.*;

public class MyRmiImpl extends UnicastRemoteObject
                       implements MyRmi
{
  public MyRmiImpl(String obj_name) throws RemoteException
  {
    server = obj_name;
  }

  //define the remote method here
  public String rmiconvert(String message) throws RemoteException
  {
    return (message.toUpperCase());
  }

  public static void main(String args[])
  {
    //create and install the Security Manager
    System.setSecurityManager(new RMISecurityManager());
```

CONTINUES

LISTING 16.6 MyRmiImpl.java (Continued)

```
  try
  {
    MyRmiImpl remote_obj = new MyRmiImpl("MyRmiServer");
    Naming.rebind("MyRmiServer", remote_obj);
  }
  catch(Exception ex)
  {
    System.err.println("MyRmiServer Error : "  + ex.getMessage());
    ex.printStackTrace();
    return;
  }
  System.out.println("MyRmiImpl server is now runningñ);
}
private String server;
}
```

■

Write the Client Program

Our applet will use the MyBean component developed earlier in the chapter and register as a listener for the `MyBeanEvent`. Note that we implement the `MyBeanListener` interface so that we can incorporate all the necessary functionality into the `convert` method. Here is the `init` method of MyRmiApplet, which performs the above tasks:

```
public void init()
{
  // assume MyBean to be in the same package
  myb = new MyBean();
  add(myb);
  // register as a listener
  myb.addMyBeanListener(this);
  myb.setSize(400,300);
  myb.setVisible(true);
}
```

Now let's examine the `convert` method step by step. First we will use an accessor method that we coded in MyBeanEvent to return `out_string`, a private member of the class. Recall that this string is actually passed to the constructor of `MyBeanEvent`. Here is the code to do this:

```
// obtain string from event using accessor method
String input = e.getString();
```

Next we construct a URL using the `getCodeBase` method in conjunction with `getHost` so that the `java.rmi.Naming.lookup` method can use this URL to perform a lookup in the registry for the remote object and obtain its reference. This lookup can be done from any host machine. Here is the code:

```
MyRmi obj = (MyRmi)Naming.lookup("//" +
            getCodeBase().getHost() + "/MyRmiServer");
```

> **CAUTION:** *It is important that the constructed URL contain the host; it will cause a security problem otherwise. If the host is not specified, the applet will, by default, try to do a lookup on the client machine. This is a breach of the Java security model, as applets live in the "sandbox" and are not allowed to access the local file system. Applets are only allowed to communicate to the host that they originated from.*

We now use the reference to the remote object to invoke the remote method `rmiconvert` and get it to convert our input string to uppercase characters.

```
String output = obj.rmiconvert(input);
```

The call to `myb.setText` in turn puts the string in the bottom TextField of MyBean. Remember to call `repaint()` to refresh the screen. The entire code for the client applet program appears in Listing 16.7.

16

LISTING 16.7 MyRmiApplet.java

```java
import java.awt.*;
import java.applet.*;
import java.rmi.*;

public class MyRmiApplet extends Applet implements MyBeanListener
{
  public void init()
  {
    myb = new MyBean();
    add(myb);
```

CONTINUES

LISTING 16.7 MyRmiApplet.java (Continued)

```java
    myb.addMyBeanListener(this);
    myb.setSize(400,300);
    myb.setVisible(true);
  }

  public void paint(Graphics g)
  {
    super.paint(g);
  }

  public void convert(MyBeanEvent e)
  {
    try
    {
      // obtain string from event using accessor method
      String input = e.getString();

      // perform name lookup in the registry
      MyRmi obj = (MyRmi)Naming.lookup("//" +
                      getCodeBase().getHost() + "/MyRmiServer");

      // invoke the remote method
      String output = obj.rmiconvert(input);
      myb.setText(output);
    }
    catch(Exception ex)
    {
      System.out.println("MyRmiApplet exception : " + ex.getMessage());
      ex.printStackTrace();
    }
    repaint();
  }

  private MyBean myb;
}
```

Use rmic

Once we have compiled all our Java source files into class files, we have to run the rmic compiler on the names of the class files containing the remote object implementations. This compiler is available with the Java Development Kit 1.1 and should be included in your local PATH variable. We will use the rmic compiler on the command line as follows:

```
rmic  MyRmiImpl
```

Recall that "MyRmiImpl" is the name of the Java class file containing our remote object implementation. We could use more than one class file as input to rmic, provided they are implementations of the remote objects. The rmic compiler in turn produces the MyRmiImpl_Stub.class and MyRmiImpl_Skel.class files as the stub and skeleton for the remote object implementation.

Put It All Together

We have now done most of the hard work and should be ready for the final touches. Before we get into all the steps necessary to get our RMI server and client programs running, you need to ensure that your CLASSPATH contains the directory where all your class files are situated.

Start the RMI Registry

The registry is started on the server by using the rmiregistry command in Windows 95 or Windows NT:

```
start rmiregistry
```

On Solaris the command would be:

```
rmiregistry &
```

The rmiregistry does not produce any output and must always be running in the background to provide the bootstrap naming service.

Recall that RMI creates the registry by default on port 1099. If you wish to use a port other than the default, you could use the following command to create a registry on, for example, port 6789:

```
start rmiregistry 6789
```

CAUTION: *The registry must be stopped and restarted if the remote interface is modified in any way; otherwise none of your changes will be incorporated into your programs.*

16

Start the Server

When we start the server we must specify the property value of `java.rmi.server.codebase`. This is necessary so that any references to remote objects instantiated by the server can contain the URL information. The stub class generated by rmic can then be dynamically downloaded to the client when required from this URL. We use the -D option of the Java interpreter to set this property value.

```
java -Djava.rmi.server.codebase=http://host/your_codebase/
    MyRmiImpl
```

This example assumes that you are able to run the program on the HTTP server. If this is not the case, then substitute "file" for "http" in the above command statement.

Start the Client

In this case we start our applet using the appletviewer due to the fact that none of the Web browsers, at the time of this writing, incorporate the necessary Java upgrade to run RMI. However, this will soon change and should not prevent us from writing distributed applications using RMI technology and Beans. We can now code our index.html file with the usual applet tag and load the applet by using the following command:

```
appletviewer http://host/your_codebase/index.html
```

Again, we can substitute "file" for "http" if necessary. If all goes well we should see the applet running as shown in Figure 16.1. Click on the button and add some text to the top TextField to see how easily RMI works. Now let's move on to discuss the Java IDL.

Introduction to the Java IDL

This section will continue to use the MyBean component developed earlier in this chapter in introducing the reader to the distributed object world of CORBA using the Beans component model and the Java IDL.

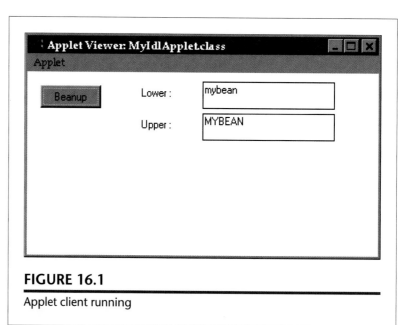

FIGURE 16.1

Applet client running

This discussion assumes that you are familiar with CORBA and the use of the IDL, which is the industry-standard interface definition language used by CORBA developers. The intent of this section is merely to get you acquainted with the implementation of the Java IDL and how it relates to the CORBA model for distributed-object computing.

Packages

At the time of writing, the Java IDL package was at alpha 2.2 release. You can download this package from the site http://splash.javasoft.com/JavaIDL/page/index.html. It is anticipated that the client-side runtimes will be bundled with a future release of the Java Development Kit; however, it is JavaSoft's intention to ship the server-side runtimes as a separate product. The following Java packages are included in this release:

- ▶ sunw.corba
- ▶ sunw.door
- ▶ sunw.idl
- ▶ sunw.orb

Since the Java IDL package falls outside the scope of the core Java classes, you must ensure that the CLASSPATH environment variable points to the directory where the classes.zip file resides. Typically this would be in the \your_idl_dir\lib location. Likewise, your PATH environment variable should include the directory \your_idl_dir\bin so the idlgen compiler is found.

16

Write the IDL File

As previously stated, it is assumed here that you are familiar with the use of the IDL; it is certainly beyond the scope of this chapter and even the book to delve into that subject matter. As a start, you must decide which methods you want to make known to clients and then proceed to write the IDL file. We create a file called MyIdl.idl with the following code:

```
interface MyIdl
{
  string idlconvert(in string mesg);
};
```

Here we specify idlconvert as the method to be invoked remotely.

Using idlgen

The file that we wrote called MyIdl.idl is now compiled using idlgen, which generates Java interface definitions and Java client stubs and server skeletons. Once we have all the required Java source files, we can use the javac compiler to produce the bytecode. The idlgen compiler will map the IDL file to the Java equivalent using a mapping specification developed by JavaSoft. This mapping is still in the process of finalization and is evolving with the development of the Java language. We use the following command for idlgen on Solaris:

```
idlgen -fclient -fserver -e MyEnviron.env MyIdl.idl
```

and this one on Windows 95 and NT:

```
idlgen -fclient -fserver -fno-cpp -e MyEnviron.env MyIdl.idl
```

The idlgen options are described below (only those which are applicable are listed).

▶ -fclient requests that idlgen generate the client side of the IDL file specified.

▶ -fserver requests that idlgen generate the server side of the IDL file specified.

▶ -fno-cpp: is used if you do not have a C++ preprocessor named "cl" on your PATH. The idlgen compiler requires this to preprocess IDL files.

▶ -e MyEnviron.env specifies an environment file to be used to supply attributes for the translation from IDL to Java. This file is an alternative to the #pragma directives used in the IDL files themselves. Our file MyEnviron.env contains the following:

```
// default values applicable to every file
default: RepositoryPrefix="JavaSoft.COM" RepositoryVersion="1.0";
```

Note that if no module is specified in the IDL file, the idlgen tool will automatically create the default package name "idlGlobal" and place all generated Java source files in this subdirectory. Any modules specified in the IDL file are mapped to Java packages. Using our file MyIdl.idl, the idlgen compiler will generate the following list of ORB independent files:

▶ MyIdlHolder.java

▶ MyIdlOperations.java

▶ MyIdlRef.java

▶ MyIdlServant.java

▶ MyIdlSkeleton.java

▶ MyIdlStub.java

Figure 16.2 illustrates how the various stubs and skeletons are used to build our distributed application.

Write the Implementation Class for the Remote Method

Our implementation class, `MyIdlImpl`, must implement the `MyIdlServant` interface. This is one of the generated Java files listed above. We then use the method `idlconvert` to convert our user input string to uppercase characters. Listing 16.8 shows the code for the implementation class.

Write the Server Program

Our server program will service a specific port and listen for requests for the `published` method. The following code will specify which port to use and also request that all network traffic connections be logged to an error stream.

```
// use port 4800 to accept incoming Java-to-Java
connections
sunw.door.Orb.initialize(4800);
// log all connection opens and closes
sunw.door.Orb.logConnections(true);
```

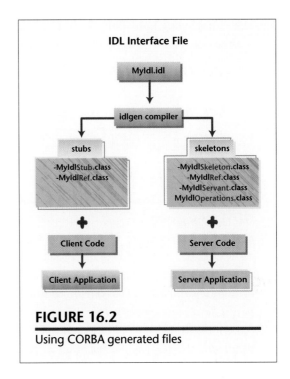

FIGURE 16.2

Using CORBA generated files

LISTING 16.8 The Implementation Class `MyIdlImpl`

```
public class MyIdlImpl implements idlGlobal.MyIdlServant
{
  public MyIdlImpl() {
  }

  public String idlconvert(String message)
  {
    String result = message.toUpperCase();
    return result;
  }
}
```

The call to the `sunw.door.Orb.initialize` method to create and initialize our server object does a lot of work behind the scenes:

▶ It creates a `java.net.ServerSocket` object to listen on the specified port.

▶ It checks that a security manager is running.

▶ It creates a `SingletonServer` object.

▶ It binds "door-orb" as the naming context.

NOTE: *The present release of the Java IDL is based on the Door Object Request Broker (ORB) architecture. This is a lightweight RPC protocol implemented on top of TCP/IP. The net effect of this is that you can only communicate with Java servers. However, the designers of the Java IDL system have ensured scalability by using a portable Java ORB core which will accommodate new ORB protocols. In fact, JavaSoft is currently developing a Java interface to the industry-standard Internet Inter-ORB Protocol (IIOP) which will allow seamless and transparent distributed-object computing among all vendors supporting IIOP.*

Our next step is to create a reference to our remote object by using the skeleton generated by idlgen. Here is the code:

```
idlGlobal.MyIdlRef obj = idlGlobal.MyIdlSkeleton.createRef(
                                               new MyIdlImpl());
```

We then publish the method by putting the given object into the local machine name space. That way, other machines can do a lookup and resolve the name via a URL.

```
sunw.door.Orb.publish("idlconvert", obj);
```

The first argument to the `publish` method is the string "idlconvert", which describes the remote method we initially defined in the MyIdl.idl file. The second argument is the remote object to which the name is bound. The complete source code for the server program appears in Listing 16.9.

Write the Client Program

Basically, our client program consists of an applet using the same MyBean component we used in the previous section on RMI. Again we must register as a listener for the `MyBeanEvent` and implement the `MyBeanListener` interface. The first task for our applet is to check that we have a URL in the applet param tag. The `init` method of the applet does this checking.

LISTING 16.9 MyIdlServer.java

```java
public class MyIdlServer
{
  public static void main(String args[])
  {
    // use port 4800 to accept incoming Java-to-Java connections
    sunw.door.Orb.initialize(4800);
    // log all connection opens and closes
    sunw.door.Orb.logConnections(true);

    // create and publish a MyIdl IDL objRef
    try
    {
      idlGlobal.MyIdlRef obj = idlGlobal.MyIdlSkeleton.createRef(
                                        new MyIdlImpl());

      sunw.door.Orb.publish("idlconvert", obj);
    }
    catch(Exception ex)
    {
      System.err.println("MyIdlServer Error : " + ex.getMessage());
      ex.printStackTrace();
      return;
    }
    System.out.println("MyIdlServer is now running");
  }
}
```

```java
    url = getParameter("url");
    if(url == null)
    {
      usage();
      NoUrl = true;
    }
```

As part of our applet `start` method we obtain a reference to our remote object by using the `MyIdlStub` class generated by idlgen:

```java
    remote_target = idlGlobal.MyIdlStub.createRef();
```

Once we have this reference, we take the URL format string obtained from the applet's param tag and try to resolve it to an object, which in our case is the `remote_target`.

```
sunw.corba.Orb.resolve(url, remote_target);
```

This step may involve loading the appropriate vendor's ORB package. Clients can then find the CORBA service because it is registered with an ORB that provides an object identification service. You must ensure that the URL uses the format that the Java IDL expects. A valid URL has the following format:

```
idl:package_name://host_name[:port]/relative_name
```

where

- ▶ "idl" is mandatory as the first part of the URL.

- ▶ *package_name* is "sunw.door" in our particular case but will vary depending upon the ORB being used.

- ▶ *host_name* is the name of the server.

- ▶ *port* is the actual port used and is optional.

- ▶ *relative_name* is the name of the published method, which is "idlconvert" in our case.

Because we implement the `MyBeanListener` interface, we can place all the necessary functionality in the `convert` method. Here is the code which makes the call to the Java CORBA server:

```
String output = remote_target.idlconvert(input);
```

You can see the complete source code listing for the client applet program in Listing 16.10.

LISTING 16.10   MyIdlApplet.java

```java
import java.awt.*;
import java.applet.Applet;

public class MyIdlApplet extends Applet implements MyBeanListener
{
  public synchronized void init()
  {
    // get the URL
    url = getParameter("url");
    if (url == null)
```

CONTINUES

LISTING 16.10 MyIdlApplet.java (Continued)

```
  {
    usage();
    NoUrl = true;
  }
  // add our Bean component and register as a listener
  myb = new MyBean();
  add(myb);
  myb.addMyBeanListener(this);
}

public void start()
{
  // return if no URL is passed in the param tag
  if(NoUrl)
    return;
  showStatus("Now connecting to MyIdlServer at " + url);
  myb.setSize(400, 300);
  myb.setVisible(true);

  try
  {
    try
    {
      remote_target = idlGlobal.MyIdlStub.createRef();
      sunw.corba.Orb.resolve(url, remote_target);
    }
    catch(Exception ex)
    {
      System.err.println(ðUnable to resolve ð + url + ð : ð + ex);
      return;
    }
  }
  catch (Throwable th)
  {
    System.err.println("MyIdlApplet.start caught : " + th);
    th.printStackTrace();
  }
}
```

CONTINUES

LISTING 16.10   MyIdlApplet.java (Continued)

```java
  public void stop()
  {
    remote_target = null;
  }

  // here we implement the method from the MyBeanListener interface
  public void convert(MyBeanEvent e)
  {
    try
    {
      if(remote_target != null)
      {
        // use accessor method to obtain information from the event
        String input = e.getString();
        // make the call to the method serviced by the CORBA server
        String output = remote_target.idlconvert(input);
        myb.setText(output);
      }
    }
    catch(Exception ex)
    {
      System.err.println("Unable to invoke method : " + ex);
      ex.printStackTrace();
    }
    repaint();
  }

  private void usage()
  {
    System.err.println(
      "URL missing : must be in the following format :");
    System.err.println(
      "<param name=url value=idl:sunw.door://myhost:4800/idlconvert>ñ);
  }

  private MyBean myb;
  private idlGlobal.MyIdlRef remote_target;
  private boolean NoUrl = false;
  private String url;
}
```

16

Put It All Together

Once we have compiled all our Java source files into class files and set our CLASS-PATH variable to where these files are located, we can begin setting up our distributed-computing environment.

Start the Server

We start the server on our host machine using the usual `java` command and the class file MyIdlServer:

```
java MyIdlServer
```

Write the HTML Code for the Applet

Before we can load our applet, we need to write the HTML code for our index.html file. The HTML code fragment shown in Listing 16.11 should be all that's necessary to start the applet in a Web page.

LISTING 16.11   The HTML Code for the index.html File

```
<applet
    code=MyIdlApplet.class
    width=400 height=200>
<param
    name=url
    value="idl:sunw.door://myhost:4800/idlconvert">
</applet>
```

We must substitute the appropriate machine host name for *myhost* and ensure that the port number (4800 in the example) corresponds to the port on which our server is listening. Lastly, note that "idlconvert" is the name that was published in our server program.

Start the Client Applet

At this point in time, we are limited to using the appletviewer to load the applet because Web browsers have not yet fully incorporated the Java CORBA technology. The following command starts our applet from the current directory:

```
appletviewer index.html
```

Since we are using the same MyBean component as in the RMI example, the applet should be the same as in Figure 16.1.

16

Summary

The world of distributed-object computing is at the forefront of a new era and the advent of JavaBeans provides us with a quantum leap into the next generation. Using powerful technologies such as RMI and Java CORBA, you will be able to exploit the potential of distributed-object computing to its fullest extent by building upon the knowledge gained from this chapter.

16

Chapter *17*

Bridging JavaBeans to ActiveX

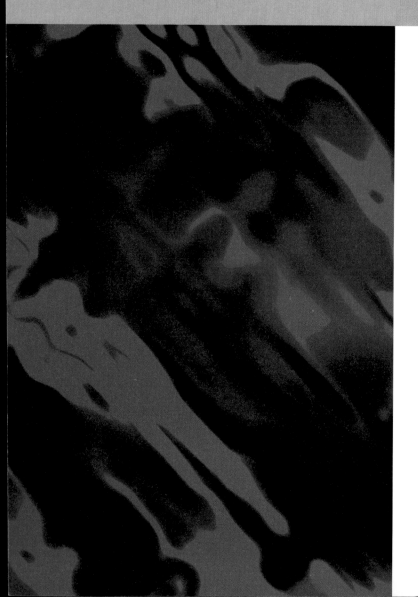

- ► **ActiveX Bridge Basics**
- ► **Using Beans in Visual Basic**

Even though Java and JavaBeans have enjoyed their fair share of media attention, you would be hard-pressed to not have heard something in the past year about ActiveX, Microsoft's foray into component software. There has been a great deal of debate surrounding ActiveX and how it compares to JavaBeans, since they both tackle essentially the same problem. I'm not really interested in debating which technology is better because in reality they are both strategically positioned to thrive in different ways. It's my contention that JavaBeans and ActiveX can co-exist peacefully.

Fortunately, I'm not the only person who feels this way. OK, maybe I am, but Microsoft and Sun are at least scared enough of each other to make serious efforts at supporting each other's technology. In this chapter you'll learn about Sun's ActiveX Bridge, which allows JavaBeans components to be used as ActiveX components. The ActiveX Bridge allows you to use JavaBeans in applications such as Visual Basic and Microsoft Office, which currently operate solely on ActiveX components. The latter part of this chapter is devoted to using Beans in Visual Basic. But first, you need to understand some of the basics of the ActiveX Bridge.

In this chapter, you'll learn

▶ The basics of the ActiveX Bridge

▶ How to package Beans as ActiveX components

▶ How to use Beans in Visual Basic

ActiveX Bridge Basics

The ActiveX Bridge is a set of classes and utilities that allow JavaBeans components to be used as ActiveX components in ActiveX-based environments such as Visual Basic. The ActiveX Bridge marks a serious commitment on Sun's part to support the ActiveX technology. This opens up many opportunities for JavaBeans developers and ultimately lessens the concerns over which technology is better. If you can use them interchangeably, who cares? I'm not saying we are to the point of not caring just yet, but the ActiveX Bridge marks a large leap forward nonetheless.

The Bridge consists of a few different parts:

▶ Bridge classes

▶ The ActiveX Packager utility

▶ Example Beans

▶ Documentation

17

> **NOTE:** *As of this writing, the latest release of the ActiveX Bridge is beta 2. Feel free to check JavaSoft's Web site (http://splash.javasoft.com/beans) for the latest version.*

The Bridge classes consist of special Java and C++ classes that act as a translator between JavaBeans and ActiveX. The ActiveX Packager is a utility that builds extra functionality into a Bean so that it is capable of being used as an ActiveX component. The example Beans are two Beans from the BDK that have already been run through the Packager. The documentation consists primarily of a tutorial on how to use a Bean in Visual Basic. You'll work through a similar tutorial a little later in this chapter.

With the ActiveX Bridge, JavaBeans components are capable of firing events that can be caught by ActiveX containers and acting as servers for ActiveX method invocation. The first of these capabilities allows a Bean to fire events that are handled in ActiveX containers such as Visual Basic forms. For example, a Bean button click could be handled and responded to with Visual Basic code. The second capability allows ActiveX environments such as Visual Basic to call Bean methods.

> **NOTE:** *If this discussion seems biased toward Visual Basic as an ActiveX development tool, it's because Visual Basic is currently the most thoroughly tested environment for the ActiveX Bridge. It also makes an interesting environment for JavaBeans integration because it is a very popular visual development tool with no direct support for Java or JavaBeans. However, if you aren't using JavaBeans on a Windows platform, please stay with me throughout this chapter because you'll learn some interesting things that could be applicable eventually (since ActiveX is currently being ported to other platforms).*

The ActiveX Bridge is designed to be as automatic as possible. Ideally, a Bean would require no additional overhead to masquerade as an ActiveX component. The key word here is "ideally"! Back in the real world, we have to deal with the realistic issues involved in integrating two very different technologies. The ActiveX Bridge actually goes a long way toward making the JavaBeans/ActiveX merger a straightforward one. All things considered, Beans require little additional overhead to be usable as ActiveX components.

With the ActiveX Bridge, Beans require three elements to operate in an ActiveX environment:

- ▶ A type library

- ▶ A registry file

- ▶ Java stub classes

First off, it's important to note that these elements are all generated automatically by the ActiveX Packager. A *type library* is a binary file that describes the properties, methods, and events of a Bean in ActiveX terms. You can think of a type library as ActiveX's rough equivalent of a Bean information class. The registry file contains information about the Bean, such as the path to the type library. The Java stub classes comprise the actual Bridge between a Bean and ActiveX. These classes are generated and added to the JAR file for a Bean by the ActiveX Packager.

Bridging Properties

All Bean properties are accessible under ActiveX. The ActiveX Bridge automatically invokes the proper accessor methods for JavaBeans properties. Bound and constrained properties are also supported through similar facilities in ActiveX. Native Java property types are automatically mapped to comparable ActiveX property types. Additionally, some JavaBeans properties are naturally mapped to standard ActiveX properties. Since it is standard for ActiveX property names to begin with a capital letter, all JavaBeans property names are capitalized by the Bridge.

Bridging Methods

All public JavaBeans methods can be called from ActiveX, with the exception that overloaded methods aren't fully supported in the beta 2 release of the Bridge. In ActiveX, the overloaded method with the most arguments is the only one accessible. Method arguments and return values are automatically processed and translated appropriately by the Bridge. Exceptions thrown by a method are caught by the Bridge and returned to the ActiveX container in a special package.

Bridging Events

JavaBeans events are fully supported by the Bridge, but they are merged together under one interface. In other words, the Bridge doesn't support multiple event interfaces. This could be a problem if different interfaces contain methods with the same name.

Another big issue regarding events and the ActiveX Bridge is the differing approaches to event processing used by JavaBeans and ActiveX. JavaBeans events are based on the Java AWT event model, which relies heavily on event information being represented by an immutable event object, which is an object that can't be modified. ActiveX events, on the other hand, are represented by native data types that are sometimes writeable. The ActiveX Bridge supports both types of events; it refers to the ActiveX event type as "cracked," which alludes to the fact that the information is broken up into separate entities. You can specify whether you want cracked or uncracked events when packaging a Bean with the ActiveX Packager.

Using Beans in Visual Basic

Perhaps the most interesting way to get to understand the ActiveX Bridge is by using it with an existing development tool that relies heavily on ActiveX components. Visual Basic is a very powerful and popular development tool that uses ActiveX components throughout. Visual Basic has no concept of a Java class, much less a JavaBeans component, which makes it an ideal candidate for experimentation with the ActiveX Bridge. The rest of this chapter is devoted to using Beans in Visual Basic via the ActiveX Bridge.

Although the ActiveX Bridge automatically installs a couple of demo Beans for testing purposes, it would be much more fun to try out the Bridge with some of your own Beans. More specifically, you're going to try out the Bridge by using the Image Button and Needle Gauge Beans in Visual Basic. All Beans must be appropriately packaged before being used with the Bridge, so before you can add your Beans to the Visual Basic environment you must package them up with the ActiveX Packager.

Packaging Beans

Beans are packaged for ActiveX using the ActiveX Packager. The ActiveX Packager is an application written in Java, which means you have to execute it in a Java interpreter. To run the ActiveX Packager using the standard JDK interpreter, issue the following command:

```
java sun.beans.ole.packager
```

NOTE: *The ActiveX Bridge requires a dynamic link library,* `packager.dll`, *to execute properly. To give the Bridge access to this DLL, you need to add the path containing the DLL to your system path. Under the default installations of the BDK and ActiveX Bridge, this path is* \bdk\bridge\bin.

When you execute this command, the ActiveX Packager's Step 1 window will appear (see Figure 17.1). The ActiveX Packager is presented as a wizard-style interface with five different steps. The first step involves selecting the JAR file containing the Bean to be packaged. You simply click the Browse button to select the desired JAR file. It's important to note that the ActiveX Packager only operates on JAR files; you can't specify Java classes directly. For this example, you need to select the file ImageButton.jar, which is the JAR file containing the Image Button Bean. After selecting this file, click the Next button to move on to the next step.

The second step of the Packager requires you to select a specific Bean within the given JAR file (see Figure 17.2). In this example, there is only one Bean in the

JAR file, so this step is trivial. However, JAR files are capable of holding multiple Beans, in which case this step would be critical for selecting a specific Bean.

The third step asks for the ActiveX name to be used for the Bean (see Figure 17.3). This is the name that will be used when the Bean is referenced as an ActiveX component. The ActiveX Packager usually extracts an acceptable name, as you can see in Figure 17.3. Notice that the package information has been stripped from the name. This is in agreement with ActiveX, since ActiveX doesn't really support the Java package construct.

The fourth step of the ActiveX Packager requires you to specify an output directory for the resulting ActiveX support files (see Figure 17.4). The support files consist of registry and type library files, which are required for all ActiveX components. It's usually fine to accept the default option for this step.

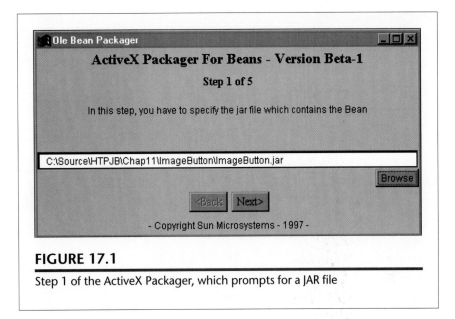

FIGURE 17.1

Step 1 of the ActiveX Packager, which prompts for a JAR file

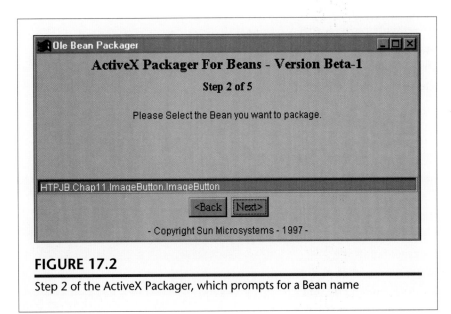

FIGURE 17.2

Step 2 of the ActiveX Packager, which prompts for a Bean name

The fifth and final step of the packaging process (see Figure 17.5) involves specifying whether the Bean's events are to be cracked or uncracked for the ActiveX Bridge. You learned about cracked and uncracked events a little earlier in the chapter. For this example, uncracked events are fine, so just accept the default value. To package the Bean with the specified settings, click the Start Generation button.

After you click the Start Generation button, the packaging process begins and you are presented with a window detailing its status (see Figure 17.6). The packaging process primarily consists of generating and compiling various support classes, along with adding information to the Windows registry. When the Packager finishes, you are presented with a window notifying you that changes were made to the registry (see Figure 17.7).

At this point you have a Bean packaged and ready to go as an ActiveX component. One really interesting thing about the ActiveX Bridge is that the Packager builds the ActiveX support classes for the Bean directly into the JAR file containing the Bean. This allows you to distribute one JAR file for a Bean that can be used as a

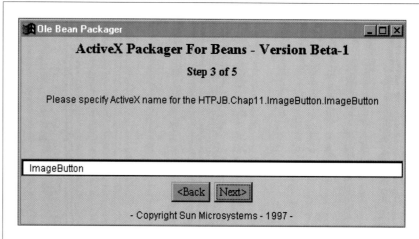

FIGURE 17.3

Step 3 of the ActiveX Packager, which prompts for an ActiveX name to be used for the Bean

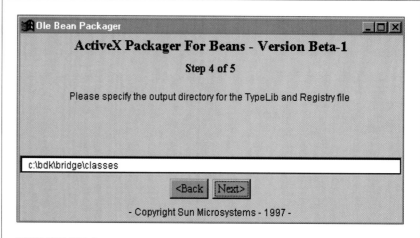

FIGURE 17.4

Step 4 of the ActiveX Packager, which prompts for an output directory for ActiveX support files

JavaBeans component or as an ActiveX component via the Bridge support files.

Now that you have the hang of using the ActiveX Packager, you must use it again to package the Needle Gauge Bean from Chapter 12. You will be using this Bean along with the Image Button Bean in the next couple of sections.

Adding Beans to Visual Basic

Beans packaged for ActiveX integration can be used in any environment that supports ActiveX components. Visual Basic is one of these environments, since it relies heavily on ActiveX components for application construction. Because Visual Basic is a development tool, you can create, customize, and connect Beans with it. Ironically, Visual Basic allows you to actually do more with Beans than the BeanBox, since Visual Basic allows you to attach code to events.

The first step in using Beans in Visual Basic is adding them to the Visual Basic environment. This is accomplished by selecting Custom Controls from the Tools menu. You will be presented with a Custom Controls dialog box containing a list of all the controls (components) that can of be used by Visual Basic (see Figure 17.8). Notice that the controls have checkboxes next to them, and only some of them are checked. The controls that

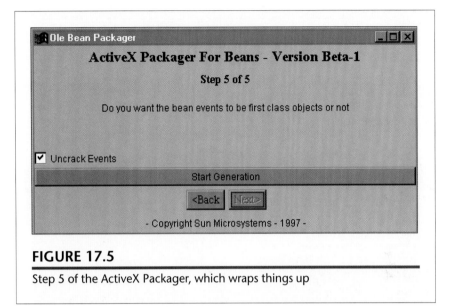

FIGURE 17.5

Step 5 of the ActiveX Packager, which wraps things up

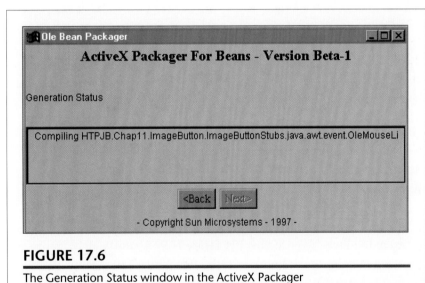

FIGURE 17.6

The Generation Status window in the ActiveX Packager

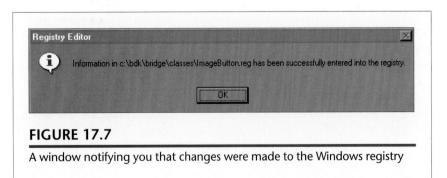

FIGURE 17.7

A window notifying you that changes were made to the Windows registry

17

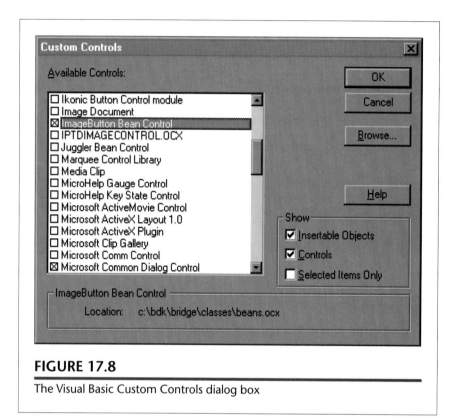

FIGURE 17.8

The Visual Basic Custom Controls dialog box

are checked are currently being used in the Visual Basic environment. This dialog box allows you to determine which controls are included in the Visual Basic toolbar by checking or unchecking them. To add the Image Button Bean to Visual Basic, all you have to do is check it in the dialog box.

The addition of the Image Button Bean is immediately reflected in the Visual Basic toolbar (see Figure 17.9). Unfortunately, the ActiveX Bridge doesn't automatically allow Visual Basic to use the standard icons for the Bean. This is primarily due to the fact that Visual Basic isn't equipped to work with GIF images. However, you can convert the icons for the Bean to Windows icons and specify their locations in the registry entry for the Bean. A future release of the ActiveX Bridge is expected to help automate this task. The Bean's icons aren't critical for trying out the Bean in Visual Basic, so let's move on and not worry about them.

FIGURE 17.9

The Visual Basic toolbar with the Image Button Bean added

TIP: *If you just can't stand the thought of not having the Bean's icon displayed correctly in the Visual Basic toolbar, feel free to convert the GIF image* *and modify the registry entry for the Bean on your own. For more information about how this is done, please refer to the ActiveX Bridge documentation.*

You now have the Image Button Bean added to Visual Basic and ready to be put through its paces. Before getting into that, though, you need to add the Needle Gauge Bean to Visual Basic using the same approach. This is necessary because you are going to use both of these Beans together in the next section.

Working with Beans in Visual Basic

Finally, the moment you've been waiting for! If you're like me, you're probably at least a little skeptical about the whole notion of using a Bean as an ActiveX component. Can you really and truly use a Bean in an application that clearly knows nothing about JavaBeans? Absolutely, read on!

To add an Image Button Bean to the current form, just click on the Bean in the toolbar and then click and drag in the form window. You should see something similar to Figure 17.10. You're probably thinking the image looks a little strange. The beta 1 release of the ActiveX Bridge, which is the latest as of this writing, has some painting problems in the design mode of Visual Basic. Nevertheless, it works quite well in runtime mode, as you will soon see.

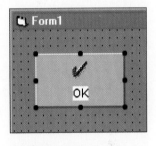

FIGURE 17.10

An Image Button Bean added to a Visual Basic form

Probably the most interesting thing to notice about the Image Button Bean in the context of Visual Basic is the Properties window (see Figure 17.11). This window is Visual Basic's version of the BeanBox's PropertySheet window. You can easily see the Bean's properties as you created them in Chapter 11, along with some other properties that probably aren't so familiar. ActiveX components are required to support a variety of standard properties such as `DragMode` and `Enabled`; these properties are added to the Image Button Bean through the ActiveX Bridge.

You're probably itching to see if the Bean can really be manipulated through Visual Basic. Let's try a little experiment before continuing with the example. Try double-clicking the Bean to open a code window. Then select the `actionPerformed` method from the Procedure drop-down list. You are now editing the event response method for the `actionPerformed` event, which is fired whenever the button is clicked. Add the following line of code to the method:

```
MsgBox "Howdy!"
```

This code is Visual Basic code that displays a dialog box containing the message "Howdy!". Figure 17.12 shows what the code window should look like with this line of code added. Before trying out this code, go ahead and make one change to the Bean that you will need later: set the Label property to "Bigger".

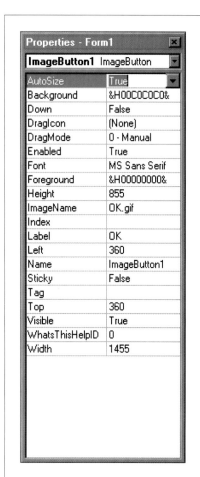

FIGURE 17.11

The Visual Basic Properties window for the Image Button Bean

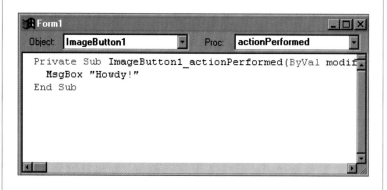

FIGURE 17.12

The Visual Basic code window containing the `actionPerformed` method

Don't worry, this will make more sense a little later in the chapter. Once you've done this, try running the project by selecting Start from the Run menu. The resulting form window in runtime mode is shown in Figure 17.13.

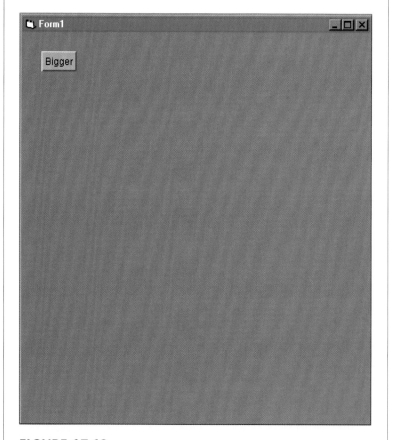

FIGURE 17.13

The example form window in runtime mode

> **NOTE:** *The current version of the ActiveX Bridge as of this writing, beta 2, has an apparent problem loading and displaying images in Beans. This is evident in Figure 17.13, which shows an Image Button Bean in runtime mode with no image displayed. A future release of the Bridge will no doubt address this problem.*

To test out the code you added, just click the button. Figure 17.14 shows the resulting output. As you can see, the "Howdy!" message is displayed in a small dialog box containing an OK button. This dialog box is entirely a Visual Basic construct, meaning that you have successfully integrated a Bean with Visual Basic code!

Getting back to the larger example, exit out of runtime mode and add another Image Button Bean to the form. Then change the label property for this Bean to "Smaller". Figure 17.15 shows what the form should look like after this step. Now add a Needle Gauge Bean to the form just below the buttons. Figure 17.16 shows the form window after this step.

Guess what's next? That's right, you're going to connect the buttons to the gauge using event response methods. Double-click the first button to edit its `actionPerformed` method, and then replace the `MsgBox` code with the following line of code:

```
NeedleGauge1.Value = NeedleGauge1.Value + 1
```

This code increments the value property of the Needle Gauge Bean, which causes the needle to rotate clockwise. Figure 17.17 shows the code window with this line added. Now edit the `actionPerformed` method for the second Image Button Bean and add the following code:

```
NeedleGauge1.Value = NeedleGauge1.Value - 1
```

FIGURE 17.14

The message box displayed when the Bigger button is pressed

17

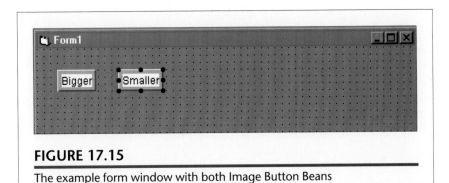

FIGURE 17.15

The example form window with both Image Button Beans

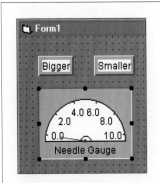

FIGURE 17.16

The example form window with both Image Button Beans and a Needle Gauge Bean

No surprises here! As you can see, this code decrements the value property of the Needle Gauge Bean, causing the needle to rotate counter-clockwise. That pretty well wraps up everything you need to do to connect the Beans in Visual Basic. Go ahead and try running the example by selecting Start from the Run menu. As you can see, this is a very good example of how easy it is to use JavaBeans components within an ActiveX-based environment.

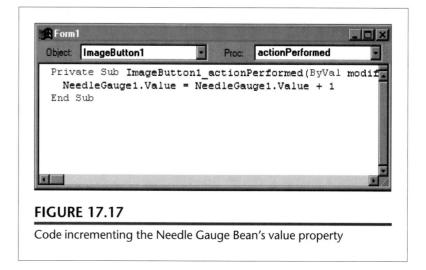

FIGURE 17.17

Code incrementing the Needle Gauge Bean's value property

Summary

In this chapter, you learned about the ActiveX Bridge for JavaBeans, which allows Beans to be used as ActiveX components. This is a significant breakthrough for JavaBeans because it provides a means of using Beans in ActiveX environments such as Visual Basic. Speaking of Visual Basic, you saw firsthand in this chapter how Beans can be integrated with Visual Basic via the ActiveX Bridge. The interesting thing about integrating Beans with Visual Basic is that you can use standard Visual Basic property sheets and forms to create and customize Beans.

Although you learned the practical side of using the ActiveX Bridge in this chapter, hopefully you also gained a little insight into the strategic implications of the Bridge. It's interesting that Sun felt the need to create the Bridge in the first place. Sun was smart in realizing that JavaBeans has a better chance of success if it directly supports competitive component technologies. The reality is that although Sun firmly believes JavaBeans is a better technology than ActiveX, it wanted to hedge its bets by making JavaBeans usable in as many contexts as possible. Sun also is busy working on bridges to other component technologies.

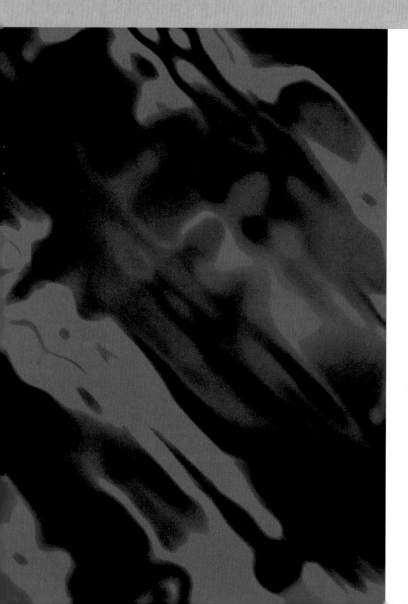

Chapter 18

Into the Future with JavaBeans

- ▸ Room to Grow

- ▸ 100% Pure Java

- ▸ JavaOS

- ▸ HotJava Views

- ▸ Java Electronic Commerce

When discussing a technology like Java that evolves at the speed of the Web, it's not enough to be merely up to date. You also need to have a well-focused picture of what's to come, extending at least a year or two into the future, which in the case of Java means covering many prospective developments whose outlines are already clear.

These future developments will address the main concerns of professional developers and corporate buyers, the two groups whose faith—or at least effort and investment—is most needed if Java is to reach its full potential in applications other than Web-page animation.

In this chapter, we'll be looking at innovations that reinforce Java's strengths in portability, low-cost deployment, efficient application support, and secure commercial transaction capability. Specifically, we will examine:

- ▶ 100% Pure Java
- ▶ JavaOS
- ▶ HotJava Views
- ▶ Java Electronic Commerce

Room to Grow

In *How To Program Java*, I described the JavaBeans component model as one of Java's coming attractions. Java's designers got that component model out the door with commendable speed, even though its implications (as we saw in Chapters 1 and 2) rippled through the length and breadth of the Java APIs.

Java astonished its critics by surviving the far-reaching enhancements of version 1.1, despite their breakneck pace, without showing any of the signs of desperation that appear when a good idea has trouble growing into a technology with staying power. It's clear that Java is not going to be a 90-day wonder, or even a three-year phenomenon that winds up on people's lists of "remember this one?"

Java won't suffer the fate of some other impressive programming technologies, such as Objective-C and Prolog, that never achieved the widespread impact predicted by their proponents. Unlike those technically promising tools that achieved only narrow (if modestly profitable) acceptance, Java has found the backing of people and organizations with the resources, and the will, to improve it in the ways the market demands.

18

100% Pure Java

One of the pressures on Java comes from the tension between the ideal and the practical. There's a "macro," long-term benefit from preserving the ideal of platform neutrality; there's a "micro," short-term practical benefit from using the full facilities of the one platform that's in front of any given user at any given time.

Proponents of individual platforms, in particular Microsoft Windows, have found an easy target in the limitations of the Java Abstract Windowing Toolkit. Applications that limit themselves to this cross-platform graphical interface package fall notably short of native applications in variety of fonts, for example, and in the sophistication of many other user interaction options. This has been used as an argument for treating Java, not as a full-fledged platform, but as merely a modern (and superbly productive) programming language for accessing platform-specific facilities such as ActiveX controls.

It's a testament to the basic rightness of the Java model that such "embrace and extend" approaches have been technically easy to deliver, in ways that have made them quite seductive. It's been possible, for example, to make an ActiveX component look to Java code like an ordinary Java class. It's also been possible to manipulate Java classes on platforms using Microsoft's Component Object Model as if they were just another species of language-neutral COM component. This bidirectional ActiveX/JavaBeans capability was demonstrated by Microsoft in April 1997.

But to the extent that Java-based products include platform-specific components such as ActiveX controls, and to the extent that programmers resort to Java's facilities for incorporating platform-specific native code (rather than writing classes that only work through the Java Virtual Machine), end-users are ultimately cheated. The short-term focus of platform-specific extensions gets in the way of achieving the long-term, evolutionary benefits that users would receive from a more competitive market (one with broader options for microprocessor designs, operating environments, and hardware form factors).

If the computing world is to get away from the "Beige Box" model of Windows-on-X86 computing, and to enjoy the stunning price and performance advantages of modern RISC processors (like those that power mass-market entertainment systems), there needs to be a base of Java code that really does run on any conforming Java Virtual Machine. If an implementation of the JVM can pass Sun's verification suite, consisting of more than 8000 tests as of Spring 1997, it shouldn't matter whether the underlying host is an Intel-compatible chip, an Alpha microprocessor, or a multiprocessor constellation based on still-prospective technology. Applications that assume what they're explicitly promised by the JVM specification would then find large markets, without the redundant effort that faces developers who try to offer multiplatform product lines today. The resulting

base of code would motivate platform vendors to offer first-rate Java implementations that would, in turn, attract more buyers for those multiplatform applications.

The process begins by creating end-user confidence in a base of genuinely portable packaged software. This is the goal of the 100% Pure Java Initiative.

Defining 100% Pure

To carry the logo of the 100% Pure Java program, a software product will have to be written entirely in the Java language. Perhaps this seems obvious, but the Initiative documents take pains to spell it out: "While Java bears some superficial resemblance to C and C++, this should not be construed to mean that pure Java code may include C or C++ code," warns the defining white paper.

This prohibition also applies, of course, to the writing of modules in any other language. Using Java's native method interface to incorporate non-Java executable modules compromises the features that most dramatically elevate programmer productivity and end-user convenience.

Specifically, the use of native methods limits the effectiveness of Java's garbage collection, the automatic memory-management facility that eliminates many of the most common causes of error in C and C++ programming. It also fatally weakens the inherent security of Java's bytecode validation process, by which a Java Virtual Machine determines that a program does not attempt to manipulate instructions that lie outside the program's own region of memory. Finally, it nullifies the more advanced and finely grained controls that are accessible through the `SecurityManager` mechanism. Native method calls completely bypass this distinctive feature of the Java technology.

Native code is neither technically nor practically suited to network-based deployment through Web page applets, since native code assumes a particular client hardware type, which cannot be guaranteed in the Internet environment. Furthermore, native code (of which ActiveX components are an example) can take uncontrolled liberties with client system resources.

The market's acceptance of ActiveX suggests that this dangerous freedom is not widely viewed as a fatal problem, especially if code can be established as "trusted" through cryptographic signing or other means of verifying its source and its freedom from malicious or accidental alterations. Even so, the fragmentation of Java into dialects that require specific platforms would violate the most attractive promises that are being made by Java's proponents in the name of all Java applets. It might be a grave strategic error to blur those promises in users' minds by introducing exceptions to the rules.

The guidelines for the 100% Pure Java Initiative do allow a product to include native code as a parallel option, provided that the same feature is also implemented in Java. This would let a developer offer the end-user a choice. An application's user-definable preference settings might specify the Java implementation of a feature (with all of Java's advantages) as the default, but allow the user to choose the native implementation for its higher performance and/or richer access to platform-specific features. A product must, though, be capable of full function without the use of native method calls to bear the 100% Pure Java mark.

More than just conformance, the 100% Pure Java program will seek to guarantee end-user convenience by requiring that participating software include all needed Java API classes in the distributed package. The standard Java API libraries are already furnished as part of any licensed Java implementation, generally by the vendor of the operating system or other operating environment in question. In March of 1997, Sun also gave application vendors the option of bundling a Java Runtime Environment with a distributed application, giving end-users an up-to-date Java Virtual Machine and class libraries but not including the development tools that make up the balance of Sun's Java Development Kit.

Finally, the 100% Pure Java guidelines also dictate that provisional Standard Extension API packages must be distributed as needed by application products. With the Java API classes, extensions, and runtime support all coming in one package, end-users can be confident that they won't have to waste their time tracking down needed libraries before they can run an application.

To complete the package that gives end-users confidence in a logo-marked product, 100% Pure Java products will have to pass Sun's certification suite as mentioned above. Sun has reserved the right to require recertification, using an updated suite, at any time for a product to retain its certified status.

JavaOS

The user gets many benefits from 100% Pure Java, but so does the implementer of systems software such as an operating system. The use of diverse programming languages creates a great deal of complexity that must be overcome by the facilities of a general-purpose operating system. This often comes with a price tag of enlarged memory requirements and reduced application performance. An operating system gains many efficiencies when it can be designed to host only Java-based applications.

How does an operating system benefit from an all-Java applications base? When a Java Virtual Machine is implemented in software, as it is on any general-purpose microprocessor (as opposed to a Java-specific microJava, picoJava, or similar chip), the Java Virtual Machine is itself merely one of the running applications. The Java bytecode stream that the Java Virtual Machine reads from a Java .class file is data to the JVM, in the same way that a spreadsheet formula is data to a spreadsheet program even if it seems like code (a machine-readable description of a behavior) to the user.

Early Participants in the 100% Pure Java Program

As of the time this chapter was prepared, the following companies had committed to participation in the 100% Pure Java effort:

Activerse Inc.	HOME Account Network, Inc.
Active Software	IBM Corporation
AgentSoft, Ltd.	Industrial Technology Research Institute (ITRI)
AllPen Software, Inc.	Information Builders, Inc. (IBI)
Apple	Informix
Applix	I-Kinetics
Aquas, Inc.	Infoscape
Arachnid Software	Infospace
Art Technology Group	InterNetivity, Inc.
Bandai	InterSoft Argentina
BEA Systems, Inc.	IONA Technologies
BHR Software	JUSTSYSTEM
BlackWatch	Jyra Research, Inc.
Bluestone	Karadigm Software, Inc.
Brainstorm Technologies	KL Group, Inc.
BulletProof Corp.	Kinetix
Centura	KIVA Software Corp.
Competency Center for Java,	LG Electronics
Singapore	Lotus/cc:mail
Connect! Corporation	Marimba
Contigo Software	Metrowerks
Corel Corp.	Microline Software
Crystal WebWorks, Inc.	Micromuse
CyberCash	Microtec Microware Systems Corp.
Cyberexpress	Mitsubushi Electronics Corp. II
D Cube	NCD
Dimension X	NetDynamics, Inc.
EarthWeb, Inc.	NetFactory, Inc.
ELcom Systems, Inc.	Net-It
EPS, Inc.	Netscape
FTP Software	Nomura
Fujitsu, Ltd.	Novell, Inc.
FutureTense, Inc.	Novera Software, Inc.
GemStone Systems, Inc.	Novita Object Design, Inc.
Graham Technology	OKI Electric Industry Co., Ltd.
Health Systems Integration, Inc.	OpenConnect Systems, Inc.
HDS Network Systems, Inc.	Open Horizon, Inc.
Hewlett Packard	Open Software Associates
Hitachi	Oracle

18

Early Participants in the 100% Pure Java Program (Continued)

As of the time this chapter was prepared, the following companies had committed to participation in the 100% Pure Java effort:

ParaGraph International	Sybase, Inc.
Parc-Place Digitalk	Taligent, Inc.
Persoft	Texas Instruments
PictureTalk	Thought, Inc.
Pierian Spring Software	Toshiba Corp.
Platinum Technology, Inc.	TransactNet, Inc.
Progress Software	Trifox
Random Noise	TriTeal
Resonate	TVObjects
Sanga International	Visigenic Software
Santa Cruz Operation (SCO)	VisualTek Solutions
Sarrus Software, Inc.	Wind River Systems
ShowBase Media, Inc.	Wright Strategies
Soft Mountain	Wyatt River Software
Spyglass	Wyse Technology
Stock Smart	

If the Java Virtual Machine is being hosted on a general-purpose operating system that may also be hosting other applications, then that operating system must make a number of conservative assumptions. It has to manage the scheduling of time on the processor, allocating that critical resource among the various concurrent tasks, and perhaps allowing for the possibility that some of those tasks were not written to optimize their performance in a multitasking environment. It has to protect applications from encroaching on each other's portions of the global address space. And it has to couple applications to the operating system's device drivers for graphical display interaction, file system interface, printing, and other services.

In a hybrid environment, where the JVM is potentially just one of several running applications, the situation resembles that illustrated in Figure 18.1. Note that the execution environment is dominated by layers that correspond to native, platform-specific code. There are relatively few chances to take advantage of Java's "write once, run anywhere" economies.

If the application base consists entirely of Java applications, the task of the operating system becomes vastly simpler. For example, Java technology precludes the use of the arbitrary pointer manipulations that pervade generic C and C++ programming. This means that data structures belonging to separate concurrent tasks, as well as data structures within a task, need not take paranoid measures to protect themselves against either accidental or malicious mischief.

With an applications base that's entirely written in the disciplined style of Java, the addressing scheme that the processor uses to refer to locations in memory can be based on a single set of identifying numbers (known as an *address space*), rather than requiring the multiple address spaces used by general-purpose operating systems. Multiple address spaces degrade system performance because they force the processor to spend a great deal of time in laborious context switching as it rearranges its internal housekeeping information to shift its attention from one protected region of memory to another.

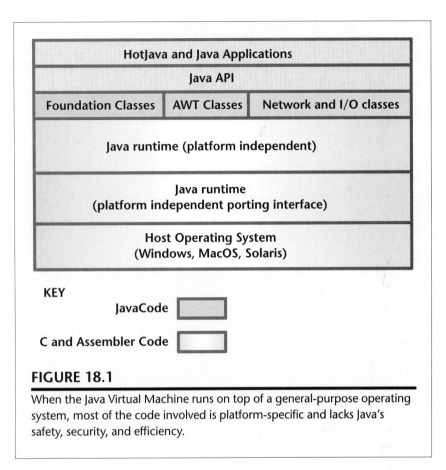

FIGURE 18.1

When the Java Virtual Machine runs on top of a general-purpose operating system, most of the code involved is platform-specific and lacks Java's safety, security, and efficiency.

By eliminating the need for multiple address spaces, a Java-based operating environment avoids the need for a hardware memory-management unit. A hardware MMU has been a part of every X86-family processor from the Intel 286 through the Pentium and its successors. Where an MMU is available, that's an added benefit for the Java-based system, since the MMU can be used to streamline memory-mapping and virtual-memory facilities (virtual memory uses mass storage to expand the effective capacity of a computer beyond the amount of physical memory on board). But many of the most time-consuming operations involved in running concurrent tasks simply cease to be required when all of the applications are running under Java's rules.

Much of the burden of delivering applications on more than one platform can also be eliminated by putting most of the device interface logic in portable Java routines, leaving only critical kernels to be written in native code. Again, this requires the certainty that only Java-based applications need be hosted. The resulting situation, with Java code dominating the environment instead of native code, is demonstrated in Figure 18.2.

18

Running applications that respect Java's rules, and use only the JVM's capabilities, is the charter of JavaOS. Sun describes JavaOS as "a small and efficient operating system that executes Java applications directly on hardware platforms." The first release of JavaOS went out to licensees just as this book was being completed. Proving the possibility of a wide-open processor marketplace, the initial release of JavaOS supported the SPARC, X86, and information-appliance StrongARM processor families.

JavaOS is layered for ease of deployment and maintenance. The operating system kernel and the Java Virtual Machine are coded natively for the particular hardware platform. The Window and Graphics systems, JavaOS Device Drivers, and JavaOS Network Classes are written in Java and portable to all target environments.

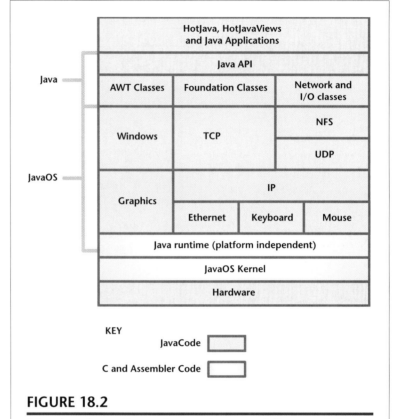

FIGURE 18.2

A Java-based operating environment can use platform-neutral Java code for all but the lowest-level tasks and can rely on Java's disciplined respect for boundaries between concurrently running programs.

The core services of the operating system are handled by the minimal kernel. This boots the operating system when the machine is activated, handles interrupts during operation, and performs tasks such as thread switching, trap execution, and fast-track data transfer between various hardware subsystems. Handling these critical functions with native code maximizes the performance of concurrent applications and of foreground/background operating modes, such as downloading files while also performing interactive tasks.

The functions of the Java Virtual Machine are already familiar to any Java developer. This module performs the class loading, bytecode verification, bytecode interpretation, thread scheduling, and other higher-level operations that give Java its distinctive strengths as a productive programming platform.

Though Java was not originally conceived of as an Internet-centered technology, its facilities for making the Internet a transparently accessible resource have had much to do with its rapid acceptance. That tradition, if we may use this word for something that's still so new, continues with the JavaOS Network Classes. These give applications in a JavaOS environment full access to TCP/IP, UDP, and ICMP protocols, with either DNS or NIS available to handle host-name lookup and session-management tasks (such as logging in and checking user passwords).

Graphical interface operations are divided between the JavaOS Window System, which manages access to the display subsystem (including the display of user interface elements and the handling of overlapping windows) and the JavaOS Graphics System, which provides the API calls for low-level elements such as lines, arcs, and polygons. Filling and font rendering are also handled in this layer, which calls on the Abstract Windowing Toolkit to maximize reuse of code.

The proof that this is worth the effort will come from end-users' satisfaction with the performance of low-cost JavaOS-based computers, delivering the functions of much more heavily configured hardware that's burdened by a less streamlined operating system. According to Sun, a complete network computer implementation (including the HotJava browser, class libraries, and over a megabyte of fonts) requires 4MB of disk space or ROM and 4MB of RAM. Sun estimates that JavaOS and HotJava will use less than 2.5MB of that 4MB complement of RAM, leaving the rest for caching Web pages, images, and other rich data, and the bytecode of executing applications.

HotJava Views

For optimal user interaction with the lean, mean JavaOS machine, Sun has rethought the design of the graphical user interface to produce the new environment called HotJava Views. HotJava Views doesn't have a "desktop," it doesn't use the conventional notion of files, and it doesn't make a distinction between applications and documents. What it does is focus on the needs of what Sun calls the "Transaction User," who doesn't employ the large numbers of voluminous applications that are typical of many Windows-based PC users today.

Since applications need to be loaded into a JavaOS-based "network computer" from central storage, across the network, Sun doesn't recommend this type of system for the current Windows "power user." In many cases, however, the resources of Windows are tremendous overkill for the user with only basic needs for personal productivity tools combined with one or two task-specific applications. The latter is the target user of JavaOS, HotJava, and the HotJava Views productivity suite.

18

HotJava Views includes viewing tools for mail, schedule, and personnel information as well as the other usual facilities of an Internet or intranet browser. It avoids the performance overhead of managing overlapping windows by switching between full-screen displays for each of its functions. The user switches among these displays with the Selector, a column of graphical icons along one side of the screen. A typical display from HotJava Views appears in Figure 18.3.

Ironically, one of us (Coffee) has long since adopted a similar configuration for his Windows Explorer desktop, with the Task Bar at the edge of the display and narrowed to the point that only the icons stay visible. Pardon us, therefore, if we say that Sun's designers showed excellent taste.

The applications within the HotJava Views suite reflect the designers' focus on the features that will be most needed. This parsimony is essential if a limited-memory network computer is going to be responsive enough to be accepted by users.

The HotJava Views electronic mail program, for example, eliminates the overhead and learning curve required to manage multiple folders of saved messages, providing instead one folder for saving received messages for future reference and another folder for automatically keeping copies of messages sent. Reducing the number of commands left the mail program with so few functions that a single bar of icons could handle them all. Having taken for granted the notion of pull-down menus, the designers expressed some trepidation about eliminating them. For the mail program, though, this proved to be the best approach.

Menus were retained in other programs with more required functions, such as the calendar manager, but the HotJava Views user interface

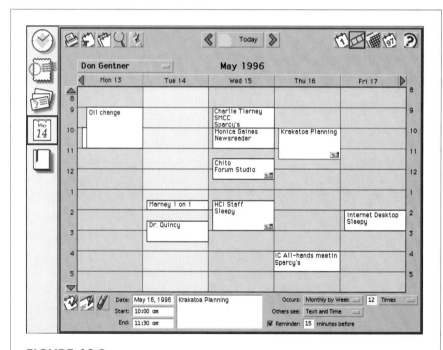

FIGURE 18.3

HotJava Views minimizes user-interface complexity with full-screen displays and icon-based navigation and control, rather than using the multiple windows and elaborate menus of Windows or other "fat desktop" graphical user interfaces.

moves menus away from the top of the screen to wherever their choices are most relevant. This maximizes usability despite the compactness of the display, and reduces the chance of having users fail to discover some useful function merely because they never penetrated far enough into the depths of a distant menu tree.

Without the capability to show two applications at once using overlapping windows, the designers needed to come up with a new approach to integrating application functions. Drag-and-drop transfer of information, for example, isn't possible when only one application is visible at a time.

HotJava Views retained the intuitive appeal of multiple windows without their performance overhead by introducing pop-up "reduced" displays of the kind shown in Figure 18.4. These present some relevant subset of a full-screen display, as needed, to accept a transfer of information from the application that's currently shown in full-screen mode. The passive desktop background goes away, replaced by a screen that's always devoted to the user's foreground application but with integration among all of the other concurrent tasks.

By eliminating the passive desktop, the HotJava Views environment eliminates the user's expectation of being able to see and manipulate files as discrete data objects. Instead, HotJava Views' applications all become viewers of data, with active behaviors for manipulating that data; in other words, they become objects with direct user interaction on the front end, and with the possibility of applying robust database technologies at the back end (which ought to be the evolutionary goal of mainstream PC applications as well).

Since objects in HotJava Views are only visible when they're doing something, the de-

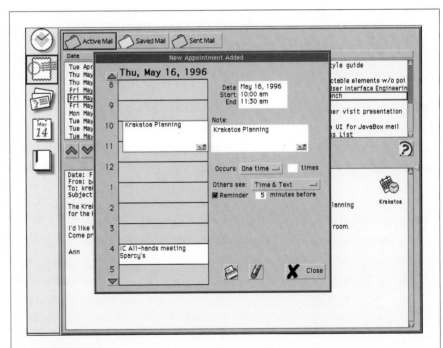

FIGURE 18.4

The use of pop-up "reduced" displays rather than free-form overlapping windows gives HotJava Views a familiar and intuitive look without the hardware overheads and user learning barriers of an open-ended "electronic desktop."

18

signers decided to eliminate the troublesome distinction between single-click (select) and double-click (perform default interaction) operations. A single click on any object opens it into its data viewing mode. The arcane rules for multiple selections (Shift-click for continuous extension of a set, Control-click for discontinuous extension, and the like) have been eliminated by precluding all multiple selection.

HotJava Views is not for the power user, but merely saying this begs the question of how many users ever wanted to reach that level of mastery. How many power users got that way as a defense against the complexity and unreliability of today's PCs, with their individual variations that make each user his or her own system administrator?

The designers of HotJava Views make it clear that what they're producing is a successor to the 3270 terminal, but with richer graphical interaction; a successor to the X Window "display server" (also known as a terminal), but with far more local processing power for non-display functions and therefore with more consistent application performance. Their insights are relevant to the would-be developer of a rich collection of JavaBeans components that can become the basis for an enterprise suite of efficiently delivered, easy-to-use applications.

Java Electronic Commerce

In the words of Deep Throat, the anonymous source in the 1970s Watergate scandal, "Follow the money." The software foundation that becomes the preferred habitat of Internet-based commercial transactions will enjoy a compelling advantage in attracting the best toolmakers and the most innovative developers, not to mention the most affluent users (whose buying power will make the entire process feed on itself).

In pursuit of these advantages, Java's designers are developing new Java facilities under the umbrella label of the Java Electronic Commerce Framework. This is very much a work in progress, with current information available on the Web at http://www.javasoft.com/products/commerce/.

Java Electronic Commerce is a comprehensive phrase for an entire model of automated billing and payment transactions, addressing the concerns that naturally arise with regard to reliability, confidentiality, authentication of participants' identities, and other vital issues. At the lowest level, though, the code has to hit the road, and we encounter the new Java Commerce APIs.

The Commerce APIs include interfaces such as `Action`, which defines the methods needed to participate in a transaction, with two-phase commit to ensure that both parties either complete the process or abort. They also define classes such as `Wallet`, which organizes persistent data such as the "instrument" structures that encapsulate permissions to participate in certain types of transaction.

The Commerce APIs were in a "pre-alpha" stage at the time that this book was completed. For additional information, consult the JavaSoft Web site named above.

Summary

JavaBeans components are attractive because they can run wherever Java runs. In this chapter, we've seen that this potential market is being enlarged by the 100% Pure Java Initiative and by the proliferation of cost-effective information appliances based on JavaOS.

Innovative refinements to the overly complex Windows-style GUI can deliver JavaBeans-based applications to users without the steep learning curve of today's GUI environments, which are only considered intuitive by users who are already on their second or third generation of personal computer. The vast market of potential users who are still bewildered by Windows, or even the Macintosh, may become more reachable with these more focused and less overwhelming designs, as exemplified by HotJava Views.

The acid test is whether these users will want to do business by means of such software, lowering costs in the retail and financial sectors in the process. Java's designers are trying to stay abreast of growing mass-market acceptance of electronic commerce with the Java Commerce APIs and the associated management-education effort that comes with the Java Electronic Commerce Framework.

18

Appendix

Using the CD-ROM

The CD-ROM accompanying this book contains lots of software and useful information. This appendix describes the contents of the CD-ROM and how to install and use each portion of it.

Examples from the Book

All of the example source code covered throughout the book, including associated resources and executable class files, is provided on the CD-ROM. This source code serves as a very good basis for developing Beans of your own. The following chapters have source code associated with them that is included on the CD-ROM:

- ▶ Chapter 6: Echo Key Bean and Count Up application
- ▶ Chapter 7: Arrow Bean
- ▶ Chapter 8: Arrow Bean serialization
- ▶ Chapter 9: DefaultEvent and MyBeanInfo support classes
- ▶ Chapter 10: Arrow Bean customizer and Bean information class
- ▶ Chapter 11: Image Button Bean
- ▶ Chapter 12: Needle Gauge Bean
- ▶ Chapter 13: Clock Bean
- ▶ Chapter 14: Image Enhancer Bean
- ▶ Chapter 15: Timer Bean

APPENDIX

All of this example source code is provided on the CD-ROM under the `\Examples` directory. The code for each chapter is contained in a .ZIP file located in a subdirectory beneath the `\Examples` directory. To install the code for a particular chapter, just extract the .ZIP file for the chapter. Make sure you extract the contents of each .ZIP file so that they keep their relative paths. This is important because the source code files are organized in a hierarchical structure that must correspond with the package names used in the code.

Software

Although example source code is very important, you probably expected the CD-ROM to come with some useful software. Well, you expected right! The CD-ROM comes with the following software packages, several of which are indispensable for JavaBeans development:

▶ Java Development Kit (JDK) Version 1.1.1

▶ JavaBeans™ Development Kit (BDK) Version 1.0

▶ Sun's Java Workshop 1.0 Try-andBuy Version 1.0

▶ HTML version of the book *How To Program Java*

JDK Version 1.1.1

The Java Development Kit, or JDK, is the standard suite of development tools for Java. It includes a command-line Java compiler, debugger, disassembler, applet viewer, and archiver, among other tools. The JDK also includes the complete source code for the Java API, which includes the JavaBeans API. To put it simply, the JDK is a must for every serious Java developer.

To install the JDK from the CD-ROM, follow the directions outlined in the HTML page for the platform on which you are installing the JDK. For Windows, take a look at the `Inst_win.htm` page, which is located in the `\Jdk\Win_32` directory on the CD-ROM. For Solaris, check out the Inssolar.htm page, which is located in the `\Jdk\Sparc` directory on the CD-ROM.

Java™ Development Kit Version 1.1 Binary Code License

This binary code license ("License") contains rights and restrictions associated with use of the accompanying software and documentation ("Software"). Read the License carefully before installing the Software. By installing the Software you agree to the terms and conditions of this License.

1 **Limited License Grant.** Sun grants to you ("Licensee") a non-exclusive, non-transferable limited license to use the Software without fee for evaluation of the Software and for development of Java™ compatible applets and applications. Licensee may make one archival copy of the Software. Licensee may not re-distribute the Software in whole or in part, either separately or included with a product. Refer to the Java Runtime Environment Version 1.1 binary code license (http://www.javasoft.com/products/JDK/1.1/index.html) for the availability of runtime code which may be distributed with Java compatible applets and applications.

2   **Java Platform Interface.** Licensee may not modify the Java Platform Interface ("JPI", identified as classes contained within the "java" package or any subpackages of the "java" package), by creating additional classes within the JPI or otherwise causing the addition to or modification of the classes in the JPI. In the event that Licensee creates any Java-related API and distributes such API to others for applet or application development, Licensee must promptly publish an accurate specification for such API for free use by all developers of Java-based software.

3   **Restrictions.** Software is confidential copyrighted information of Sun and title to all copies is retained by Sun and/or its licensors. Licensee shall not modify, decompile, disassemble, decrypt, extract, or otherwise reverse engineer Software. Software may not be leased, assigned, or sublicensed, in whole or in part. **Software is not designed or intended for use in on-line control of aircraft, air traffic, aircraft navigation or aircraft communications; or in the design, construction, operation or maintenance of any nuclear facility. Licensee warrants that it will not use or redistribute the Software for such purposes.**

4   **Trademarks and Logos.** This License does not authorize Licensee to use any Sun name, trademark or logo. Licensee acknowledges that Sun owns the Java trademark and all Java-related trademarks, logos and icons including the Coffee Cup and Duke ("Java Marks") and agrees to: (i) to comply with the Java Trademark Guidelines at http://java.com/trademarks.html; (ii) not do anything harmful to or inconsistent with Sun's rights in the Java Marks; and (iii) assist Sun in protecting those rights, including assigning to Sun any rights acquired by Licensee in any Java Mark.

5   **Disclaimer of Warranty.** Software is provided "AS IS," without a warranty of any kind. ALL EXPRESS OR IMPLIED REPRESENTATIONS AND WARRANTIES, INCLUDING ANY IMPLIED WARRANTY OF MERCHANTABILITY, FITNESS FOR A PARTICULAR PURPOSE OR NON-INFRINGEMENT, ARE HEREBY EXCLUDED.

6   **Limitation of Liability.** SUN AND ITS LICENSORS SHALL NOT BE LIABLE FOR ANY DAMAGES SUFFERED BY LICENSEE OR ANY THIRD PARTY AS A RESULT OF USING OR DISTRIBUTING SOFTWARE. IN NO EVENT WILL SUN OR ITS LICENSORS BE LIABLE FOR ANY LOST REVENUE, PROFIT OR DATA, OR FOR DIRECT, INDIRECT, SPECIAL, CONSEQUENTIAL, INCIDENTAL OR PUNITIVE DAMAGES, HOWEVER CAUSED AND REGARDLESS OF THE THEORY OF LIABILITY, ARISING OUT OF THE

USE OF OR INABILITY TO USE SOFTWARE, EVEN IF SUN HAS BEEN AD-
VISED OF THE POSSIBILITY OF SUCH DAMAGES.

7   **Termination.** Licensee may terminate this License at any time by destroying all copies of Software. This License will terminate immediately without notice from Sun if Licensee fails to comply with any provision of this
License. Upon such termination, Licensee must destroy all copies of
Software.

8   **Export Regulations.** Software, including technical data, is subject to U.S.
export control laws, including the U.S. Export Administration Act and its
associated regulations, and may be subject to export or import regulations
in other countries. Licensee agrees to comply strictly with all such regulations and acknowledges that it has the responsibility to obtain licenses to
export, re-export, or import Software. Software may not be downloaded,
or otherwise exported or re-exported (i) into, or to a national or resident
of, Cuba, Iraq, Iran, North Korea, Libya, Sudan, Syria or any country to
which the U.S. has embargoed goods; or (ii) to anyone on the U.S.
Treasury Department's list of Specially Designated Nations or the U.S.
Commerce Department's Table of Denial Orders.

9   **Restricted Rights.** Use, duplication or disclosure by the United States government is subject to the restrictions as set forth in the Rights in
Technical Data and Computer Software Clauses in DFARS 252.227-7013(c)
(1) (ii) and FAR 52.227-19(c) (2) as applicable.

10   **Governing Law.** Any action related to this License will be governed by
California law and controlling U.S federal law. No choice of law rules of
any jurisdiction will apply.

11   **Severability.** If any of the above provisions are held to be in violation of
applicable law, void, or unenforceable in any jurisdiction, then such provisions are herewith waived to the extent necessary for the License to be
otherwise enforceable in such jurisdiction. However, if in Sun's opinion
deletion of any provisions of the License by operation of this paragraph
unreasonably compromises the rights or increase the liabilities of Sun or
its licensors, Sun reserves the right to terminate the License and refund
the free paid by Licensee, if any, as Licensee's sole and exclusive remedy.

JDK Version 1.1.1 Copyright 1997 Sun Microsystems, Inc. 2550 Garcia Ave.,
Mtn. View, CA 94043-1100 USA, All rights reserved.

BDK Version 1.0

Designed to be used in conjunction with the JDK, the JavaBeans™ Development
Kit, or BDK, provides tools necessary to create and test JavaBeans components. The
most important tool in the BDK is the BeanBox, which allows you to test Beans in
a visual environment. As of this writing, the BDK is the only environment to fully

support JavaBeans development. Hopefully, by the time you read this there will be some third party development tools supporting JavaBeans.

To install the BDK, execute the installation application for the platform you are using. For Windows, execute `Feb97.exe`, which is located in the `\Bdk\Windows` directory on the CD-ROM. For UNIX, execute `Feb97.sh`, which is located in the `\Bdk\Unix` directory on the CD-ROM.

BDK Binary Code License Version 1.0

This License ("License") contains rights and restrictions associated with use of the accompanying software. Read the License carefully before using the software. By using the software you are agreeing to the terms and conditions of this License.

1 **Limited License Grant.** Sun grants to you ("Licensee") a nonexclusive, nontransferable, worldwide, royalty-free license to use the Beans Developer's Kit Version 1.0 (the "Software") for the purpose of developing Java Beans.

2 **Redistribution of Demonstration Files.** Sun grants Licensee the right to use, modify and redistribute the Beans example and demonstration code, including the Bean Box ("Demos"), in both source and binary code from provided that (i) Licensee does not utilize the Demos in a manner which is disparaging to Sun; and (ii) Licensee indemnifies and holds Sun harmless from all claims relating to any such use or distribution of the Demos. Such distribution is limited to the source and binary code of the Demos and specifically excludes any rights to modify or distribute any graphical images contained in the Demos.

3 **Restrictions.** The Software is confidential, copyrighted proprietary information of Sun and title to all copies is retained by Sun and/or its licensors. Licensee shall not make copies of Software, other than a single copy of Software in machine-readable format for back-up or archival purposes and, if applicable, Licensee may print one copy of on-line documentation, in which event all propriety rights notices on Software and on-line documentation shall be reproduced and applied to all copies. Licensee shall not, decompile, disassemble, decrypt, extract, or otherwise reverse engineer Software. Except as provided in Section 2 above, Software may not be transferred, leased, assigned, or sublicensed, in whole or in part. No right, title or interest in and to any trademarks or trade names of Sun or Sun's licensors is granted hereunder. **Software is not designed or intended for use in on-line control of aircraft, air traffic, aircraft navigation or aircraft communications; or in the design, construction, operation or maintenance of any nuclear facility. Licensee represents and warrants that it will not use or redistribute the Software for such purposes.**

4 **Trademarks and Logos.** Licensee acknowledges that Sun owns the Java trademark and all Java-related trademarks, logos and icons including the Coffee Cup and Duke ("Java Marks") and agrees to: (i) to comply with the Java Trademark Guidelines at http://java.sun.com/trademarks.html; (ii) not do anything harmful to or inconsistent with Sun's rights in the Java Marks; and (iii) assist Sun in protecting those rights including assigning to Sun any rights acquired by Licensee in any Java Mark.

5 **Disclaimer of Warranty.** Software is provided "AS IS," without a warranty of any kind. ALL EXPRESS OR IMPLIED REPRESENTATIONS AND WARRANTIES, INCLUDING ANY IMPLIED WARRANTY OF MERCHANTABILITY, FITNESS FOR A PARTICULAR PURPOSE OR NON-INFRINGEMENT, ARE HEREBY EXCLUDED.

6 **Limitation of Liability.** SUN AND ITS LICENSORS SHALL NOT BE LIABLE FOR ANY DAMAGES SUFFERED BY LICENSEE OR ANY THIRD PARTY AS A RESULT OF USING OR DISTRIBUTING SOFTWARE. IN NO EVENT WILL SUN OR ITS LICENSORS BE LIABLE FOR ANY LOST REVENUE, PROFIT OR DATA, OR FOR DIRECT, INDIRECT, SPECIAL, CONSEQUENTIAL, INCIDENTAL OR PUNITIVE DAMAGES, HOWEVER CAUSED AND REGARDLESS OF THE THEORY OF LIABILITY, ARISING OUT OF THE USE OF OR INABILITY TO USE SOFTWARE, EVEN IF SUN HAS BEEN ADVISED OF THE POSSIBILITY OF SUCH DAMAGES.

7 **Termination.** Licensee may terminate this License at any time by destroying all copies of Software. This License will terminate immediately without notice from Sun if Licensee fails to comply with any provision of this License. Upon such termination, Licensee must destroy all copies of Software.

8 **Export Regulations.** Software, including technical data, is subject to U.S. export control laws, including the U.S. Export Administration Act and its associated regulations, and may be subject to export or import regulations in other countries. Licensee agrees to comply strictly with all such regulations and acknowledges that it has the responsibility to obtain licenses to export, re-export, or import Software. Software may not be downloaded, or otherwise exported or re-exported (I) into, or to a national or resident of, Cuba, Iraq, Iran, North Korea, Libya, Sudan, Syria or any country to which the U.S. has embargoed goods; or (ii) to anyone on the U.S. Treasury Department's list of Specially Designated Nations or the U.S. Commerce Department's Table of Denial Orders.

9 **Restricted Rights.** Use, duplication or disclosure by the United States government is subject to the restrictions as set forth in the Rights in Technical Data and Computer Software Clauses in DFARS 252.227-7013(c) (1) (ii) and FAR 52.227-19(c) (2) as applicable.

10 **Governing Law.** Any action related to this License will be governed by California law and controlling U.S federal law. No choice of law rules of any jurisdiction will apply.

BDK Version 1.0 Copyright 1997 Sun Microsystems, Inc. 2550 Garcia Ave., Mtn. View, CA 94043-1100 USA, All rights reserved.

ActiveX Bridge Beta 2

With a little help from a software layer known as the ActiveX Bridge, JavaBeans components can be used as ActiveX components. The ActiveX Bridge provides all the overhead required to pull this off. Using the ActiveX Bridge, you can use a Bean in a purely ActiveX environment such as Visual Basic. The ActiveX Bridge works in concert with the BDK.

As of publication of this book, the ActiveX Bridge is still in beta. As Sun does not allow for re-distribution of beta software, we could not include the ActiveX Bridge on the CD that accompanies this book.

To install the ActiveX Bridge, go to the AcitiveX Bridge, beta 2, download site: http://java.sun.com/beans/bridge/download.html

Sun's Java Workshop 1.0 Try-and-Buy Version 1.0

Java Workshop is Sun's visual development environment for Java. Built entirely in Java itself, Java Workshop executes within a Web environment, which is unique for a development tool. This makes it particularly well suited to network team development, although it is also very useful as a stand-alone tool.

To install Java Workshop, refer to the `Jws.txt` text file in the `\Jws` directory on the CD-ROM. This text file provides specific installation instructions for both Windows and UNIX systems.

Sun's Java Workshop 1.0 Try-and Buy Version 1.0 Copyright 1997 Sun Microsystems, Inc. 2550 Garcia Ave., Mtn. View, CA 94043-1100 USA, All rights reserved.

HTML Version of the Book *How to Program Java*

Although a decent degree of Java knowledge is expected in this book, you may find yourself rusty in some areas. For this reason, the CD-ROM includes the complete electronic version of the book *How to Program Java*. If you are relatively new to Java, you may want to read through *How to Program Java* to get a solid Java foundation before digging into the details of JavaBeans in this book.

To access the HTML version of the book *How to Program Java*, just open the `Welcome.htm` page, which is located in the `\Htp_java` directory, in a Web browser. This page serves as the table of contents for the book.

Index

Italicized page numbers denote figures.

100% Pure Java, 330–334

3D effects, painting for Image Button Bean, 189

A

Abstract Windowing Toolkit (AWT), 86
  and inheritance-based event handling, 101–103
  and tight coupling of Java 1.0 events, 87–88

accessor methods
  of Beans, 53
  code example for raised property of Clock Bean graphical clock, 231
  for Image Button Bean, 185–187
  for Image Enhancer Bean, 249–250
  relationship to Image Button Bean, 181–182

action events, firing with Timer Bean, 273–274

action listeners
  used with Timer Bean, 279, 280
  using to customize Beans, 168, 169

action method of old inheritance model in Java 1.0, 92

ActiveX Bridge
  basics, 315
  bridging events with, 317
  bridging methods with, 317
  bridging properties with, 317
  DLL (dynamic link library) for, 318

problems with loading and displaying images in Beans, 325
  requirements for operating in ActiveX environment, 316–317
  role of Java stub classes, 317
  role of registry file, 317
  role of type libraries, 317
  selecting Bean within JAR (Java ARchive) file, 318–319
  selecting JAR (Java ARchive) file containing bean to package, 318

ActiveX Bridge beta 2, downloading, 316

ActiveX Bridge classes, composition of, 316

ActiveX components, using Java Beans components as, 315

ActiveX Packager, 318–320

Ada 95, 16

adapter classes, relationship to inner classes in JDK 1.1, 98

adapters in JDK 1.1, 92, 95–98, 169

Add Java Component menu command in PowerJ, 46–47

address space, used in JavaOS, 335

alpha filter, supported by Image Enhancer Bean, 248

alpha property
  determining maximum value for Image Enhancer Bean, 251
  used with Image Enhancer Bean, 248

alpha values, scaling, 263

animations
  determining frame rates for, 272–273
  displaying with Beans, 75–77
  timing, 271, 272–273

INDEX